Windows 8.1 Plain & Simple

Joli Ballew
Nancy Muir

ISBN: 978-0-7356-8127-9

Third Printing: April 2014

Printed and bound in Canada.

Microsoft Press books are available through booksellers and distributors worldwide. If you need support related to this book, email Microsoft Press Book Support at *mspinput@microsoft.com*. Please tell us what you think of this book at *http://www.microsoft.com/learning/booksurvey*.

Microsoft and the trademarks listed at *http://www.microsoft.com/about/legal/en/us/IntellectualProperty/Trademarks/EN-US.aspx* are trademarks of the Microsoft group of companies. All other marks are property of their respective owners.

The example companies, organizations, products, domain names, email addresses, logos, people, places, and events depicted herein are fictitious. No association with any real company, organization, product, domain name, email address, logo, person, place, or event is intended or should be inferred.

This book expresses the author's views and opinions. The information contained in this book is provided without any express, statutory, or implied warranties. Neither the authors, O'Reilly Media, Inc., Microsoft Corporation, nor its resellers, or distributors will be held liable for any damages caused or alleged to be caused either directly or indirectly by this book.

Acquisitions and Developmental Editor: Kenyon Brown
Production Editor: Kristen Brown
Editorial Production: Lisa Greenfield and Rich Kershner
Technical Reviewer: Simon May
Copyeditor: Richard Carey
Indexer: Bob Pfahler
Cover Design: Twist Creative • Seattle
Cover Composition: Ellie Volckhausen
Illustrator: S4 Carlisle Publishing Services

For my friend, mentor, and (retired) agent, Neil Salkind, PhD.

Contents

Acknowledgments

This was a fun book to write, what with all of the images, steps, callouts, and red pointy lines! Of course, all I had to do was write the words, take the shots, and detail what I wanted to show; many other people contributed and were responsible for the final product you hold in your hands now. And although I don't know all of them and can't thank them personally, there are a few I know by name.

Kenyon Brown served as my acquisitions and developmental editor, and brought me on to this project. He held my hand while I learned the ropes and was pretty patient with me; there was a lot to learn, having never written a Plain & Simple book before. Kristen Brown was my production editor, and she was in charge of making sure everything was placed correctly on the page, that the various people working on the book were available when needed, and was responsible for ironing out any differences that came up between the participants (although I can't recall any, now that I'm thinking about it). Ultimately, Kristen was responsible for the book going to press. Thanks to Simon May for his excellent technical editing and Richard Carey for the excellent copyediting, too. There are always mistakes to be corrected, no matter how careful one is.

I'd also like to mention that while all of this was going on, I was still in charge of my 93-year old father, his two dogs, and my two cats and their two hamsters, among the other myriad tasks associated with daily living. I teach at Brookhaven Community College (part of the Dallas County Community College District) and serve as the Microsoft IT Academy Coordinator there, too. I have a pretty popular YouTube channel to keep up with as well.

If you can imagine it, I was writing another Windows 8.1 book for Microsoft Press at the same time I was writing this one. Looking back, I'm not sure how I did it, to be honest! Luckily I have help with the daily chores; Cosmo and I are celebrating 20 years together, my daughter is very patient with my busy schedule and works around it so I can see my new granddaughter, and they are all okay with me going to bed at eight-thirty or nine p.m. and rising early to write quietly. Thanks, everyone!

About this book

1

Knowing how to use your Windows operating system is key to a successful computing experience. Even if you've been using Windows for years, there are a lot of new features and interface changes to get used to. This is true even if you are only moving from Windows 8; Windows 8.1 is packed with lots of enhancements and additions, including new apps, a redesigned Start button, an Apps view, lots of customization options, and more.

This book is designed to give you a simple-to-use visual reference that has you using Windows 8.1 right away. This book will help you understand the new Windows 8.1 Start screen, apps, and available touchscreen capabilities. This book will also direct you quickly to some of the more traditional features so that you can use your existing knowledge of Windows to ease your learning curve.

Whether you've used Windows before or are just starting out, this easy-to-understand book takes you through tasks step by step with a friendly visual interface that makes learning intuitive.

In this section:

- A quick overview
- A few assumptions
- What's new in Windows 8.1?
- The final word

A quick overview

Windows 8.1 Plain & Simple is divided into sections; each section has a specific focus with related tasks. To help you understand how to move around and use the book, you might want a quick overview of the book's structure. This section is Section 1.

Section 2, "Meet the Windows 8.1 interface," and Section 3, "Providing input," provide an introduction to the Windows 8.1 interface and the basic skills you need to navigate its features. You discover how to start and shut down Windows, get help, and how to provide input with your mouse, keyboard, or fingers by using a touchscreen.

Section 4, "Managing a computing session," covers how to use the Settings charm to control volume and brightness, how to change the time zone, manage power, display an on-screen keyboard, and connect to a network.

Section 5, "Customizing the appearance of Windows," leads you through common tasks associated with personalizing your computer by modifying settings for colors, backgrounds, and more. You learn how to organize and customize tiles on the Start screen, as well.

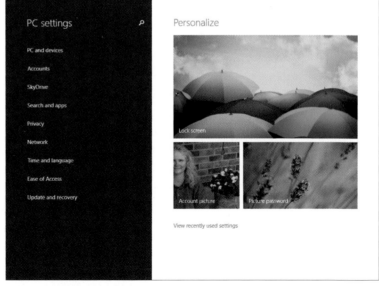

Section 6, "Searching for anything," covers all the tools Windows 8.1 offers for searching content both on your computer and online.

Section 7, "Using the Maps app," introduces you to the useful Maps app to help you find your way. If you've never used apps before, this is a great place to start.

Section 8, "Going online with Internet Explorer 11," gets you online, connecting to the Internet and learning to use the new features of the Internet Explorer 11 browser to navigate the web.

In Section 9, "Using Calendar and People," provides steps for managing your contacts and time by using the People and Calendar apps.

Section 10, "Using Mail and Skype," lets you communicate with the people you know using email, text, voice, and video.

In Section 11, "Buying apps at the Windows Store," you learn how to shop at the Windows Store for apps, sort, apps, and view your own apps.

In Section 12, "Playing music," you'll learn all about using the Music app to play music, obtain music, and create playlists, including buying music at the Xbox Music store. The Music app finds your music and makes it available here automatically.

Section 13, "Viewing pictures and video," provides instructions for viewing your own pictures and videos and making purchases at the Xbox Video store.

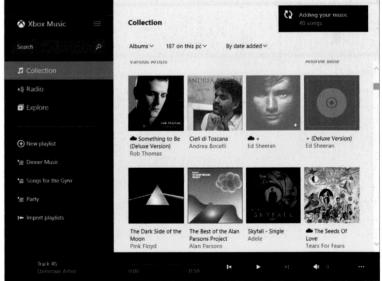

In Section 14, "Working with desktop apps," you learn about using applications, such as finding, opening and closing an app, inserting pictures, and entering and formatting text. You'll also discover the ins and outs of saving and printing files.

Section 15, "Working with devices and networks," provides the practical content that helps you connect with a network, manage your security and privacy, and maintain Windows to keep it trouble-free.

Section 16, "Working with users and privacy," shows you how to work with user accounts and security tools such as Family Safety, Windows Firewall, and Windows Defender.

Section 17, "Sharing settings and files in the cloud," helps you keep your data safe and secure, and available from anywhere.

Section 18, "Managing data," shows how to use File Explorer to manage the data you keep. You'll learn to find, rename, move, copy, paste, and delete files, as well as how to create compressed folders and back up your data.

Section 19, "Working with Accessibility settings," shows how to reconfigure the mouse for left-handed use, how to change the speed the mouse moves, and how to adjust volume. You'll also explore some of the accessibility features such as Magnifier, Narrator, and Speech Recognition.

Section 20, "Maintaining and troubleshooting your computer," includes information about how to configure Windows Updates, resolve problems with hardware, get help in various ways, and refresh and reset your PC.

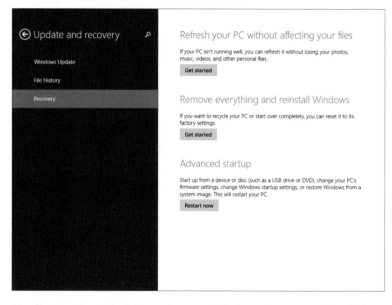

Finally, Section 21, "Upgrading to Windows 8.1," provides information you'll need to successfully upgrade to Windows 8.1 and Section 22, "Getting help," offers suggestions about how to get more help. The appendix, "Windows 8.1 keyboard shortcuts," gives you a handy list of keystroke shortcuts.

A few assumptions

In writing any book, it's important to make a few assumptions about your readers. I assume that you are basically computer literate, meaning that you have used a computer before and know how to turn it on and turn it off, how to use a mouse, and how to select text and objects. I also assume that you have worked with some kind of software before and know what a menu, dialog box, and tool button are. I do not assume that you have used a touchscreen before because this is a relatively recent addition to computers.

I assume that you use computers either at work or at home, or both, and that you have access to an Internet connection and have experience using one web browser or another. Other than that, I try to give you all the steps you need to get things done in an easy-to-understand way, no matter what your technical background.

What's new in Windows 8.1?

The biggest changes in Windows 8.1 (from Windows 8), involve the new Start screen customizations, as well as the integration of SkyDrive. There is an improved Apps view too, and a redesigned PC Settings hub.

Like Windows 8, Windows 8.1 makes excellent use of online resources and third-party apps, somewhat akin to the way the average smartphone does. With an Internet connection, you'll find that on-screen elements update you in real time about everything from stocks and weather to activity on your social networking sites. Because you're probably connected with many people in a variety of ways, Windows 8.1 gives you the ability to share content with others easily. Also, a Microsoft Account allows you to access your content from wherever you are.

If you've used File Explorer before, you'll find that it now includes a ribbon, with tools similar to those you might have used in a recent version of Microsoft Office.

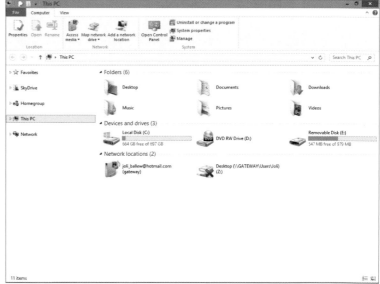

Using a touch-enabled system

In this book, I provide instructions based on traditional keyboard and mouse input methods. If you're using Windows 8.1 (or Windows RT) on a touch-enabled device, you might be giving commands by tapping with your finger or with a stylus. If so, substitute a tapping action any time I instruct you to click a user interface element. Also note that when I ask you to enter information in a text box or address window, you can do so by typing on a keyboard, tapping in the entry field under discussion to display and use the on-screen keyboard, or even speaking aloud, depending on your computer setup and your personal preferences.

Here's a brief introduction to touch gestures:

- Tap, which involves touching and releasing the screen, much like pressing a keyboard key with your finger. You tap to select buttons and options.

- Pinch, in which you slide your thumb and index finger together on the screen, usually to zoom in.

- Stretch, which involves spreading your thumb and index finger apart on the screen, usually to zoom out.

- Slide, in which you tap and hold down on something on the screen, drag to move it, and then release.

- Swipe, which consists of a quick finger drag and release, either across or up or down the screen. Swiping is often used for scrolling and selecting.

- Tap and hold, which involves tapping then holding briefly on an item, often to see a contextual menu. You might also use tap, hold, and release to show options such as the option to resize or uninstall a tile on the Start screen.

The final word

Your computer has become vital to your productivity and entertainment, so why shouldn't your computing experience be pleasant and fun? In this book, I try to offer short tasks to get you working with Windows 8.1 quickly and painlessly. I keep the technical terminology and explanations to a minimum, all within a visually appealing book that immediately connects you to what you see on screen. My goal is to get you less focused on the tool and more focused on what you can do with it to make your life simpler.

I hope you find the structure and design of this book easy to navigate and helpful as you get up to speed with all the wonderful new features in Windows 8.1.

Meet the Windows 8.1 interface

2

The first thing you'll notice when you power on your Windows 8.1-based computer is its new interface. You'll immediately see a lock screen and then a Start screen, both features now included as part of all Windows 8-based devices. The lock screen offers up-to-date information about new email, the time and date, and even your network status, and protects your computer from unauthorized access. When you bypass the lock screen, you'll see the Start screen, a brand-new look and approach to using your computer. The Start screen is simple and clean in appearance and offers tiles that represent the various apps installed on your computer.

In addition to the Start screen, there is also the traditional Windows desktop. The desktop provides the familiar computing experience, and opens when you need to run desktop apps including Paint, WordPad, Control Panel, Microsoft Office Word, PowerPoint, Excel, and so on. As with any other version of Windows, you can create shortcuts to files or applications on the desktop; use the taskbar to manage open windows and applications; install applications; and access the Recycle Bin. You can use File Explorer to manage your data and access your network too. And yes, there is a Start button, although it's a little different than what you might be used to. You'll learn about all of this and more here.

In this section:

- Starting Windows 8.1
- Exploring the Start screen
- Accessing Apps view
- Understanding tiles
- Using charms
- Overview of the desktop
- Using the Start button
- Overview of File Explorer
- Booting to Apps view
- Booting to the desktop
- Switching from a local account to a Microsoft account

Starting Windows 8.1

When you first turn on your computer (or laptop or tablet) or when your computer has gone to sleep after an interval of inactivity and you wake it up, you will see the lock screen. The lock screen displays a picture as well as other information such as date and time. You must bypass the lock screen and enter a password or PIN to get to the Start screen.

Start your computer and log on to Windows 8

1 Press the power button to start your computer.

2 Click once with the mouse, tap a key on the keyboard, or drag the bottom of the lock screen upward.

3 If multiple user accounts exist, click the user you want to log on as.

4 Enter your password or PIN.

> ✓ **TIP** The lock screen will likely appear after a certain interval of inactivity and also appears when you choose to lock your computer or put it to sleep manually. To lock your device quickly, use the keyboard combination Windows logo key+L.

Exploring the Start screen

The Start screen offers tiles you click to open apps. These apps let you do things like check the weather, read email, and get directions to a place. Beyond that, there is a scroll bar that appears along the bottom of the screen (when you position your cursor there) to let you access tiles that run off the screen on the right. There is a down-facing arrow there too; click this arrow to access all of the apps on your computer. There is an account settings button in the upper-right corner for changing

users or your account picture and for signing out or locking the device.

In addition, and hidden by default, are charms that you can display whenever you need them. One way to show the charms is to use the keyboard combination Windows key + C. Charms offer access to various settings and options. You'll learn a lot about charms in a few moments.

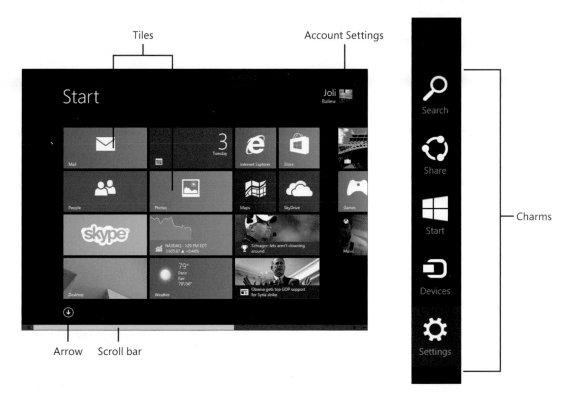

Tiles · Account Settings · Charms · Arrow · Scroll bar

Accessing Apps view

The Start screen holds certain tiles by default. You'll see Mail, Maps, SkyDrive, Games, Finance, and so on, and these apps come with Windows 8.1. You can personalize what is shown here and add and delete tiles, as you'll learn in Section 4. For now what's important is to understand that not every tile you have access to is shown on the Start screen. They just won't all fit there. To access the rest of the tiles and to see all of the apps installed on your computer, you need to access the Apps view.

3

Access all of your app tiles

1 If you are not on the Start screen, press the Windows key on your device or keyboard.

2 Move the cursor on the screen to invoke the down arrow.

3 Click the down arrow that appears.

4 Use the scroll bar to see all of the available tiles.

5 Click the up arrow to return to the Start screen.

5   4

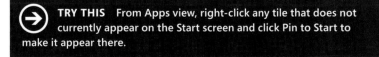

TRY THIS   From Apps view, right-click any tile that does not currently appear on the Start screen and click Pin to Start to make it appear there.

Understanding tiles

Tiles make apps available in a graphical way so that opening an app is intuitive. You don't have to locate an app in any kind of menu or list; you need only to find the tile and click it. If you own a touchscreen device, tiles are even more convenient because you can simply tap a tile to open an app.

Beyond convenience, some tiles offer up-to-date information that you might find helpful. These are called Live tiles. The News app can show breaking news, the Mail app can show the number of unread emails in your Inbox, and the Sports app can show the latest scores and news.

Pre-Installed Live Tiles   Tiles You've Added

Pre-Installed Tiles

TRY THIS A Live tile is a tile that shows changing information on the Start screen, such as the News tile flipping through headlines or the Mail tile showing a number representing the number of unread emails. Right-click a Live tile to turn this feature off.

Using charms

Charms allow you to access features that let you search, share, access the Start screen, view devices that are installed on your computer, and configure settings, among other things. Charms are hidden and can be accessed in a number of ways. For the most part, when you click a charm, you are taken to a subpanel on which you can access commonly used settings that are

relevant to the current view or open app. Here you'll explore the Settings charm. This charm always offers access to network settings, sound, brightness, the option to turn off notifications temporarily, options to power down your device, and to access an on-screen keyboard no matter from where you access it.

Display and use charms

1 Press Windows logo key+C to display the charms.

2 Click Settings.

3 Click the sound icon.

4 Move the slider to increase or decrease the volume.

5 Click Power to see the options.

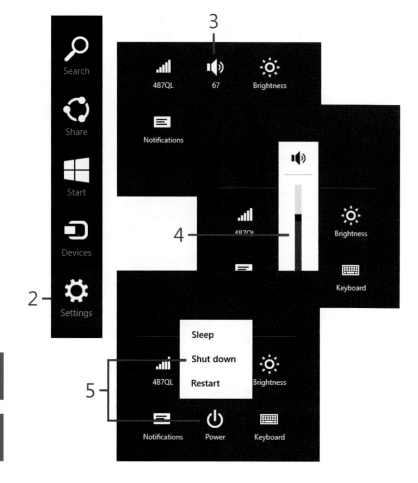

TIP To hide the charms (if they don't go away on their own after performing a task), click outside of the charms list.

TIP To get to the Settings charm quickly, use the keyboard combination Windows Logo key + I.

Overview of the desktop

The Windows 8.1 desktop opens automatically when you opt to use desktop apps such as Paint, WordPad, Control Panel, Task Manager, the Command Prompt, and third-party applications you've installed from CDs, DVDs, and the Internet. Although you can open these types of apps from the Start screen, they open on the desktop because they are desktop apps. You can also open the desktop from the Desktop tile that is available on the Start screen.

The Windows 8.1 desktop has many features you will be familiar with if you've used previous versions of Windows, such as the desktop background, desktop shortcuts, the Recycle Bin, and the taskbar. You can also access the new Start button, the Notification area, and File Explorer.

Recycle Bin

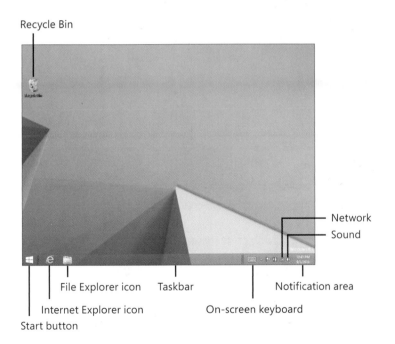

Network
Sound

File Explorer icon   Taskbar   Notification area

Internet Explorer icon   On-screen keyboard

Start button

Desktop tile

Using the Start button

The desktop offers a Start button that, when clicked, takes you back to the Start screen. This behavior is different than what you might be used to. You don't click the Start button to access a list of programs anymore. However, you can right-click the Start button to gain access to areas of your computer that you might need, including the option to shut down your computer, access Control Panel, to open Device Manager, and so on.

Use the Start button

1 Press Windows logo key+D to open the desktop.

2 Right-click the Start button to view Shut Down or Sign Out and other options.

3 Click outside the menu to close it.

4 Click the Start button once to return to the Start screen.

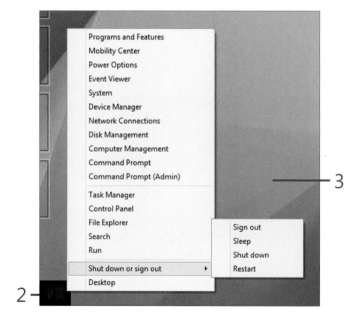

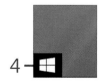

> **TRY THIS** Position your cursor over the bottom left corner of the Start button, and then slowly move the cursor upward. A sidebar appears that holds thumbnails for your other open apps. Click any thumbnail to go there.

Overview of File Explorer

File Explorer opens on the desktop. It will look familiar if you've used another version of Windows. File Explorer gives you access to all the drives of your computer, including your hard drive, DVD drive, and external and USB drives. File Explorer is also the best way to manage the data you store on these drives, and makes it easy to create folders and subfolders, copy and move data,

access data on a network, and manage files you keep online, in SkyDrive. You can even "map" a network drive so that you can access the data on it as if it were actually stored on your own PC. To access File Explorer, press Windows logo key+E. You can also click the file folder icon on the desktop's taskbar. (See Section 18, "Managing data," for more about using File Explorer.)

Ribbon   Search

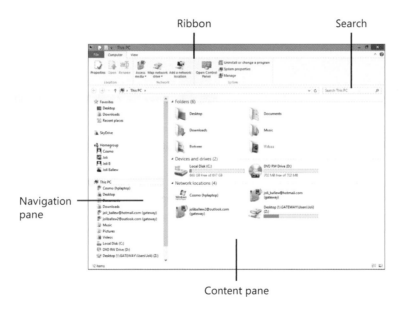

Navigation pane

Content pane

> **TRY THIS** Click This PC in the Navigation pane, and then double-click the Pictures folder. If you have pictures on your computer, this is where they are likely stored. Click the Back arrow to return to the previous screen.

Booting to the Apps view

By default, when you power on your computer, unlock it, or wake it from sleep, the Start screen appears. This might be fine with you, or you might want to go directly to the Apps view instead. The Apps view offers access to all of the tiles available on your computer, which might be preferable.

Set up to show Apps view instead of the Start screen

1 Press Windows logo key+D to open the desktop.

2 Right-click the taskbar and click Properties.

3 Click the Navigation tab.

4 Select Show The Apps View Automatically When I Go to Start.

5 Click OK.

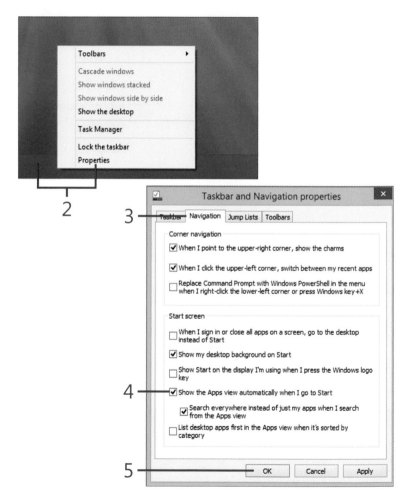

> ⚠ **CAUTION** If you select the option to Show The Apps View Automatically When I Go to Start, anytime you try to access the Start screen using any method, the Apps view will appear instead.

Booting to the desktop

By default, when you power on your computer, unlock it, or wake it from sleep, the Start screen appears. This might be fine with you, or you might want to go directly to the traditional desktop instead. This is fine and won't cause any problems; you can always access the Start screen by clicking the Start button that appears on the desktop.

Set up to boot directly to the desktop

1 Press Windows logo key+D to open the desktop.

2 Right-click the taskbar and click Properties.

3 Click the Navigation tab.

4 Select When I Sign In or Close All Apps on a Screen, Go to the Desktop Instead of Start.

5 Click OK.

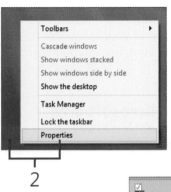

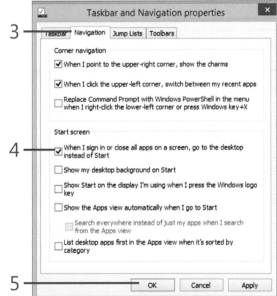

TIP If you use a tablet or small laptop, it's probably best not to configure the setting to boot directly to the desktop. The Start screen and related apps are better viewed on small screens than traditional applications and the desktop.

Switching from a local to a Microsoft Live account

There are two common ways to log on to a Windows 8.1 device. You can use a local account or a Microsoft account. A Microsoft account is preferred. When you use a Microsoft account, certain information about you and your preferences is stored on the Internet, and when you log on to any Windows 8-based computer with that account, your settings and relevant data are synced, meaning that the look and feel of your computer follows you everywhere. A Microsoft account also enables you to store data in the cloud, on SkyDrive, and use apps like Calendar and the Windows Store, among others. You can't do any of these things with a local account. If you use a local account, switch now to a Microsoft account.

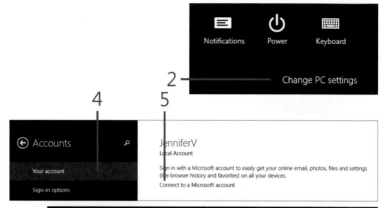

Set up to log on by using Microsoft Live

1 Press Windows logo key+I.

2 Click Change PC Settings.

3 Click Accounts (not shown).

4 Click Your Account.

5 Click Connect To A Microsoft Account.

6 Type your current password, and click Next (not shown).

7 Enter your username and password.

8 Click Next and enter any final configuration options as prompted.

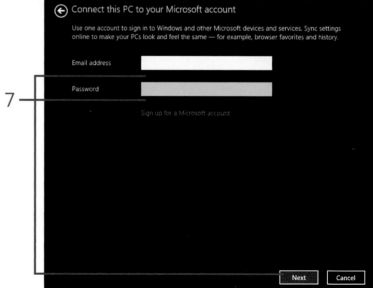

> **TIP** If you don't yet have a Microsoft account, you can obtain one during this process by clicking the Sign Up For A Microsoft Account link.

> **TIP** In most instances, you should opt to use a Microsoft account instead of a local account. You'll need a Microsoft account to use many of the apps effectively, to sync settings, and to store data online in SkyDrive easily.

Providing input

3

There are many ways to input data into and interact with a computer. The most common are to use a mouse and keyboard. Windows 8.1 is no different; all of the mouse and keyboard techniques you already know will work here too. So, there's no reason to worry if your computer screen or device isn't touch-compatible, and there's nothing new to learn about input methods, except perhaps, a few keyboard combinations that you might not be familiar with. (One to commit to memory is pressing the Windows logo key + C to bring up the hidden charms that you can use to make changes to how your computer works.) As you read through this chapter, understand from the start that all of the ways you've interacted with a computer before are still available, and that touch is not a requirement for Windows 8.1.

If you do have a touch-capable device though, Windows 8.1 offers novel ways to interact with your computer. If you have compatible hardware, you can use touch techniques such as tapping, swiping, pinching, flicking, dragging, and tapping and holding to get things done and to move around in Windows 8.1. Each of these touch options has a mouse and/or keyboard counterpart, and you can mix and match techniques as desired.

In this section:

- Comparing input options
- Using touch to get things done
- Swiping edges
- Zooming in and out
- Snapping apps
- Using a touchscreen keyboard
- Displaying charms
- Using keystroke shortcuts
- Right-clicking and the long tap
- Displaying and managing recently viewed apps

Understanding input options

As noted in the Introduction, you can perform common computing tasks by using a keyboard and/or mouse, or by using a compatible touch technique. You don't need a touch-compatible device, just as you don't need a keyboard and mouse to use

Windows 8.1. To understand how this works, here you'll open the Search charm and resulting Search window by using three different methods.

Explore the three most common input methods

1 To use a mouse:

  a Position your cursor in the top or bottom right corner of the screen.

  b When the charms appear, move the cursor upward.

  c Click the Search charm.

2 To use a physical keyboard, press Windows logo key+Q.

3 To use touch:

  a Position your thumb or finger in the middle of the right side of the screen.

  b Touch the monitor and flick inward.

  c Tap the Search box.

  d Use the Search box to type what you're looking for.

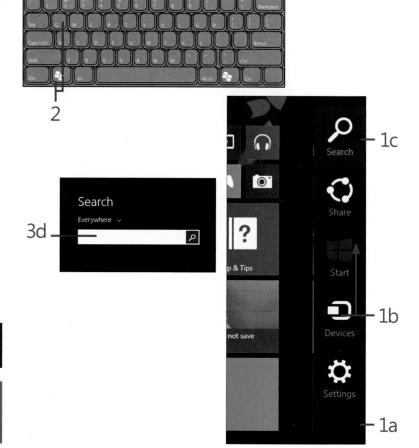

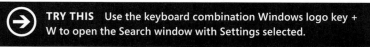

> **TRY THIS** Use the keyboard combination Windows logo key + W to open the Search window with Settings selected.

> **TIP** In the Search box, note the arrow by Everywhere. Click that arrow to narrow your search by selecting Settings, Files, Web images, or Web videos instead.

Overview of touchscreen gestures

With a touchscreen device, you use your finger to tap buttons, tiles, or other objects; to swipe to display toolbars or scroll through a document or a webpage (also called a flick); and to pinch to zoom in or out. Sometimes you can tap and hold, a technique that might produce what you'd get with a right-click of a mouse. You'll learn more about these techniques in this chapter, but this overview will help you get started.

Use touch to get things done

1 With the Start screen displayed, tap a tile such as Maps.

2 Swipe from the right side of the screen inward to show the charms.

3 Tap the Start charm to return to the Start screen.

(continued on next page)

> **TRY THIS** At the Start screen, tap, hold, and release any tile to see options such as Resize and Pin to Start.

Use touch to get things done *(continued)*

4 Tap another tile, such as Finance.

5 Swipe from the top of the screen downward to hide the app and go back to the Start screen.

6 From the Start screen, spread apart two fingers, place them on the screen, and pull them together to zoom out to see more tiles.

7 With the tiles minimized, put two fingers together, put them on the screen, and pull outward to return the tiles to their original size.

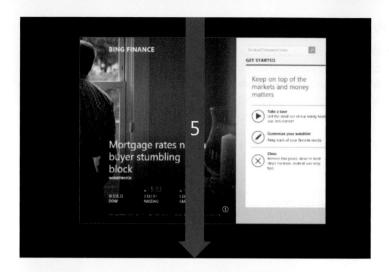

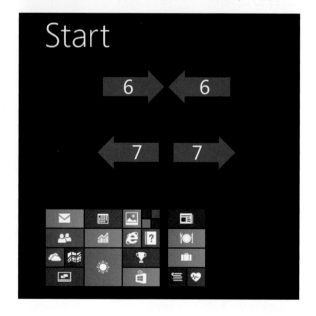

Swiping edges

In Windows 8.1, you can swipe from the edges of the screen to cause certain things to happen. You can swipe in from the right edge to display charms, which give you access to various settings and access to the Start screen; you can swipe in from the left to switch to a previously used app; you can swipe down from the top of the screen to close an app. Often you can swipe up from the bottom to show an app's toolbar(s).

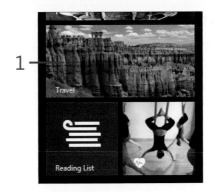

Swipe the screen

1 Tap the Travel app tile on the Start screen.

2 Swipe up from the bottom to display the Travel toolbars.

3 Tap the Windows key to return to the Start screen. A touch-only device will have a physical Windows button on it.

4 Tap the Maps app tile on the Start screen.

5 Swipe in from the left to access the previously used app.

6 Swipe down from the top to hide the app.

> ✓ **TIP** You can use your mouse to click tiles and to drag an app downward to hide it. To display charms, you simply move your mouse to the upper-right or lower-right corner without clicking. In many apps, you can display toolbars by simply right-clicking.

> ✓ **TIP** Swiping is sometimes referred to as flicking.

Zooming in and out of the display

You can use your fingers to zoom in and out while using certain apps, such as data displayed on a webpage in Internet Explorer, or a location you've found in Maps. You can even zoom out on the tiles on the Start screen. To zoom, you use a pinching motion with at least two fingers.

Zooming in or out

1 Open the Maps app.

2 With the Maps app displayed, position your thumb and forefinger apart, place them on the screen, and pinch them toward each other to zoom out.

3 Put your thumb and forefinger together, place them both on the screen, and pinch them away from each other to zoom back in.

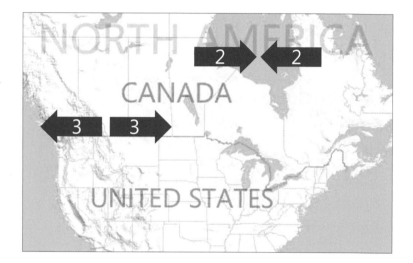

 TRY THIS Practice this pinching motion on the Start screen and in the Internet Explorer app.

Snapping apps

Snapping apps helps you to organize more than one app on your screen to view their contents side by side. Depending on your hardware, you can snap up to four apps at once.

Snap an app

1 From the Start screen, tap the Weather tile.

2 Tap the Windows key to return to the Start screen.

3 From the Start screen, tap the Sports tile.

4 Position your mouse in the top-left corner of the screen, move the cursor downward, and click and drag the desired app into place.

5 When the app is in position to take up half of the screen, let go.

6 To snap apps with your finger, flick in from the left side, somewhat slowly, and let go when the app is close to halfway on the screen.

> ⚠ **CAUTION** To snap apps, your screen resolution must be set to 1366x768 or higher. The higher the resolution, the more apps you can snap (up to four).

Using a touchscreen keyboard

If you have a touch-only device, you'll have to get comfortable with the touch keyboard quickly. A touch keyboard will appear when you tap inside a box, window, or other item that allows text to be input. For the most part, the touch keyboard works like a regular keyboard, complete with a Shift key, Ctrl key, and

an Enter key. While this keyboard opens by default on touch-only devices when needed, there is a keyboard available from the desktop as well. If you need to enter text by using touch and no touch keyboard appears, you can access one here.

Use the touch keyboard

1 From the Start screen, begin typing **WordPad**.

2 Tap the WordPad app in the search results.

3 Tap the keyboard button on the taskbar.

4 Tap keys to enter a word.

5 Tap the Symbol/Number key.

6 Tap keys to enter punctuation or numbers.

7 Tap the Symbol/Number key again to display the letter keyboard.

8 Tap the Expand/Shrink button to expand the keyboard.

9 Tap the Close key to hide the keyboard.

> ✓ **TIP** While using the touch keyboard, note that the qwerty and uiop keys have a number on them as well as a letter. To input the related number, quickly swipe up on its key. For example, you swipe up on the Q key to input the number 1.

> ✓ **TIP** If you want a keyboard to appear on the Start screen, access the Settings charm from the Start screen. Then click Keyboard, and click Touch Keyboard And Handwriting Panel.

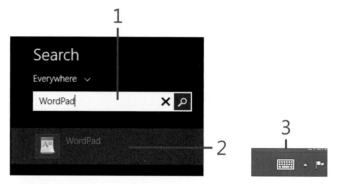

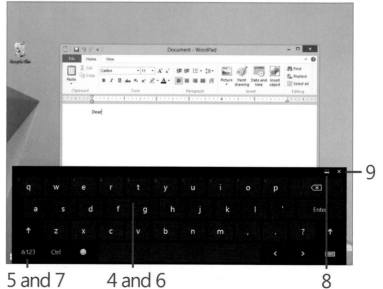

5 and 7   4 and 6   8

Displaying charms

Charms are buttons for accessing common device settings. For example, there is a charm (named Start) that displays the Start screen, as well as one (named Search) that displays the Search feature. You can use the Settings charm to change system volume, put your device to sleep or turn it off, and connect to a network, among other things. You can display the charms by using your mouse, keyboard, or touchscreen.

Display charms

You can display the charms by using any of the following three techniques:

- Swipe your finger inward from the right edge of the screen.

- Press Windows logo key+C on your keyboard.

- Move your mouse to the upper-right or lower-right corner of the screen.

 TIP You can display the charms from both the desktop and the Start screen by using any of these methods.

Using keystroke shortcuts

If you don't have a touch-capable computer or device, there's no reason to worry. Your physical keyboard also provides a great way to get things done with keystroke shortcuts. This involves pressing one key and then, while holding down that key, pressing another key. By using these special keystroke combinations, you can access the Search feature, move from one open app to another, display the charms, and much more.

Examples of keystroke shortcuts

- Press the Windows logo key to display the Start screen.

- Press Windows logo key+C to display the charms.

- Press Windows logo key+Q to display the Search feature for apps.

- Press Windows logo key+R to go to the desktop, and enter a program or file name to run.

- Press the Windows logo key to return to the Start screen.

- Press Windows logo key+Tab to display recently used apps.

Windows
logo key

 SEE ALSO See Appendix B, "Keyboard shortcuts," for a more complete listing of useful keystroke shortcuts.

Right-clicking and the long tap

Right-clicking has traditionally been a way to display command menus that are contextually relevant to where you click. For example, if you right-click selected text in a Word document, you can see commands such as Cut and Copy. If you right-click an empty area of the desktop, you'll see options, including one to change the screen resolution. You can perform a long tap (tap and hold) to get the same results. In Windows 8.1, there are new right-click and long tap features. For example, you can use a similar technique on a tile on the Start screen to access options to resize an app tile, change how the tile looks, or to add or remove it from the Start screen.

Use right-click

1 On the Start screen, right-click or tap, hold, and release (this may take some practice) the Weather tile to display the related options.

2 Right-click or tap the tile again to deselect it.

3 Click or tap outside the app to return to the Start screen.

4 Click or tap the Desktop tile.

5 Right click or tap, hold, and release an empty area of the desktop.

6 Click or tap outside of the resulting menu to return to the desktop.

TRY THIS While in any app, right-click to see its toolbar. While on a webpage, right-click to see a contextual menu that includes options to copy what's on the page, open a link, or save a picture, among other things.

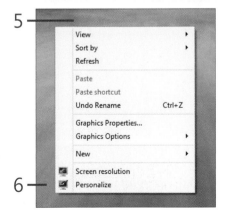

Finding recently viewed apps

In Windows 8.1, you might not close apps that often. You will likely open apps and then return to the Start screen or search for another app or file to open, leaving multiple apps open at one time. When you do this, you can display all open apps in a list and jump back to one easily. By moving your mouse to the upper-left edge of the screen, you can go to the most recently opened app quickly. You can also right-click any thumbnail to close the app, or to snap it right or left.

View, open, and manage recent apps

1 From the Start screen, open multiple apps.

2 Move your mouse to the upper-left corner of the screen.

3 Slide your mouse down the left edge of the screen.

4 Click a thumbnail to go to a recently viewed app.

5 Repeat steps 1–3.

6 Right-click any thumbnail to close an app or to insert it (snap it) when you have another app already snapped.

> ✓ **TIP** Currently open desktop apps like Paint and WordPad are displayed on the taskbar in the desktop. You can click the icon on the taskbar to maximize it.

Managing a
computing session

4

The most common Windows 8.1 settings are available from the Settings charm, which provides tools for managing a computing session effectively. You can change the brightness of the screen, increase or decrease the volume, and power down the device, among other things. The main purpose of the Settings charm then, is to offer a quick and easy way to access these common configurations that you will need in most computing sessions.

In this section:

- Exploring the Settings charm
- Controlling volume
- Adjusting brightness
- Changing the time zone
- Managing power
- Displaying a keyboard
- Connecting to a network

Exploring the Settings charm

The most commonly used session-related settings for Windows can be reached from the charms, which you can display along the right edge of any screen. Clicking the Settings charm displays a group of commonly used settings that include volume and brightness, among other things.

Explore the Settings charm

1 Press the Windows logo key+C to display the charms.

2 Click the Settings charm.

3 Note the options listed at the bottom of the Settings pane (listed in the table below in order from top-left to bottom-right).

Settings charms

Charm	Results
Network	Displays a list of available networks; lets you connect and disconnect from networks.
Sound	Displays a slider for increasing and decreasing volume. You can also mute sound quickly.
Brightness	Displays a slider to adjust screen brightness.
Notifications	Offers settings for hiding notifications for 8 hours, 3 hours, or 1 hour.
Power	Displays three commands: Sleep, Shut Down, Restart.
Keyboard	Offers settings for language and displaying a touch keyboard.

> **TRY THIS** Try the Windows logo key + I to open the Settings charm by using the keyboard. Flick in from the right-side of the screen on a touch-compatible device to access all of the charms.

Controlling volume

Some individual desktop apps, such as Music, have their own volume controls. However, the Windows system volume is a master control. If you set the system volume to 50 percent, app volume controls can't make the volume any louder than that. Setting an app volume to 80 percent would mean that it's playing at 80 percent of the Windows system volume setting. It's quite common to want to adjust the system volume or mute sound entirely, which you can do by using the Volume slider.

Adjust system volume

1 Press Windows logo key+I.

2 Click the Volume button; it will likely have a number on it to denote the current setting.

3 Click and drag the slider to raise or lower volume.

4 Click the volume icon at the top of the slider to mute the volume.

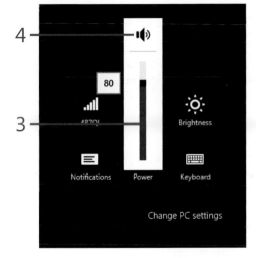

> ✓ **TIP** When the master volume is high, so are the system sounds, such as the sound that plays when a new email arrives. You can lower the system sounds to minimize the impact of those sounds while listening to music or playing a movie at a high volume. To do this, open the desktop, click the volume icon on the taskbar, and click Mixer. Move the slider for System Sounds as desired.

Adjusting brightness

There are many reasons why you might need to adjust the brightness of your display. You might want to lower it while reading an e-book or raise it while working indoors in a dark room. While running a device like a laptop or tablet on battery power, you can lower the brightness to lengthen battery life. You might need to reconfigure brightness settings when you move from one environment to another, such as from an office or cubicle to a taxi, train, or subway.

Set brightness

1 Press Windows logo key+I.

2 Click the Brightness button.

3 Click and drag the slider to increase or decrease brightness.

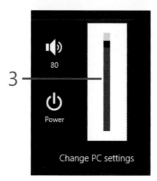

> **→** **TRY THIS** If you have a laptop, look for keys on the keyboard that have the Brightness icon on them. Some keyboards offer this on the navigation arrows that are located on the right side of the keyboard, near the bottom, while others offer this on the Function keys that run across the top.

Changing the time and date

Your computer uses a specific time zone to display clocks on the desktop's taskbar, set calendar applications to the correct date, run scheduled maintenance tasks, and so on. The time zone you select (or the time zone your computer has selected for you) keeps track of the time automatically. Depending on the device you use, the settings you've configured, and whether or not location services are enabled, the time might update on its own when you travel to different time zones. However, no matter what the settings, often the correct time is required for certain apps to work properly (or work at all), so it's important to know how to change the time zone when applicable.

Change the time zone

1 Press Windows logo key+I.

2 Click Change PC Settings.

3 If you see a back arrow, click it. Click Time and Language (not shown).

4 From the Date and Time tab, choose the correct time zone from the Time Zone field.

5 If desired, turn on or leave on the option to adjust for daylight savings time automatically.

6 Ensure that Set Time Automatically is enabled.

> ⚠️ **CAUTION**   To change the date and time, you must be logged on with an Administrator account. Even then, you must turn off the option to set the time automatically before you click Change, if you want to access the options to pick a new date and time.

> ✓ **TIP**   You can configure multiple clocks on the desktop's taskbar. To do this, click the time and date in the Notification area, click Change Date And Time Settings, and click the Additional Clocks tab.

> ⚠️ **CAUTION**   If you see a Back arrow when you open PC Settings, click it. That will return you to the PC Settings home page.

Managing power

Windows puts your computer to sleep after a specific amount of idle time, which saves battery power if you have a laptop or tablet and conserves energy if you are connected to a power outlet. While the computer is asleep, a black screen hides your work until you wake it. Sleep is a power option.

There are two other power options. You can restart your computer, which you'll need to do when you install or run certain apps or need to put certain changes into effect. You can also shut your computer down, for example, if you need to move your desktop computer to a new location or if you won't be using your computer for a while.

Put to sleep, shut down, or restart your computer

1 Press Windows logo key+I.

2 Click the Power button.

3 Click the Sleep, Shut Down, or Restart command, depending on what you want to do.

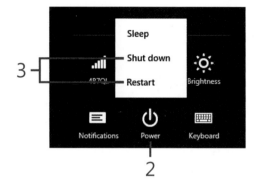

TRY THIS Right-click the Start button from any screen, and point to Shut Down or Sign Out. Then, click Sign Out, Sleep, Shut Down, or Restart as desired.

Displaying a touch keyboard

If you have a touch device, you'll need access to the touch keyboard. You can find this from the Settings charm. You can tap the virtual keys to type. This keyboard also offers a handwriting panel, which allows you to enter text by "writing" with your mouse, finger, or a stylus.

Display the keyboard and handwriting panel

1 Press Windows logo key+I.

2 Click Keyboard.

3 Click Touch Keyboard And Handwriting Panel.

4 Click the keyboard icon to switch to another format.

5 Click the Handwriting Panel icon.

6 Click or tap to write something in the resulting handwriting panel.

7 Click the Hide button to hide the keyboard.

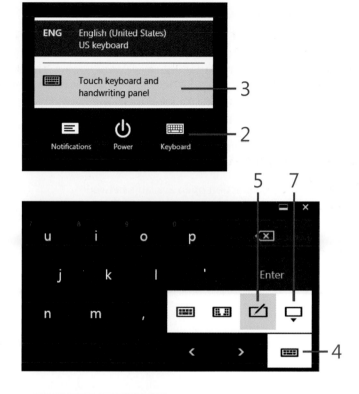

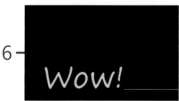

> ✓ **TIP** Use the keyboard format setting to display a split screen. This style of screen makes it easier to type on a smaller device such as a Windows 8.1 tablet, where you might use both your thumbs to hit keys on different edges of the screen.

Connecting to a network

A network is a group of computers. There are public networks and private networks. For the most part, networks are used to share data, resources, and/or an Internet connection. At home and in the office, you'll connect to a private network. At libraries and coffee shops, you'll connect to a public one. The Settings charm offers a way to connect to networks easily.

Connect or disconnect from a network

1 Press Windows logo key+I.

2 Click the Network button.

3 Click a network connection or an available network.

4 If you aren't connected, click the Connect button.

5 As applicable, type any passcode or passkey; choose what to share on the network when prompted.

> ⚠️ **CAUTION** You won't be able to connect to a private network without the password, sometimes called a passkey. You will probably be able to connect to public networks without a key, although on occasion a key will be required. You might also have to access a webpage and accept terms of use before you can join.

Customizing the appearance of Windows

5

There are many ways to customize your computer to make it uniquely yours. To name a few, you can change the color and background of the Start screen and rearrange the tiles; you can change the picture on the lock screen and customize the notifications you see there; and you can apply a theme to the desktop. If you log in with a Microsoft Account, those changes will, by default, follow you from computer to computer.

Almost all of the personalization options are either available from PC Settings or Control Panel, so there's no need to cover every option available. In this chapter, you'll explore only a few. This will allow you to make additional changes to customize your computer to meet your every need, simply by exploring the other options available to you from these two areas of Windows 8.1.

In this section:

- Pinning an app
- Unpinning an app
- Changing a tile's size
- Repositioning tiles on the Start screen
- Applying a new Start screen background
- Choosing a lock screen image
- Choosing lock screen apps
- Selecting an account picture
- Creating a desktop shortcut
- Changing the desktop's theme
- Selecting a desktop background
- Changing the screen resolution

Customizing the Start screen

The Start screen is your new home screen in Windows 8.1. The Start screen contains tiles that represent installed apps such as SkyDrive, Photos, and Maps. You can also pin tiles for individual items such as contacts, pictures, links to webpages, and so on. Here you'll learn how to pin an app.

Pin an app

1 From the Start screen, move the cursor to show the down arrow.

2 Click the arrow that appears.

3 Locate a tile that isn't currently on the Start screen that you'd like to have there, and right-click it.

4 If desired, right-click additional tiles to select them too.

5 Click Pin To Start.

> ✓ **TIP**   When you install apps from the Windows Store, they do not appear on the Start screen by default. If you want them there, repeat these steps to add them.

> ✓ **TIP**   If you select a tile to add to the Start screen and try to pin it, but the tile already appears there, Unpin from Start and Find in Start are available instead of Pin to Start.

Unpin an app

1 Display the Start screen by pressing the Windows logo key.

2 Right-click a pinned app.

3 Click Unpin From Start.

✓ **TIP** You can unpin multiple apps at once using this method. To do this, in step 2, right-click additional app tiles before performing step 3.

✓ **TIP** You can pin a desktop app to the desktop taskbar by right-clicking it and choosing Pin To Taskbar. To unpin the app, right-click it on the taskbar, and in the menu that appears, choose Unpin This Program From Taskbar. This works only for desktop apps, not apps like Maps, Weather, SkyDrive, and so on.

Modifying tiles on the Start screen

Tiles on the Start screen come in different sizes by default. Some are larger, and others are smaller. You might want to make tiles you use most often larger and tiles you use less often smaller.

Change a tile's size

1 Right-click a tile.

2 Click Resize.

3 Click the desired size.

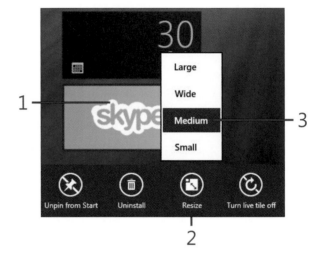

 TIP When you make smaller tiles larger, more information can be shown on the tile. The logo on the tile may change too.

 TIP If you like to keep a lot of tiles on the Start screen, consider reducing the size of most of them so that you don't have to scroll as much to find what you need.

Reposition tiles on the Start screen

You can reposition tiles on the Start screen. You can move your most used tiles to the far left so that you won't have to scroll to find them, and you can move tiles you use less often to the far right so that they are out of the way, yet still easily available.

1 Display the Start screen.

2 Click a tile, and drag it to a new location.

3 Release your mouse button.

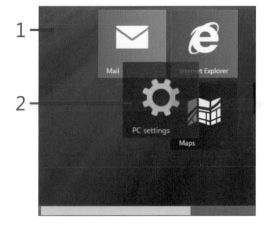

TIP PC Settings, shown in this image, isn't on the Start screen by default. To add it there, on the Start screen type PC Settings, and in the results right-click PC Settings and click Pin to Start.

TRY THIS! After you have used Windows 8.1 for a while, take inventory of the apps that are represented by tiles on the Start screen. Decide which you never use, and unpin them from the Start screen. Locate apps you've acquired that you use often, and pin them to the Start screen. Move the tiles around so that the information or apps you need every day appear to the far left and you don't have to scroll to find them.

Changing the Start screen background

You can change the look of the Start screen background. You can choose a new design and a new color scheme, and you can even use the background you've selected for your desktop. You access the options from the Settings charm.

Apply a new Start screen background

1 From the Start screen, press Windows logo key+C.

2 Click Settings.

3 Click Personalize.

4 As desired:

   a Click a design.

   b Click a new background color.

   c Click a new accent color.

   d Click the desktop background (the last tile in the design list)

> **TIP** When you change the background color, the color that appears in the Personalize window changes to match it, as does the background you'll see when you open other items, such as PC Settings.

> ⚠ **CAUTION** If you access the Settings charm while on the desktop instead of from the Start screen as detailed here, you won't see the Personalize option. Instead you'll see Personalization. If you click Personalization, the Control Panel will open instead of the Personalize options you see here.

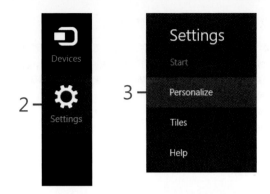

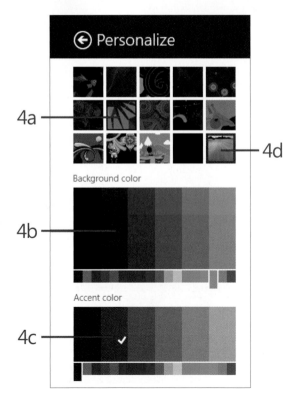

Personalizing the lock screen background

The lock screen appears when you first start your computer, when you lock your computer, or when your computer goes to sleep after a period of inactivity and you wake it back up. You can personalize this screen in few ways. This screen displays a background image that you can switch to another standard Windows lock screen image, or you can use an image of your own. You can also choose what notifications to display on the lock screen, such as the time, date, and weather. You can also change the image that appears with each user name, using your own image or another picture of your choosing.

Choose a lock screen image

1 Press Windows logo key+C.

2 Click Settings.

3 Click Change PC Settings.

4 Click any Back arrows, should they appear.

5 From the PC Settings screen, click PC And Devices. Lock Screen will be selected.

6 Click a picture.

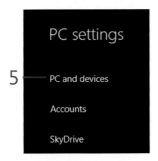

> **TRY THIS** If you want to use your own picture for your lock screen image, click the Browse button in step 6, locate the picture you want to use, and then click Choose Picture.

Setting up lock screen apps

By default, Windows 8.1 displays (on the lock screen) the date and time, notifications of any new email from the Mail app, and other information, including your network connection status. You can remove these or add your own.

Choose lock screen apps

1 Press Windows logo key+C.

2 Click Settings.

3 Click Change PC Settings.

4 Click any Back arrows, should they appear.

5 From the PC Settings screen, click PC And Devices. Lock Screen will be selected.

6 Locate Lock Screen Apps.

7 To stop showing a notification for an app, click its tile and choose Don't Show Quick Status Here.

8 To show a notification for an app that isn't configured, click the + sign.

9 Click the app to show.

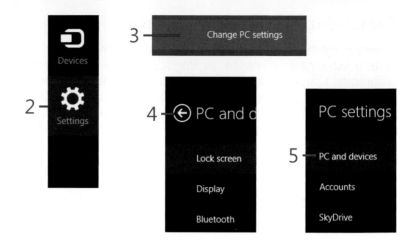

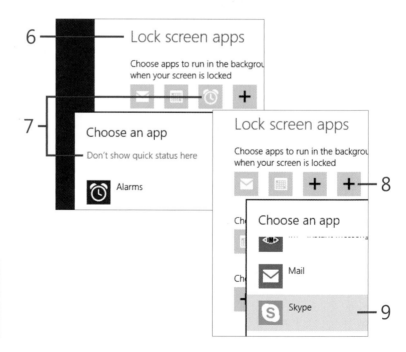

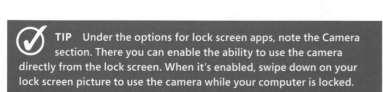

TIP   Under the options for lock screen apps, note the Camera section. There you can enable the ability to use the camera directly from the lock screen. When it's enabled, swipe down on your lock screen picture to use the camera while your computer is locked.

Modifying the account picture

After you bypass the lock screen, you are presented with a picture and password field for any logged in user or, if nobody is currently logged in, for all users. If you assign a picture to a user account, that image will be displayed instead of the default silhouette. Adding a picture for each account is a nice way to personalize Windows and quickly find your own account in a group of users.

Select an account picture

1 From the Start screen, click your account name.

2 Click Change Account Picture.

3 Click Browse. Note that you might already have an account picture applied.

(continued on next page)

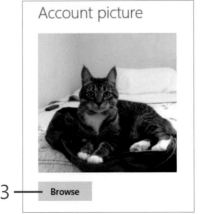

Account picture

TIP Note the options to lock your computer, sign out, and possibly switch users when you click your account name on the Start screen.

Select an account picture *(continued)*

4 As applicable, click a folder or subfolder to locate the picture to use.

5 Click an image.

6 Click Choose Image.

TIP While in the Accounts settings, note the other two tabs: Sign-In Options and Other Accounts. Explore these features if time allows.

TRY THIS While at the main PC Settings screen, note the search icon. It looks like a magnifying glass. Click it to search for a specific option or setting in PC Settings instead of browsing the tabs.

Putting shortcuts on the desktop

You can place shortcuts on the desktop to access frequently used documents or applications. This is the desktop equivalent of pinning tiles to the Start screen. After you create a shortcut, you simply double-click the shortcut to open a document or app. Shortcuts will have arrows on their icons.

Create a desktop shortcut

1 From the Start screen, move your mouse cursor and click the down arrow that appears.

2 Click File Explorer.

3 Locate the folder, document, or application you want to create a shortcut for.

4 Right-click the item, and choose Send To from the menu that appears.

5 Click Desktop (Create Shortcut).

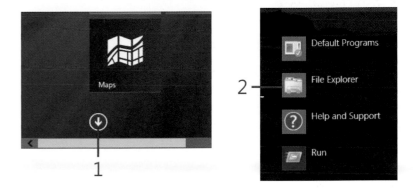

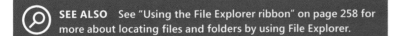

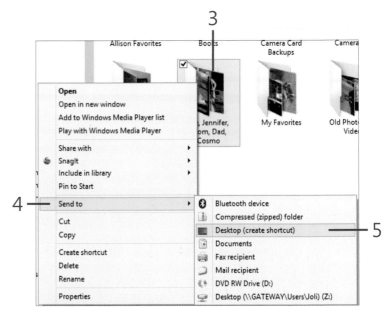

> **TIP** To delete a shortcut, right-click it and choose Delete. To rename a shortcut, right-click and choose Rename.

> **SEE ALSO** See "Using the File Explorer ribbon" on page 258 for more about locating files and folders by using File Explorer.

Choosing a desktop theme

The appearance of the desktop is a bit more customizable than the Start screen, allowing you to select preset themes or even save your own themes based on your choice of background and color. Themes apply several personalization settings at once, which means you can change almost every aspect of your desktop experience with only a few clicks of the mouse.

Change the desktop's theme

1 Use the keyboard combination Windows Logo key + D to display the desktop.

2 Right-click the desktop, and choose Personalize.

3 Click a theme to apply.

4 Click the Close button.

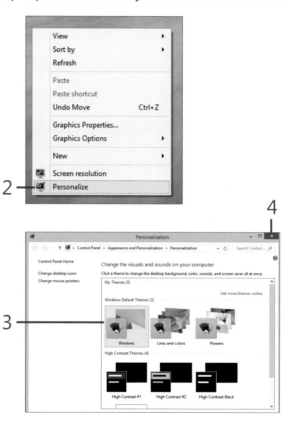

TIP You can get more themes on the Internet. With the Personalization window shown in step 3 displayed, click Get More Themes Online. A webpage opens in your browser. Use the theme categories or search feature to find a theme you like, and then click Save to download and save the theme. The theme will be available through the Personalization window of the Control Panel.

TIP You can save your own themes. Under the category of My Themes, whatever theme you are using, including any changes you have made to it, appears as Unsaved Theme. If you want to save that theme, click it and then click Save Theme. In the dialog box that appears, give the theme a name and then click Save.

Changing the desktop background

You can choose your own background for your desktop to give it a more personalized look. Windows provides some attractive pictures along with the alternative option to use a solid color for your background, or you can use any image or photo you have available in your Pictures library.

Select a desktop background

1 Use the keyboard combination Windows Logo key + D to display the desktop.

2 Right-click the desktop, and choose Personalize from the menu that appears.

3 Click Desktop Background.

4 Click Clear All if pictures are already selected due to an applied theme.

5 Click any image to apply it, or click the Picture Location drop-down list and choose from categories such as Solid Colors or your Pictures Library. Select a picture.

6 When you locate a background you like, click Save Changes.

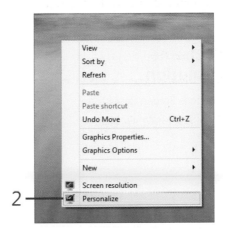

> (→) **TRY THIS** In the desktop background options, select multiple images. Then, click the option under Change picture every: and choose a setting. This lets you create a slide show on your desktop of your favorite pictures.

> (Q) **SEE ALSO** Section 13 provides information about working with photos and how to find and save photos on your computer.

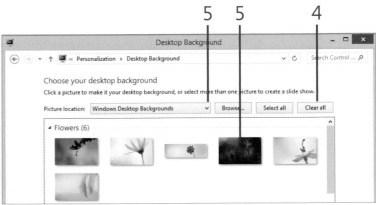

Adjusting screen resolution

Modern screens should be set to their native resolutions for best results. You can use the steps here to see how your monitor's resolution is currently configured. Note that higher resolutions make the overall screen elements smaller, while lower resolutions make them bigger.

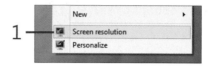

Change the screen resolution

1 Right-click the desktop, and choose Screen Resolution.

2 From the Resolution drop-down list, select the desired resolution.

3 Click OK.

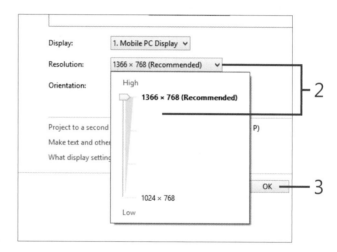

> ✓ **TIP** The higher the resolution setting, the crisper the image on your screen. However, some resolutions can distort the proportions of your screen so that items appear out of perspective. Also, not all monitors support the highest resolutions.

> ⚠ **CAUTION** Your screen resolution must be at least 1366×768 to show multiple apps on the screen at once. At 1366×768, you can snap two; at higher resolutions, up to four.

Searching for anything

6

The Integrated Search feature of Windows 8.1 is one of its most power-ful features. *Integrated* refers to the ability of Windows 8.1 to search not only your computer but also the Internet to offer a wide variety of results. Initiating a search is simple, too; you need only to type a search term (or terms) at the Start screen and browse the results offered. From the results pane you can access sorting options that help you narrow what is shown.

Beyond simple searches for data or web results, you can locate Windows administrative tools and Windows settings; data related to specific emails; photo files, and music files; and even data acquired using a specific app (like finding the nearby library while using the Maps app). You can also customize the search settings and clear your search history.

In this section:

- Searching from the Start screen
- Searching for files
- Searching for web images
- Using the Search charm
- Searching for Windows settings
- Customizing search
- Searching inside an app

Searching from the Start screen

Searching in Windows 8.1 is the most intuitive way to search you've ever experienced. You simply begin typing, and search results appear. The more you type the more specific the results become. The results appear under the Search window.

Search from the Start screen

1 From the Start screen, type **windows**.

2 Click any result, such as Windows Media Player or Windows Defender.

3 If you've opened a desktop app, close the app by clicking the appropriate Close icon, located in the top-right corner of the window.

> ✓ **TIP** To clear the search box but stay on the Integrated Search screen, click the backspace button on your keyboard to erase your current search term..

> → **TRY THIS** Repeat steps 1-3. Click the arrow beside Everywhere and click Settings. The results in the list will change. All of the results will have to do with available Windows settings you can change.

> ✓ **TIP** If you open an app instead of a desktop app in step 2, you can hide the app by dragging it downward and off the bottom of the screen.

Searching for files

If you need to find a specific file that you have saved to your computer, you can search for it from the Start screen. It's best to search using part of the name of the file, but sometimes you can also find what you're looking for by using metadata (such as a tag you've applied to a photo) or words you've included inside a document.

Search for files

1 From the Start screen, type your first name.

2 Click the arrow beside Everywhere, and click Files.

3 Note any results.

> **TRY THIS** From the results that appear after performing a search, try right-clicking any file in the list. You will likely see the option "Open file location." This will let you go to the folder that contains the file instead of opening the file in an app or on the desktop (which will happen if you click it.)

> **TIP** Most people have created files with their names in them. You should see results when you perform these steps. However, if you do not, search for a file name instead.

Searching for web images

If you want to find an image on the Internet, you don't have to open a web browser first. You don't have to navigate to a webpage that offers images from search terms either. You need only to type a search term and in the Search window and choose Web Images.

Search for web images

1 From the Start screen, type **Windows 8.1**.

2 Click the arrow beside Everywhere and click Web Images.

3 Click the first item in the results.

4 Note the results.

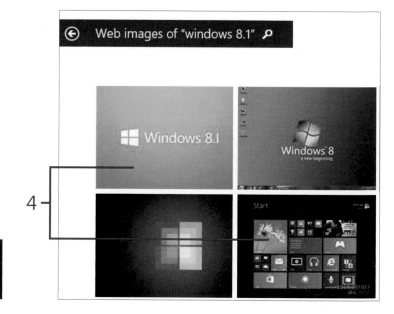

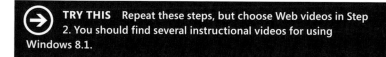

Using the Search charm

You can access the Search charm either from the Start screen or from the desktop (or other places) by displaying the charms. This method also takes you to the Integrated Search screen.

Open the Search charm

1 Press Windows logo key+C.

2 Click the Search charm.

3 Use the Search window as detailed in this chapter.

2 —

 TRY THIS If you have a touch screen, position your thumb on the right side of the screen and flick inward quickly. The charms should appear.

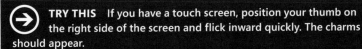 **TIP** After you type a search term in the Search pane, press Enter on the keyboard to see results from everywhere.

 TRY THIS Use the keyboard combination Windows Logo Key + S to open the Search pane.

Locating Windows settings using Search

Sometimes it can be difficult to find exactly where to make a particular change to Windows settings, such as your account picture, or to check on the status of a certain Windows feature, like the firewall. With the integrated search feature, you don't have to know. You can search for the setting.

Searching for Windows settings

1 From the Start screen, type Account Picture.

2 Click the arrow beside Everywhere, and click Settings.

3 Click Change Your Account Picture, but note the other results.

4 Return to the Start screen.

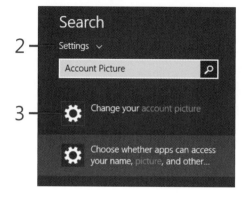

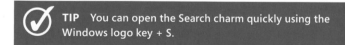

TIP You can open the Search charm quickly using the Windows logo key + S.

TRY THIS! Repeat the steps here, and type **lock screen**, **firewall**, **defender**, **mobility center**, or other computer terms you are already familiar with.

Customizing Search

There are a few settings you can configure to make your searches more efficient and to alter your search experience. You can change the search filter from Moderate (the default) to Strict or Off. You can also delete your past searches.

Customize how Search works

1 Press Windows logo key+I.

2 Click Change PC Settings.

3 Click any Back buttons if applicable, and then click Search and Apps. Note that Search is selected.

4 Click Clear to clear your search history. Click Clear again to verify.

(continued on next page)

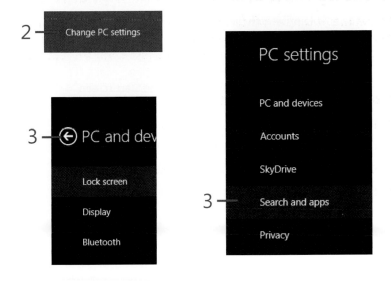

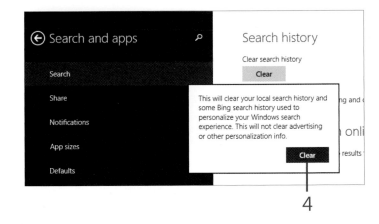

Customize how Search works *(continued)*

5 Opt to enable or disable Bing as your search engine.

6 Choose the appropriate Search experience.

7 Choose a SafeSearch setting.

8 Press the Windows logo key to return to the Start screen.

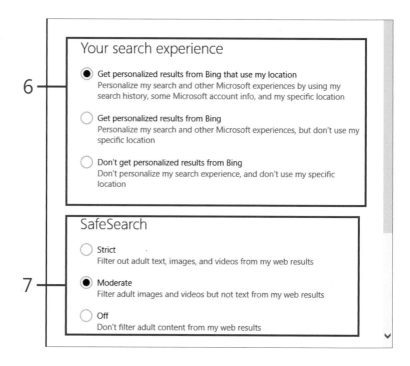

5 —

Use Bing to search online

Get search suggestions and web results from Bing

On

6 —

Your search experience

◉ Get personalized results from Bing that use my location
Personalize my search and other Microsoft experiences by using my search history, some Microsoft account info, and my specific location

◯ Get personalized results from Bing
Personalize my search and other Microsoft experiences, but don't use my specific location

◯ Don't get personalized results from Bing
Don't personalize my search experience, and don't use my specific location

SafeSearch

◯ Strict
Filter out adult text, images, and videos from my web results

7 —

◉ Moderate
Filter adult images and videos but not text from my web results

◯ Off
Don't filter adult content from my web results

> ✓ **TIP** If you opt to clear your search history you will clear your local search history and some Bing search history. It does not clear advertising or other personalization information.

Searching inside an app

You can often type a search term while in an app to get results that apply only to that app and nothing else. For example, while in Maps you can type "libraries", press Enter on the keyboard, and view libraries that are near you. (If Maps doesn't currently show your current location, right-click the screen and click either Clear Map or My Location, or both.)

Search only inside an app

1 From the Start screen, click Maps.

2 Type **libraries**.

3 Press Enter on the keyboard.

4 Note the results.

(continued on next page)

Search only inside an app (continued)

5 Click any result.

6 To clear the map, right-click the screen and click Clear Map.

5

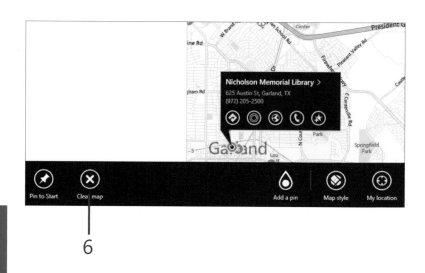

6

 TIP Remember that certain apps, including Maps, require that you have access to the Internet to return results. If you don't have access, the Search feature will search only your computer hard disk for matches in apps, files, and settings categories.

SEE ALSO See additional sections in this book, such as Section 7 about using Maps.

Using the Maps app

7

The Maps app comes pre-installed in Windows 8.1, and it offers some very easy-to-use and useful features.

Using the Maps app, you can pinpoint your computing device's current location (especially handy with laptops and tablets); get directions from point A to point B; get an aerial view of the world; and figure out how to avoid traffic on your morning or evening commute. The ability to zoom in and out for greater or lesser detail can be helpful in finding your way on a map too. You can even get information about businesses and attractions, or jump quickly to online search results or related websites to find more details.

In this section:

- Opening and navigating the Maps app
- Choosing a map style
- Searching for locations
- Displaying information about a location
- Showing traffic on maps
- Getting directions
- Adding a pin
- Marking a favorite

Opening and navigating the Maps app

You can use the Maps app for many purposes, including finding nearby locations and getting directions there. But you can also use Maps to get information about businesses such as restaurants and clubs by clicking an applicable web site, provided it is offered in the results. When perusing the Maps app, you can zoom in and out to get more or less detail with a click, quickly find your current location, and then move the map around to find nearby locations with a simple click and drag action.

Open and move around maps

1   On the Start screen, click the Maps tile.

2   If prompted, click Allow to let Maps learn your current location.

3   Position the cursor on the right side of the map, and click the + sign to zoom in.

4   Click the – sign to zoom out.

5   To view adjacent areas, click and drag on the map.

6   Right-click to display the App bars that run across the top and bottom of the screen.

7   To view the map of your current location, click My Location.

 TIP   You can zoom in and out of a map by using the scroll wheel on your mouse.

 TIP   When you right-click inside Maps, an App bar appears that runs across the top of the Map interface as well as the bottom. In most of the exercises in this chapter you need only to focus on the toolbar that runs across the bottom. However, the App bar that runs across the top offers two items: Map and Favorites. You'll learn about these later in this chapter.

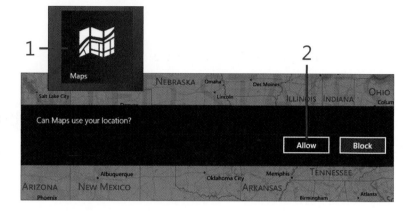

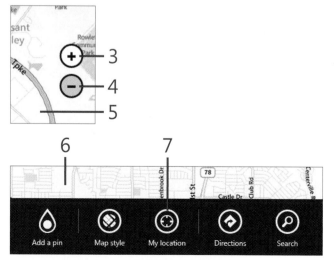

Choosing a map style

There are two map styles in the Maps app: Road View and Aerial View. The Road View is similar to a traditional road map with streets, bodies of water, and various landmarks represented as a simple two-dimensional illustration. Aerial View is an actual photo of locations from the air, showing greenery, roads, and other topographical features. The view you display depends on what information you need.

Change map style

1 With the Maps app open, right-click to display the App bar.

2 Click Map Style.

3 Click the desired view to apply it.

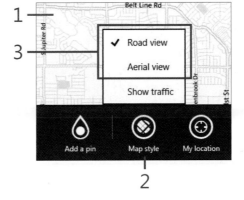

→ TRY THIS Switch to Aerial view and zoom in as far as you can to view your current location as it appears from the sky. You will likely have to click and drag to keep your location on the map screen. If you zoom in close enough, you may be able to see your own backyard, street, or a business parking lot.

✓ TIP Aerial maps aren't shown in real time. Somebody (or something) took the picture perhaps a few months or years ago, so new construction or roads might not always appear accurately.

Searching for locations

If you want to see a particular location displayed in the Maps app, you can enter an address using the Windows Integrated Search feature. The information you enter can be the name of a public landmark such as Hoover Dam, a city or town such as Denver, or a street address. To clear a map after a location has been found, right-click and select Clear Map from the toolbar.

Search for a location

1 Open the Maps app.

2 Type a search term such as "pizza."

3 Note the results, and click one, perhaps Eat + Drink.

4 Note the results; click a result to have it pinpointed on the map.

5 Click the Directions icon.

6 Choose to go by car, bus, or walk.

7 Click the right-facing arrow to get directions.

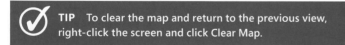

TIP To clear the map and return to the previous view, right-click the screen and click Clear Map.

TRY THIS You aren't limited to entering a generic term in the Maps search field. You can also enter a city name, a business name, and even landmarks like "The Hoover Dam."

Displaying information about a location

One of the wonderful features of the Maps app is the way it can tie into the Internet to provide details about a location or business. Maps can offer access to a company website that might offer information about its hours and payment options, or it might show customer ratings, among other things. You can almost always access a telephone number, address, and so on.

Display location information

1 With the Maps app open, type the name of a nearby business (the Search pane opens automatically) and press Enter on the keyboard.

2 Click a result.

3 With a location showing on a map, note the information offered about the establishment.

4 Hover your mouse over each icon in the information pane to see a pop-up window that displays what each button does.

 TIP If you do not want Maps to know your location and you've already allowed it, open PC Settings, click any back arrow if it appears, click Privacy, click Location, and then move the slider next to Maps from On to Off. You can do this for any other apps that use your location too.

 TIP To clear a map and start a new search, right-click and choose Clear Map.

Showing traffic on maps

If you live in a highly populated area, you can likely use the Traffic feature of the Maps app to display color codes for real-time traffic problems, as long as you have an Internet connection and the technology is available to provide it in your area. Green roads are relatively clear, yellow roads have slowed traffic, and red roads have serious problems, with traffic slowing significantly.

Display traffic

1 Open the Maps app.

2 To display the toolbar, right-click the screen.

3 Click Map Style.

4 Click the Show Traffic button.

5 To turn the feature off, repeat steps 1 to 3 and click Show Traffic again.

TIP Show Traffic isn't likely to work very well in smaller towns or rural areas where current traffic is seldom tracked, but in cities, it can show you information about traffic problems on major arteries in virtually real time to help you find the best route.

Getting directions

Looking at a map of a location can be helpful, but finding a route from one place to another is one of the major uses of a mapping program. By entering a start point and end point, the Maps app can calculate the route, tell you the total miles and time it will take to make the trip, and give you step-by-step directions.

Get directions

1 With the Maps app open, right-click and then click Directions.

2 Click in the A field, and type a starting address or location. You can leave the default My Location if desired.

3 Click in the B field, and type an ending address or location.

4 Click the arrow beside Options. (This won't be available if you opt to walk instead of drive.)

5 Configure options as desired.

6 Click the Get Directions arrow.

7 To display the route on the map, click any segment in the directions.

> ✓ **TIP** To remove the route and clear the To and From fields, right-click to display the toolbar and then click the Clear Map button.

> ✓ **TIP** To reverse the directions and switch the To and From locations, click the Direction arrows to the right of the first field (A). This is handy because on your return trip you might find that the directions differ slightly due to one-way roads or other routing anomalies.

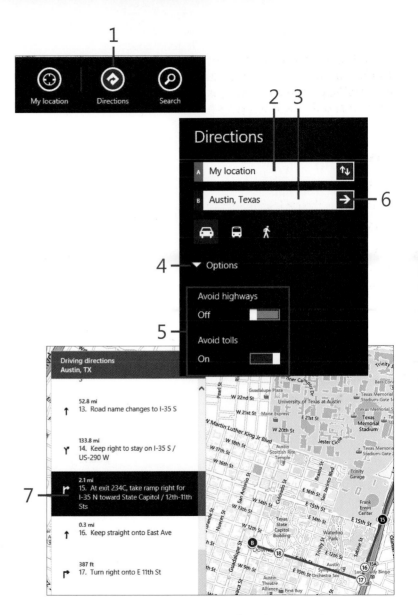

Adding a pin

You can add a pin to a map to mark it for future reference. You may want to add a pin for a location you know exists but does not appear on the map, such as a new building, park, library, and so on.

Add a pin

1 Open the Maps app.

2 Right-click the screen, and on the toolbar, click Clear Map, if applicable.

3 Right-click the screen, and from the toolbar, click My Location if the pin you want to drop is near your current location.

4 Right-click the screen, and click Add Pin.

5 Drag the new pin (an orange dot) from the App bar to the desired location.

> ✓ **TIP** After you set the pin, click the orange dot. From the resulting options you can get directions there, add it as a favorite, delete it, and more.

> → **TRY THIS** To add a location to the Start screen, click it first on the map, right-click to access the toolbar, and then click Pin To Start. Edit the name if desired, and click Pin To Start to confirm.

Marking a favorite

You can add locations to a Favorites list to more easily locate them again at a later time. When you have a list of favorites, you can manage them from the Favorites list.

Mark a favorite

1 Locate the destination to mark as a favorite on the map.

2 Click the Favorites icon. It is the icon with a star on it.

3 Right-click the screen and click Favorites (it's on the top App bar).

4 Note the new entry.

> ✓ **TIP** To remove a favorite, repeat these steps. Favorites is a toggle; clicking it again will remove it. You'll be prompted to verify this before it's removed.

> → **TRY THIS** To manage your favorites, right-click the screen and click Favorites to access the list. Right-click any item in the list to edit it. You can also remove favorites here. Click Add Home to add your own address to Favorites.

Going online with Internet Explorer 11

8

Internet Explorer is Microsoft's web browser. You use a browser to navigate around the Internet, the worldwide network of computers that makes up the World Wide Web.

Windows 8.1 includes a tile on the Start screen for the new Internet Explorer 11 app (IE 11). This app is optimized for the Windows 8.1 interface, including the ability to use it with a touchscreen computing device. The main paradigm for the new design is to show as much content as possible on the screen at any time (eliminating the clutter associated with toolbars and menus). This is a great feature, but a new one, so it'll take a little getting used to. Thus, the majority of this section is to show you how to navigate inside this new interface. After you have experienced the IE11 app, you'll explore the traditional Internet Explorer desktop app, which is still available and can be used when the IE 11 app doesn't suffice.

In this section:

- Exploring Internet Explorer 11
- Navigating among websites
- Searching on a page
- Searching with Suggestions
- Creating tabs
- Clearing your history
- Marking and accessing a favorite
- Pinning a website to the Start screen
- Starting an InPrivate session
- Switching to Internet Explorer on the desktop
- Exploring the Internet Explorer desktop app

Exploring the Internet Explorer 11 app

The biggest difference between the new Internet Explorer 11 app you'll learn about here and the traditional Internet Explorer application you might be used to is that there are no tools (such as menus and toolbars) on the screen. For example, most of the time you'll have to display the address bar to use it; it isn't always available and taking up space on the screen. You can show the Address bar and tabs with a right-click though, and hide them again just as easily. This is what helps keep the Internet Explorer app so streamlined, and what makes it perfect for use on smaller screens.

Open Internet Explorer 11

1 Press the Windows logo key on your keyboard to go to the Start screen.

2 Click the Internet Explorer tile.

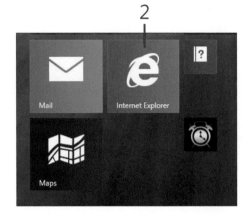

✓ **TIP**   If you open Internet Explorer from the Start screen, you open the same version of Internet Explorer as you would if you clicked the IE button on the desktop taskbar, but it's a different mode. The IE11 app is optimized for tablets and touchscreens and for those who prefer an uncluttered web browser. The one you'll find on the desktop taskbar offers the traditional look and feel of IE.

Use the address bar

1 With Internet Explorer 11 open, right-click an empty area of a web-page (one that does not have a picture or text on it).

2 Click inside the address bar that appears, and begin to type a URL, such as *www.bing.com* or *http://www.microsoft.com*.

3 Press Enter on the keyboard to go to the address you've typed, or click an entry under Suggestions.

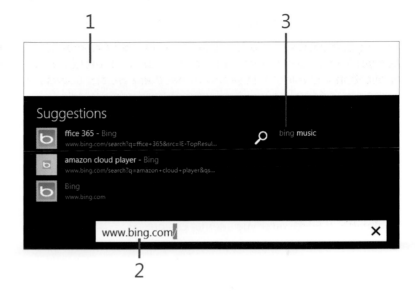

TIP When you right-click in step 1, you might see more than the address bar. You might see thumbnails of other webpages you have open. You can click one of these to go to that webpage quickly.

TIP Although there are still some exceptions, accessing most websites by using your browser no longer requires that you type the http:// or www before their names, so in the examples here, you can simply type **bing.com** or **microsoft.com** in the address bar.

Navigating among websites

When you are browsing the Internet, you will want to move from one website or webpage to another. You can do this in several ways: you can enter a URL in the address bar as covered in the previous task; move backward or forward to a previously visited site; or click a hyperlink (text or an image that is programmed to send you to another location on the Internet when you click it). You can also click options if they appear above the address bar, such as items in your search history, links to websites that are popular now, links to sites you visit often, and so on.

Move among websites

1 With Internet Explorer 11 open, use the address bar to go to *www.bing.com*.

2 In the Bing search box, type Internet Explorer 11.

3 Click the first entry in the list that appears, or, press Enter on the keyboard.

4 Click the entry that is titled Internet Explorer – Microsoft Windows – Microsoft Home Page (or something similar that points you to Microsoft's webpages).

5 Move your mouse to the left side of the screen, and click the Back button to go to the previously viewed site.

> **TRY THIS** After clicking inside the address bar, click the x that appears on the right end of it. This will delete what is currently shown there, which will make it foolproof for typing a new URL.

> **TIP** Just as there is a back arrow on the left side of the webpage to return to a previously viewed page, there is also a front-facing arrow on the right side to return you to where you just were.

Follow links

1 Open the web page *windows.microsoft.com*.

2 Click a link on the page to follow it.

3 To return to the page from which you followed the link, move your mouse cursor to the left side of the screen and click the Back button.

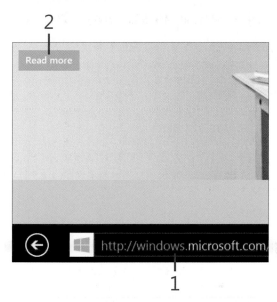

TIP If you position your mouse cursor over text or graphics and the pointer turns from a small arrow to a hand, it means there is an active link there that you can click. You can also right-click this to access options to copy the link, open the link in a new tab, open the link in a new window, and so on.

TIP Text links are colored, often (but not always) in blue to help you spot them. After you follow a link, if you return to the page it was displayed on, the link will usually appear in purple rather than blue, indicating that it's been clicked recently.

Searching on a page

Individual webpages on a website can be quite long. You can use scroll bars in your browser to move down a page, or you can search to find specific contents on a page. In Internet Explorer 11, you can use the Find On Page feature to search for and scroll through all highlighted instances of a search term on the currently active page.

Search for content on a page

1 Use the address bar to navigate to the page you want to search.

2 Right-click an area of the page. (Do not right-click a link or picture, for example.)

3 Click the Page Tools button.

4 Click Find On Page.

(continued on next page)

✅ **TIP** Sometimes you won't need to right-click to access options shown in this section, they'll already be there. If, in Step 2 for example, you already see the Page Tools options, there is no need to right-click.

Search for content on a page   *(continued)*

5 Enter a word or phrase.

6 Click the Previous or Next button to move among the results.

7 Note that the results are highlighted.

> ✓ **TIP**   When you enter a search term, such as "win," your results will include all words that contain those letters, such as Windows and winner. To narrow your search to only the word "win," simply enclose the term with quotation marks.

> → **TRY THIS**   Use the Get App For This Site selection from the Page Tools button menu (if it is available) to download any associated app for the website you are currently visiting.

Searching with Suggestions

If you want to search the entire web for a site, page, or document, you can do so in Internet Explorer 11 by typing a search term in the address bar or by using a search engine such as Bing or Google. You can go to a particular search engine by entering its URL, such as *www.bing.com*, in the address bar and pressing Enter. You can also type a search term in the address bar and choose a webpage in the Suggestions section that appears.

Search from Suggestions

1 With Internet Explorer 11 open, right-click an empty place on the screen (and not on a link or image).

2 Enter a search term, such as **Windows Phone**, in the address bar.

3 Click one of the options in Suggestions.

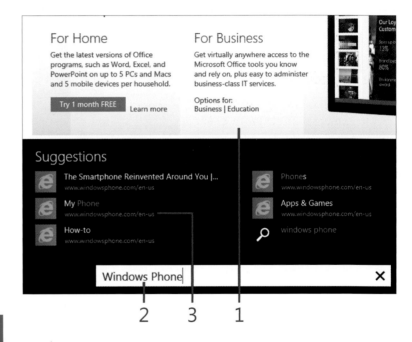

TIP If you don't want to select from the list of suggestions, just press Enter on the keyboard after you've typed your search terms in the address bar. Web results will appear and you can choose from those.

SEE ALSO To learn how to search the Internet using the Search charm, the Search Pane, and other options, refer to Section 6, "Searching for anything."

Creating tabs

Tabbed browsing is a feature that allows you to have several websites open at once so that you can move back and forth among them with a single click. In Internet Explorer 11, the tab feature has been reinvented. Tabs aren't displayed on screen; instead, you display tabs by right-clicking the screen. With the Tabs view open, you can then open new tabs, close tabs, and access tab tools.

Create new tabs

1 With Internet Explorer open, right-click an empty area of the screen (where there is no active link or image).

2 Click the New Tab button.

3 You can either:

   a Click inside the address bar and type a URL for a website, or

   b Click an item from the Frequent thumbnails.

4 If you type the URL, you might be offered a list of suggestions. If so, you can click one if desired.

> ✓ **TIP** To open a link available from a web page on a new tab, instead of clicking the link, right-click it and choose the Open Link In New Tab command.

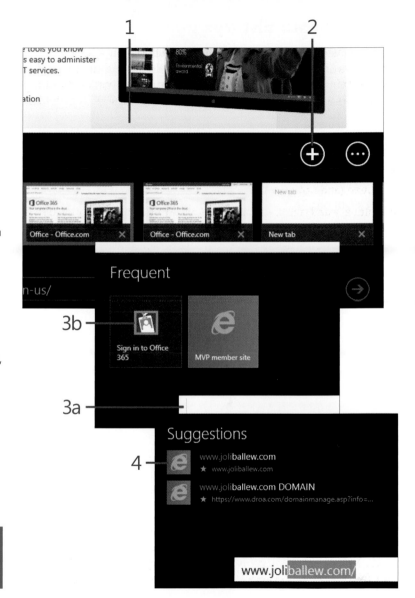

Clearing your history

After you've browsed the internet for a while, you might want to clear your history so that others who also use your computer (and your user account) can't see the sites you've recently visited. You might also want the list of sites in your History list to be empty so that you aren't prompted in any way to visit previously viewed sites as you search.

Clear your history

1 With Internet Explorer open, use the key combination Windows Logo key + I.

2 Click Options.

3 Scroll to locate History, and click Select.

(continued on next page)

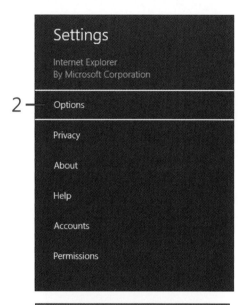

Clear your history   *(continued)*

4 Select what items to clear.

5 Click Delete.

6 Click the Back arrow to return to Options, if desired, and browse other options, or, click outside of the History pane to close it.

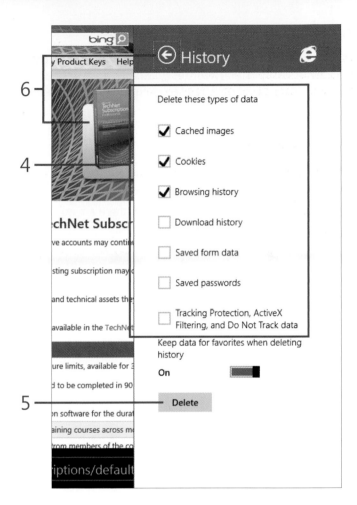

✓ **TIP** When you opt to clear your web history, you have several options, not all of which are self-explanatory. Cached images are saved to your computer so that when you access those same images from the same page, they'll load faster the next time (meaning they will load from your computer rather than from the webpage itself). Cookies are small text files that are used to personalize your web experience by remembering your name, past searches, or preferences. Form data is data you have entered into web forms, such as name and address.

Marking and accessing a favorite

If you visit a website often, you can mark it as a favorite so that you can access it easily later. Favorites you mark appear in a list of thumbnails. You click a thumbnail to go directly to the website represented by the link.

Mark and access a favorite

1 Navigate to the site you want to mark as a favorite.

2 Right-click an empty area of the screen (where there are no links or images).

3 Click the Favorites button.

4 Click the Add To Favorites button.

5 If desired or applicable, edit the name.

6 If you've previously created folders, choose the appropriate folder; otherwise, leave All selected.

7 Click Add.

(continued on next page)

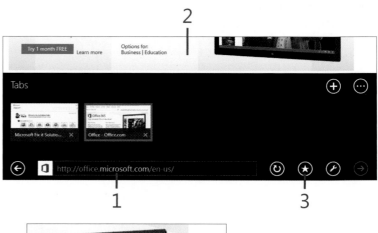

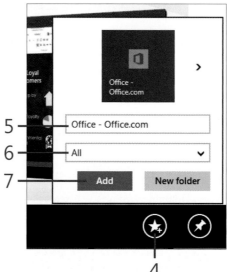

Mark and access a favorite *(continued)*

8 Click an empty area of the webpage to hide the toolbar.

9 Right-click an empty area to show the toolbar.

10 Click the Favorites icon.

11 Scroll right to locate the recently created favorite.

TRY THIS With the Favorites bar showing, right-click any thumbnail and click Edit or Remove to change it. If the Tab bar is showing instead, click the x at the bottom of any thumbnail to close the tab.

Pinning a site to the Start screen

You can pin a site to your Start screen so that you can get to it quickly. For example, if you use a search engine regularly or if you use a cloud player to play your music selections, you might want to be able to access that site on your Start screen. After it's pinned, you can click the tile for that site and go to it instantly by using Internet Explorer 11.

Pin a site

1 Go to the site that you want to pin to the Start screen.

2 Right-click an empty area of the screen (where there are no links or images).

3 Click the Favorites button at the bottom of the screen.

4 Click the Pin Site button that appears above the Favorites thumbnails.

5 If desired, edit the name.

6 Click Pin To Start.

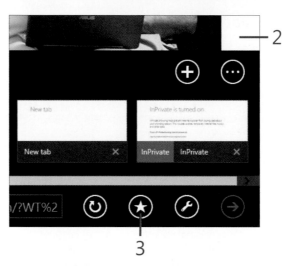

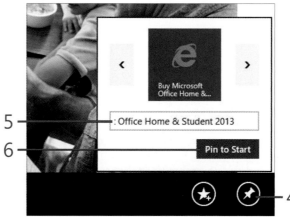

> **TIP** When you pin a website to the Start screen, it will appear on the far right side of the screen. If you visit the site often, you might want to move it farther left so that it's easier to access.

Starting a new InPrivate session

If you want to browse the web without leaving any trace of where you've been, including making sure that those sites do not appear in the History list, you will need to start an InPrivate session. When you do, nothing is saved to your computer regarding your web session.

Start a new InPrivate session

1 With Internet Explorer open, right-click an empty area of the screen where there are no links or images.

2 Click the three dots (ellipsis).

3 Click New InPrivate Tab.

4 Browse to the desired website.

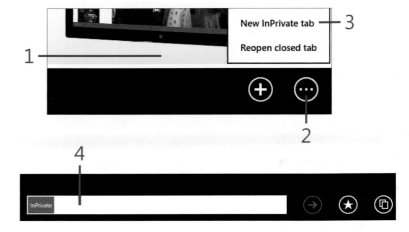

TIP If you are concerned about privacy, you might want to browse "in private" all the time to keep websites from saving information about your visits, including saving text files to your computer called *cookies*. Cookies, although generally harmless and mostly helpful, can identify you when you visit a site again to offer you a more personalized web experience, and you might not want that.

TIP If everyone who uses your computer has their own account and each logs off when they are finished using it, there should be no reason to worry why another user would access your web sessions or history.

Switching to the Internet Explorer desktop app

Sometimes, the Internet Explorer 11 app doesn't do what you want it to do. For example, it might not play certain video files.

If you run across any problem while in the app, you can switch to Internet Explorer on the desktop.

Switch to Internet Explorer on the desktop

1 Navigate to any website.

2 Right-click an empty area of the screen where there are no links or images.

3 Click the Page Tools button.

4 Click View In The Desktop.

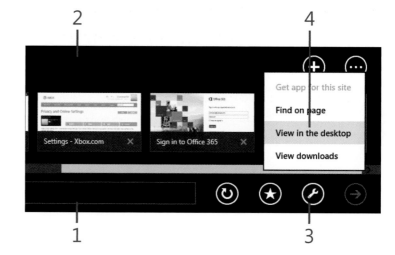

TIP Internet Explorer 11, the app, doesn't support all content. When content won't play or appear correctly on the screen, switch to Internet Explorer on the desktop.

TIP If you've used Internet Explorer in the past, Internet Explorer on the desktop will look and feel familiar to you.

Overview of the Internet Explorer desktop app

When you display Internet Explorer 11 on the desktop, you see a more traditional browser window with an address bar, tabs, and the ability to display additional toolbars. Like the IE 11 app, you'll have access to tabs and an address bar too.

Explore the Internet Explorer desktop app

1 Switch to the Internet Explorer Desktop app as detailed in the previous task.

2 Right-click the empty area above the address bar.

3 Click Menu Bar. (If time allows, explore the menus.)

4 Click the empty tab at the end of the tabs to open a new tab.

(continued on next page)

2   3

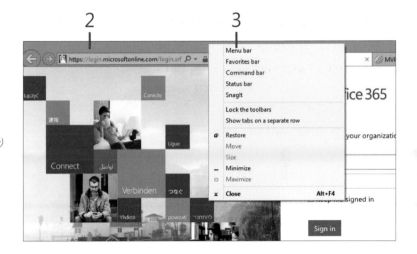

4

> ✓ **TIP** Press the Alt key on the keyboard to show the Menu bar only when you need it, if you don't want to keep it enabled all the time.

Explore the Internet Explorer desktop app

(continued)

5 Click the Favorites star to open the Favorites Center. Notice that the favorites you created earlier in this section appear here.

6 Type an address in the Address bar, and press Enter on the keyboard.

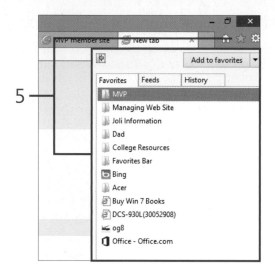

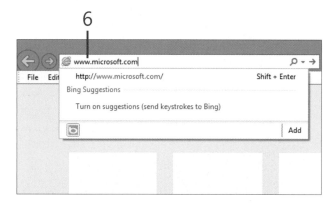

Using Calendar and People

9

The Calendar and People apps can help you organize your life and keep in touch with others. The Calendar app lets you easily create events, invite people to those events, and incorporate multiple online calendars. The People app enables you to view social networking updates for the people you maintain communications with, access and edit contact information, mark specific contacts as favorites, and even update your own social networking status, among other things.

Both the Calendar app and the People app use the Internet and other apps to provide, sync, and maintain the information available there. For example, when you access a contact's information page in the People app, you have the option to map their address (which opens the Maps app) or send them an email (using the Mail app). When you create an event in the Calendar app and opt to invite people to it, the Calendar app works with your list of contacts to provide email addresses without having to copy and paste them manually. In this section, you'll learn about all of these things and more.

In this section:

- Displaying calendar views
- Adding a calendar event
- Using reminders
- Inviting people to an event
- Editing an existing event
- Adding additional calendars
- Working with additional calendars
- Exploring the People app
- Incorporating online accounts
- Adding a new contact
- Communicating with a contact
- Culling and sorting contacts
- Viewing What's New

Displaying calendar views

The Calendar app lets you create events to help you manage your schedule. You can display the Calendar by Day, Work Week, Week, or Month view. From any view, you can quickly return to the Calendar's landing page, which includes today's date. For example, if you have scrolled six months forward to enter dates for your summer vacation, you can quickly return to today's date by right-clicking the screen, clicking What's Next, and then clicking Today.

Choose a calendar view

1 From the Start screen, click the Calendar app.

2 Right-click inside the Calendar app.

3 Click Day.

4 Right-click again.

5 Click Month. (If you don't see Month, position your cursor to the right of Week and click the arrow that appears.)

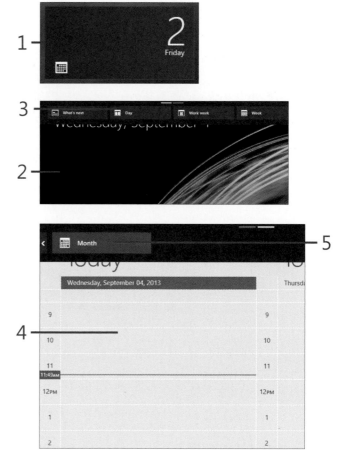

> **TRY THIS** Using Month view, use the scroll wheel on your mouse to scroll through the months in the year. If you have a touch screen, use your finger to flick through them. Look for back and forward buttons too; click to use them. The Back button appears to the left of the name of the month at the top of the page when you move the mouse.

Adding a calendar event

Using the Calendar app, you can create events such as appointments, birthdays, anniversaries, concert dates or anything else that you want to be reminded of. You can also block off a period of time, such as when you're on vacation or when you have houseguests. You can enter many details about any event you create, such as where and when it will take place, how long it will run, and if it's a recurring event. In this task, you'll create an event and configure custom start and end times.

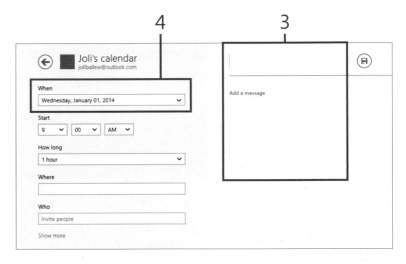

Create an event

1 In the Calendar app, navigate to the desired day and/or time.

2 In Week or Day view, right-click a time slot. (In Month view, click a date.) Click New.

3 Enter a title, and add a message about the event.

4 Confirm that the date is correct under the When heading. (Use the down arrows to make changes.)

(continued on next page)

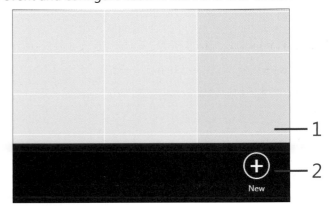

TIP Create a title for the event that is short but still details the event. You'll be able to view it better from Calendar after it's created.

Create an event *(continued)*

5 Use the selection boxes to configure the desired start time.

6 Click the selection box for the How Long field.

7 Click Custom.

8 Input the appropriate end dates and times.

9 Click the Save This Event button.

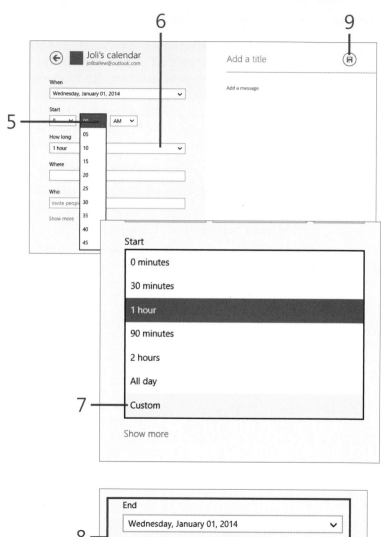

TIP You can add a basic event by simply clicking a time slot or day entry.

TRY THIS Create a new event for your birthday. Fill in the desired information, and then click Show More. One of the options there is How Often. Change the default setting, Once, to Every Year.

TIP You don't have to configure custom start and end times every time you create an event. You can choose from one of the defaults: 0 minutes, 30 minutes, 1 hour, 90 minutes, 2 hours, and All Day.

Using reminders

One reason to enter events in the Calendar app is so that you can be reminded of those events ahead of time. When you create an event, you can also apply a setting so that you are alerted prior to the event—for example, 15 or 30 minutes ahead, a day ahead, and so on. When the specified reminder time arrives, the Calendar app will send you an email about the event.

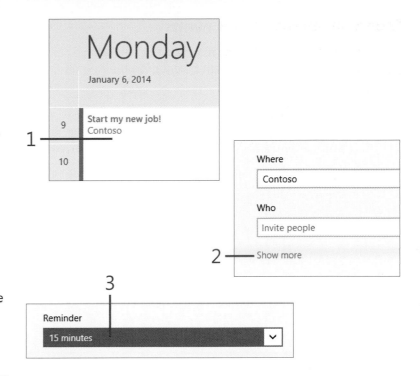

Set up a reminder

1 Click an existing event in the Calendar app.

2 Click the Show More link.

3 Click the Reminder field.

4 Click the setting for how far ahead of the event start time you'd like to receive a reminder.

5 Click the Save This Event button.

> ✓ **TIP** Sometimes it's useful to be reminded of an event a week ahead and then again a day ahead. If you want a couple of reminders about an event, you will have to set this up manually. Set the reminder that's furthest out—for example, one week. When that reminder appears in your email inbox, take a moment to go back and edit the event to add another reminder, such as one hour or one day ahead.

> ✓ **TIP** When creating a new event, you don't have to navigate to the date you'd like to create the event for first if you don't want to. You can simply click on any calendar day or time and change the When setting from the event page.

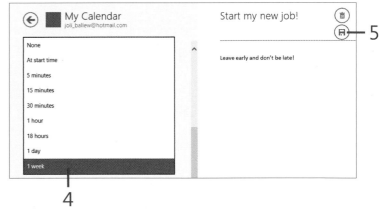

Inviting people to an event

When you set up an event such as a party or conference call, you can invite people to the event by entering their email addresses in Who field. When you do, the Calendar app will call on the Mail app to send invitations to those you've included.

Send an invite

1 In the Calendar app, click an existing event (or create a new one).

2 Fill in information if applicable.

3 Click in the Who field.

(continued on next page)

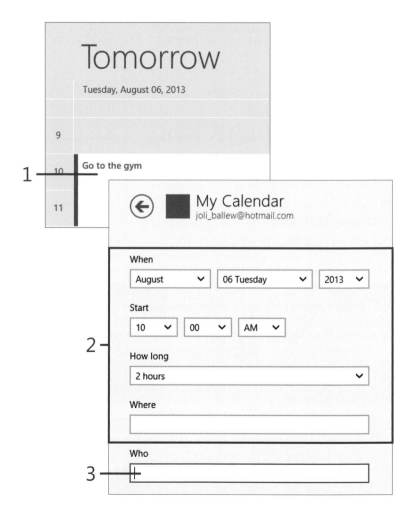

Send an invite   *(continued)*

4 Start typing an email address. If you see what you want in a drop-down list, click it: otherwise, complete the email address.

5 Click Send Invitation.

> **TIP**   If you select an email address from a list of past email contacts when inputting them in the Who field, the entry will have a blue square around it and will be accepted. If you enter an email address that Windows doesn't recognize, you'll need to click the semicolon on the keyboard to have that email address accepted into the field.

Editing an existing event

You can click an existing event to open an event's Details page and add or change information you've included there. For example, if the time of the event has changed or if you didn't know the location but now you do and want to add it, you can update these details. After you make the changes, simply save them and your event is up to date.

Edit event details

1 In the Calendar app, click an existing event.

2 Click in a field, and modify the information as needed.

3 Click the Save icon.

1

2   3

 TIP To delete an event click the Trash icon in the top right corner. Cancellations will be sent automatically.

 TIP You can copy information you've typed in the body of the event if you want to use the information elsewhere (such as posting the event to a social networking site).

Deleting an event

Change is a constant. Luckily, the Calendar app helps you keep up with changes in your schedule. If an event such as a luncheon or business meeting gets canceled, you can delete it from your Calendar, especially if you've set it up to send you a reminder. You can delete an event from its Details page.

Delete an event

1 From the Start screen, click the Calendar app.

2 Click an event.

3 Click the Delete Event button.

4 Click OK.

5 Complete the email and click Send.

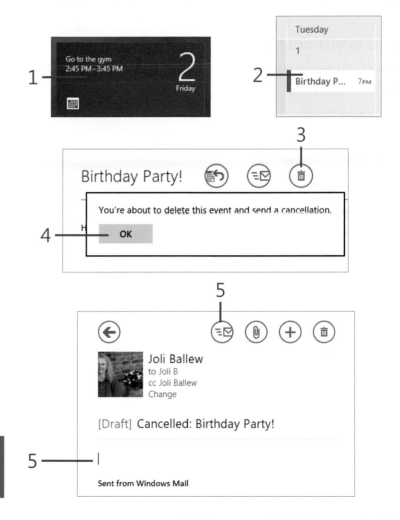

Adding additional calendars

The Calendar app is configured with one calendar, the calendar that is associated with your Microsoft account. You might have other calendars from other sources such as Exchange, Office 365, or Outlook.com. You can add these calendars from the Settings charm by adding the related account.

Add additional calendars

1 From the Start screen, click the Calendar app.

2 Use Windows Logo key + C to open the charms, and click Settings.

3 Click Accounts.

4 Click Add An Account.

(continued on next page)

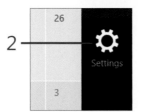

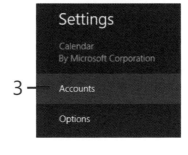

Add additional calendars *(continued)*

5 Click the type of account to add.

6 Input the required information.

7 Click Connect.

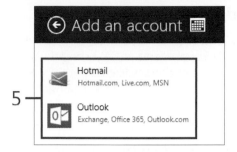

 TIP After you add an account, new entries will appear in the Calendar app in a different color. Each calendar has its own color.

Working with additional calendars

When you have more than one calendar available, you can choose which calendar to save new events to. You might want to save personal events to the calendar associated with your Microsoft account and save business events to the calendar associated with your Exchange or Outlook account. Here you'll create an event in a new way, by first selecting the calendar to use and then by adding event details.

Work with additional calendars

1 In the Calendar app, click any date or time slot.

2 Click the arrow to select a calendar for the new event.

3 Click the desired calendar.

4 Click the arrow again.

5 Click Add Details.

6 Input details as desired.

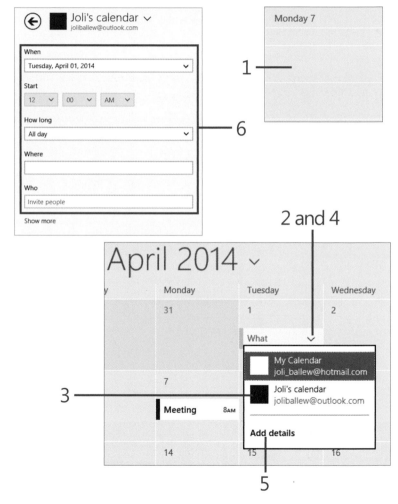

TIP You can change the color associated with a specific calendar from the Settings charm, from Options.

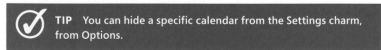
TIP You can hide a specific calendar from the Settings charm, from Options.

Exploring the People app

The People app helps you stay in touch with others by offering access to your contacts, their social updates, and the personal information they've opted to share with you. The People app has three main sections: Me, What's New, and All Contacts.

Explore the People app

1 From the Start screen, click the People app.

2 Note what's available as applicable; you might not see much if this is the first time you've used the People app.

3 Right-click the screen.

4 Click Me.

5 Click the Back arrow to return to the Home screen.

1 –

4

5 –

 TIP If you are ever lost in the People app, right-click the screen and click Home to return to the landing page.

Incorporating online accounts

The contacts available with your Microsoft account are associated with the People app the first time you sign in with it. You might also have contacts you communicate with through various social networks, like Facebook, LinkedIn, and Twitter. If you tell the People app about these other accounts, it can pull your contacts in so that you can communicate with them from your Windows 8.1–based device. Adding social account information is the best way to import contact information for the people you know.

Set up accounts

1 From the Start screen, click People.

2 Use Windows Logo key + C to display the charms, and click Settings.

3 Click Accounts.

4 Click Add An Account.

(continued on next page)

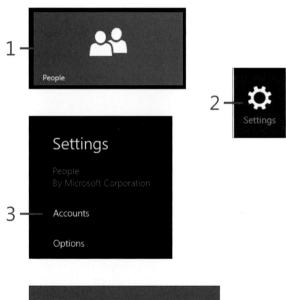

Set up accounts *(continued)*

5 Click an account type to add.

6 Provide user information.

7 Click the button to connect to the account—in this case, Connect.

5

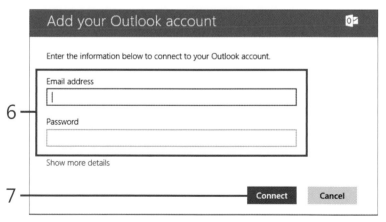

6

7

TIP If desired, repeat these steps to add all of the social accounts you belong to (that can be connected). If you decide later that you don't want to incorporate contacts from those accounts, you can hide them from the Settings charm, through Options.

TRY THIS After adding your accounts, click What's New on the People app's landing page. From there you will likely be able to access your contacts' updates on the various social networking sites.

Adding a new contact

The contacts associated with your Microsoft account are added automatically when you log in with it. More contacts can be added by adding information about the social networks you belong to, such as Facebook and Twitter, among others. You can also add contacts manually.

When you add a contact manually, you can add a name, company, email, phone, address, job title, significant other, and more. There is also a Notes field to add information such as birthday, favorite movie, or whatever you want to remember about that person. After you add a contact, you can use the People app to send various types of messages, post to that person's Facebook account, or send email. You can also map the person's location by using the Maps app.

Add a contact

1 Right-click while inside the Home page of the People app.

2 Click New Contact.

3 Enter contact information in the available fields, such as First Name and Email.

4 Under the section to add other info, click the + sign.

(continued on next page)

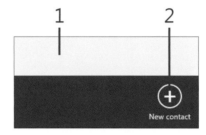

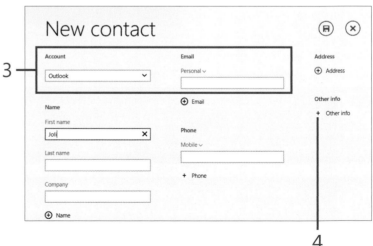

Add a contact   *(continued)*

5 Click a new type of detail to add.

6 Input the information in the new field that appears.

7 Click Save.

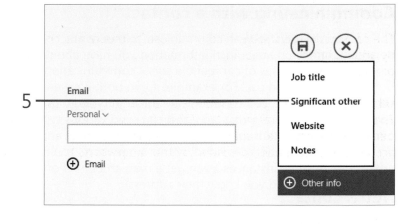

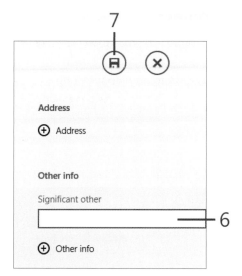

TRY THIS When entering contact information, make sure to click the + sign by Address and input a full address for Home, Work, or Other. Then, after you've saved the contact, open the Contact card and click that address. Maps will open and pinpoint the address on a map.

Communicating with a contact

The number of ways you can communicate with a contact depends entirely on how much information you have about him or her, and, what types of compatible social communications both of you have and use. For example, if you both have and use a Skype account, you communicate through typed messages, phone calls, and video calls. You can send various types of communications through Facebook, LinkedIn, Twitter, and so on too, using the outlets provided by those networks. You can email, and, in some instances, even get a map and directions to their home (provided you know their address).

Communicate with a contact

1 Right-click while inside the People app, and click Home to verify that you are at the landing page.

2 Click All Contacts (you'll probably have to scroll to the right).

3 Click any contact name.

4 Click a communication option.

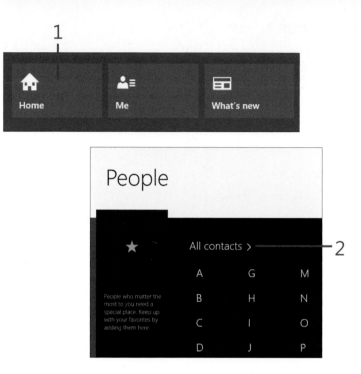

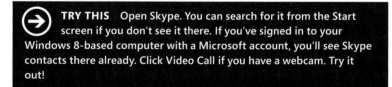

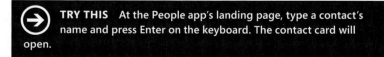

TRY THIS Open Skype. You can search for it from the Start screen if you don't see it there. If you've signed in to your Windows 8-based computer with a Microsoft account, you'll see Skype contacts there already. Click Video Call if you have a webcam. Try it out!

TRY THIS At the People app's landing page, type a contact's name and press Enter on the keyboard. The contact card will open.

Culling and sorting contacts

If you add information for all of your social networks, say Face-book, Google, LinkedIn, Outlook, Skype, and Twitter, you might have a lot of contacts in the People app. You can opt to hide contacts from some of those networks, and you can opt to sort what's left by last name or first name.

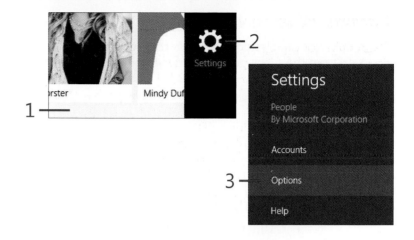

Cull and sort contacts

1 Go to the People app's home page.

2 Use Windows key + C to show the charms, and click Settings.

3 Click Options.

4 Opt to sort contacts by last name, if desired.

5 Remove the tick from the social networks for which you'd like to hide contacts.

6 Click outside the Options page to hide it.

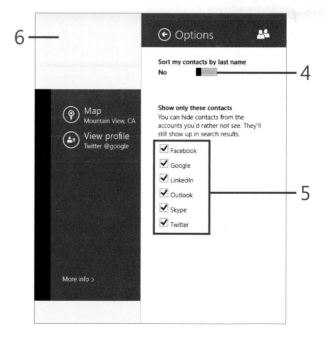

> **TRY THIS** If you have multiple entries for a contact, you can link them so that there is only one entry in the People app instead of multiple entries. To do this, click the contact to open the contact info page and click Link Contacts. You can then select the contact that you want to link it with. Click the Save icon when you're done.

Viewing What's New

The People app enables you to access contact updates that originate from the social networks you've configured to work with it. You can access updates from Facebook and Twitter, for example.

View What's New

1. In the People app, right-click the screen and click Home if you are not on the landing page.

2. Right-click again and click What's New.

3. Explore as desired, and then click the Back arrow to return to the landing page.

 TRY THIS Click any notification to see it full screen. From there you can often see others' posts, likes, and so on.

Using Mail and Skype

10

Email is a universal way to communicate with family, friends, colleagues, services providers, and businesses. Many people prefer to communicate this way over any other. With email, you have time to compose your thoughts, write them down, attach files, and keep a record of what you've sent and the replies you've received. You can also manage email messages that you want to keep by moving them to folders.

There are various ways to perform email tasks, but for the most part, either you read and manage email through a web browser (by going to the website of the email provider) or you use an email client. Windows 8.1 comes with a web browser called Internet Explorer 11, but it also comes with an email client, called Mail. Mail is likely already configured with your Microsoft account, and you'll probably prefer it over any other email management option.

When email doesn't suit your needs, you can use Skype. Skype also comes with Windows 8.1. With it, you can hold real-time text, phone, and video conversations with others. Skype is a newer way to communicate, and it's a great way to have a face-to-face conversation with someone who you can't (or don't ever) see in person.

In this section:

- Setting up an email account
- Opening your email inbox(es)
- Reading and replying to messages
- Forwarding a message
- Formatting text in a message
- Viewing and saving a photo attachment
- Creating and sending a new message
- Adding attachments
- Moving messages to folders you create
- Setting up Skype
- Adding a contact
- Saving a phone number
- Messaging with Skype
- Making a phone call to another Skype user
- Initiating a Skype video call

Setting up an email account

Mail may already set up with your Microsoft account. If that's the case, when you open Mail you'll see it there. However, you might have more email accounts than that, or, your Microsoft account might not be the one you use regularly. You may have an email account from other entities like Google, Yahoo!, AOL, Outlook, and so on as well. If you know that you have these additional account types, set them up now.

Set up an email account

1 From the Start screen, click the Mail tile.

2 Press Windows logo key+I to open the Settings charm; you'll see Settings at the top once it's opened.

3 Click Accounts.

4 Click Add An Account.

(continued on next page)

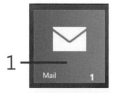

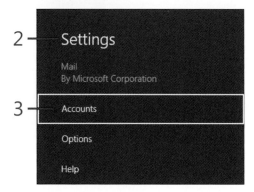

Set up an email account *(continued)*

5 Click:

  a The option that represents your email address or

  b Other account if it isn't shown. (If you click this, you may be prompted to select a type of account to add. If so, select an appropriate account type.)

6 Enter an email address.

7 Enter the password.

8 Click Connect.

5b   5a

✓ **TIP** Some accounts, like those from Google, will prompt you during setup to include (or not include) data you've associated with it, specifically data related to contacts and calendars. Click the options to include contacts and calendars, if you want to access that data from Windows 8.1.

✓ **TIP** The accounts that Mail supports are generally easy to set up, and the process is trouble-free. However, if at any point the steps here don't work (and it isn't due to a mistyped password or other mistake), contact your email provider for more specific instructions.

6

7

8

Opening your email inbox(es)

Mail obtains and holds the email you've received in a folder named Inbox. If you have multiple accounts, you'll have access to multiple Inbox folders. When you open Mail, one of those Inbox folders will open, and if you have email, it'll be accessible. You can choose a different Inbox easily and check email from multiple accounts quickly. You'll learn how to do that here.

Open your email inbox(es)

1 From the Start screen, click the Mail tile.

2 If you know you've configured more than one email account click the folder icon in the bottom left corner of the Mail interface.

3 If you performed Step 2, click the email account you want to use.

4 Click any message to read it.

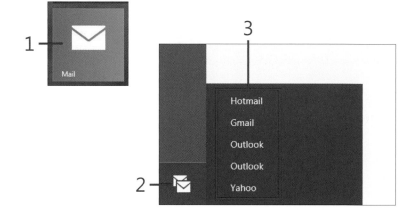

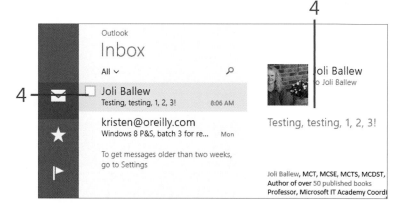

> 🔍 **SEE ALSO** The section "Reading and replying to messages," next.

> ➡ **TRY THIS** By default, all email that is in your Inbox appears, even if you've read it. You can click the arrow beside All while in an Inbox to switch to Unread. Then, what you'll see in the list are only emails you have yet to read.

Reading and replying to messages

While in the desired Inbox, you can read messages and, in most cases, reply to them. You can reply to just the sender or to the sender as well as others to whom the message was addressed.

Read a message

1 With Mail open, access the desired Inbox by using methods detailed already in this section.

2 Click the email to read in the left pane.

3 Read the message in the right pane.

1   2   3

Outlook
Inbox
All ⌄   🔍

□ Joli Ballew
  Testing, testing, 1, 2, 3!   8:06 AM

kristen@oreilly.com
Windows 8 P&S, batch 3 for re...   Mon

To get messages older than two weeks,
go to Settings

Joli Ballew   9/17/2013 8:06 AM
to Joli Ballew

Testing, testing, 1, 2, 3!

Joli Ballew, MCT, MCSE, MCTS, MCDST, Microsoft MVP
Author of over 50 published books
Professor, Microsoft IT Academy Coordinator, Brookhaven College

→ **TRY THIS** While in an Inbox for a specific account, click the Folders icon that appears in the left pane, near the top. This will take you to the account's folder list. This list contains the folders available and will include Inbox, Drafts, Sent, Outbox, and Deleted, and likely others such as Junk and Flagged. You can click any folder to access its contents.

Reply to a message

1 With a message displayed, click the Respond button.

2 Click Reply or Reply All.

3 Click Change to enter any additional email addresses.

4 Click at the top of the message pane, and type your message.

5 Click Send.

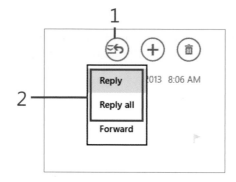

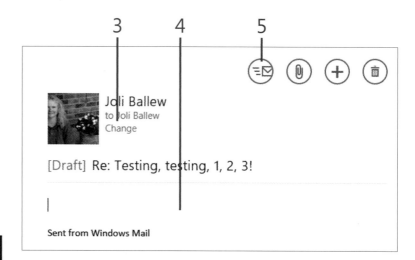

> **→ TRY THIS** Right-click any message in an Inbox that you've already read. From the options that appear at the bottom of the screen, click Mark Unread if you want an email to look like it has yet to be read. The Mark Unread icon looks like two envelopes, one of which is open and the other, closed. You can also click Flag to place a flag on the message to cause it to stand out from others in the list. This icon looks like a flag.

Forwarding a message

Sometimes when you receive a message, you want to send it on to another person. This is called *forwarding* a message. To forward an email, you must choose the Forward option, enter one or more email addresses, and send the message. You can add an additional message to the original message when you forward.

Forward a message

1 With a message displayed, click the Respond button.

2 Click Forward.

3 Enter an email address.

4 Type a message.

5 Click Send.

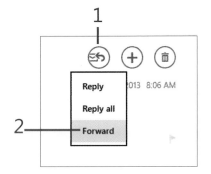

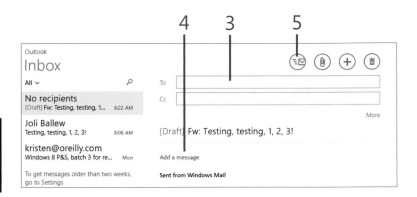

> ➔ **TRY THIS** When you reply to or forward an email, there will be a CC box available. Type email addresses here for recipients who do not need to reply to the email, but do need to be aware of it (such as a project manager or team member, for instance).

> ✓ **TIP** To remove an email address you've entered, with your cursor in the To or CC box, click the Backspace key twice on your keyboard.

Formatting text in a message

When you write text in the email body, whether it's related to a reply, forward, or even a new message you create, you have access to formatting options. However, the formatting options are hidden to keep the Mail interface clean and uncluttered. You can access these options with a right-click of the mouse.

There are two ways to work with the formatting features. One way is to configure the formatting options before you start to type. When you choose this option, the formatting you configure will be applied to everything you type until you change it. The other way to configure formatting is to apply it to text you've already added to the message. When you do this, the formatting you choose is applied only to the selected text.

Format text in a message

1 Using the methods introduced so far, select an email and opt to reply to the sender. You'll see the recipient's name at the top of the email.

2 Click inside the body of the email, placing your cursor at the top of the reply area.

3 Right-click the screen.

4 Hover your mouse over the formatting options that appear to see what each icon represents. Here, the B will make text bold.

5 Click Bold.

(continued on next page)

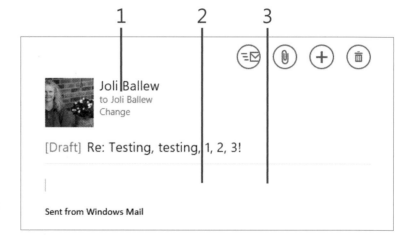

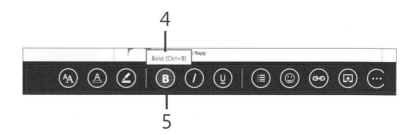

Format text in a message (continued)

6 Click where you'd like to type, and then type a few words.

7 Right-click again.

8 Click Italic.

9 Click where you'd like to type, and then type a few more words.

10 Select the words you typed by holding down the left mouse button and dragging over them.

11 At the bottom of the page, click Text Color.

12 Choose a color.

13 Click outside the text color window to apply it.

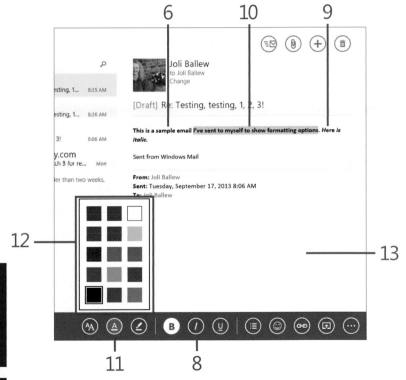

> **TRY THIS** While writing a message, right-click and choose Emoticons. This is the icon with the smiley face. Then, pick a graphic to add to your email (like a smiley face, a shape, a food item, a mode of transportation, and more). Note the options that run across the top of the options that sort the emoticons into categories. You'll need to click outside of the options to hide the emoticons pane.

> **TRY THIS** While writing a message, right-click and choose More ... You'll see options to save a draft of the email so you can finish it later, undo and redo, and clear formatting.

Opening attachments

People often attach files to an email. These files might be documents, pictures, or audio and video files. They might also be PDF files, Excel spreadsheets, or PowerPoint presentations, among other things. You generally click the attachment's icon to see the options for opening and viewing it. Depending on what is attached and what apps you have installed on your computer, you might be prompted for which app to use to open it. You might also be prompted to view it online, download it, or save it to your hard drive. Here you'll learn how to view and then save a picture that was sent as an attachment.

View and save a photo attachment

1 Open a message that contains an attachment, preferably a photo. It will have a paperclip to the right of the email.

2 If the item doesn't download automatically, click it and then click Download (or other applicable option).

3 Repeat as needed. You may see additional file types; here, "Flying over the desert" is a movie file.

(continued on next page)

> **TRY THIS** In any Inbox, position your mouse next to the messages in the middle pane and click in the check box that appears to select them. You can perform tasks on these selected items as a group, including deleting them.

View and save a photo attachment *(continued)*

4 Click the item after any downloads are complete.

5 The item will open. Slide the divider bar to the right to hide the item.

6 After all items are downloaded, click Save all, if desired. Otherwise, right-click any single item and click Save to only save the selected item.

7 In the resulting screen, name the file as applicable and click Save.

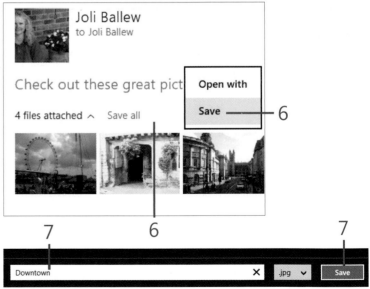

> **TIP** Attachments will open with the app configured in Windows 8.1 as the default. If you want to designate a non-default app to use to open the attachment, right-click the item and choose Open With.

> ⚠ **CAUTION** Attachments can contain viruses and malware that can infect your computer and cause problems. Therefore, don't open attachments from people you don't know, and don't opt to "Run" any file that prompts you to. When in doubt, write the person back and ask them what they meant to send, and if it is safe to open.

Creating and sending a new message

To create your own messages, open a blank email and enter information such as the email address or addresses that you want to send the message to, anybody you want to copy on the message, the subject, and the message itself.

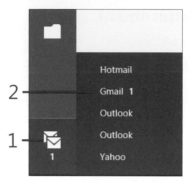

Create and send a message

1 Open Mail and choose the desired account to send from.

2 Click the email account you want to use, if applicable.

3 Click New.

4 Click More.

(continued on next page)

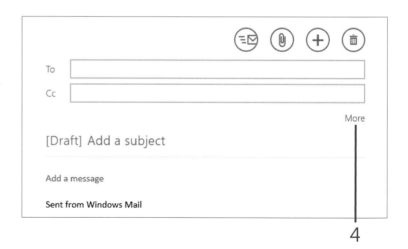

Create and send a message *(continued)*

5 Enter an address or addresses in the To line.

6 In the CC line, enter email addresses you want to publicly copy on the message.

7 In the Bcc line, enter email addresses you want blind copy on the message.

8 If desired, select a Priority. Options are Low, Normal, and High.

9 Enter a message.

10 Click Send.

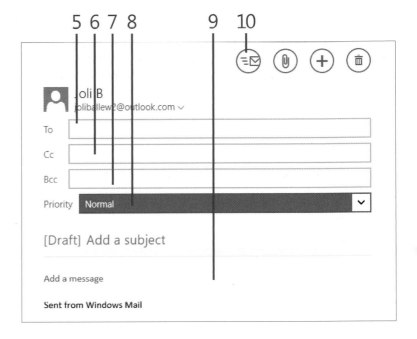

TIP If you start an email and decide you don't want to complete it, click the Trash icon at the top of the new message window.

TIP When you send a blind carbon copy to someone, the recipient gets the message but other recipients don't know that you included them in it. If you send a message with a priority of Low or High, there will be an appropriate tag on the email when it arrives at the recipients Inbox.

Adding attachments

Before you send a message you've created, you might want to add an attachment to it. This is a good way to share documents or images with others. The file that you want to attach must be available on your hard disk or on an external drive such as a USB flash drive, and you have to be able to find it!

Add an attachment to a message

1 Create a new, blank message as outlined previously in this section.

2 Click Attachments.

(continued on next page)

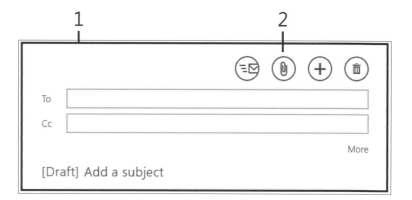

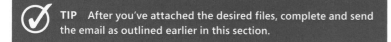 **TRY THIS** To add a hyperlink to the body of an email, right-click inside the body and from the charms that appear click the Hyperlink icon. (It looks like a chain link!) Type the address and the text to be displayed and click Insert Link.

TIP While in Mail, click the Windows key + I on the keyboard and click Options from the Settings pane that appears. Configure your default message font, font size, and color there. Those settings will be applied to all messages you compose.

TIP After you've attached the desired files, complete and send the email as outlined earlier in this section.

Add an attachment to a message *(continued)*

3 Navigate to the item to add. You might need to do one of the following:

   a Open a subfolder.

   b Click Go Up to locate a different folder.

   c Click the arrow by Sort By Name to switch to Sort By Date.

   d Click the arrow beside This PC to access another drive.

4 Click the files to attach.

5 Click Attach (not shown).

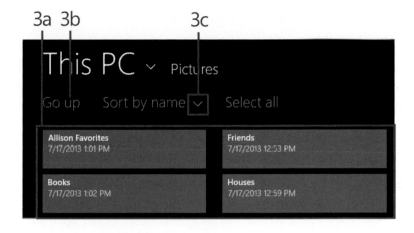

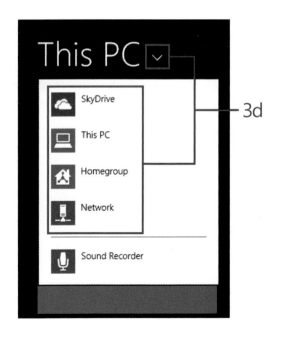

Moving messages to folders

If you left all the email messages you receive and need to keep in your Inbox, it would get quite cluttered. It's better to move messages that you want to keep into folders. Then when you want to access the message again, you can, from the folder in which it is stored. You can create folders from inside Mail, and you can also create them from the email provider's website. However, try creating new folders in Mail first; it's easier.

Move a message to a folder you create

1 With the message you want to file somewhere else open, right-click the email in the Inbox list. .

2 Click Manage folders.

3 Click Create Folder.

4 Type a name for the folder.

5 Click OK. Click OK again (not shown).

6 Drag any email from the Inbox to the left side of the screen.

7 Drop it in the folder you just created.

> ✓ **TIP** Right-click an empty area of the screen to access the available charms and click the Sweep charm (if it is available). This enables you to quickly clean up a selected inbox by selecting the option to delete all messages, messages that are older than ten days, and more.

> ✓ **TIP** To keep your email organized, create as many folders (and subfolders) as you need. When you're ready to access the folder to retrieve email you've stored there, go to the desired account's Inbox, in the left pane click the Folder icon. It is the icon in the left pane that looks like a single folder.

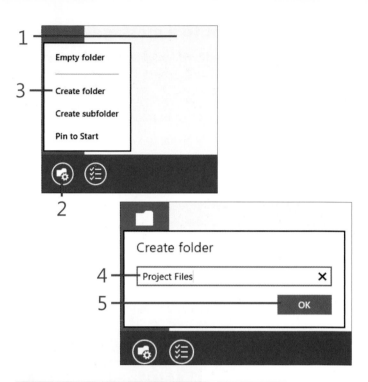

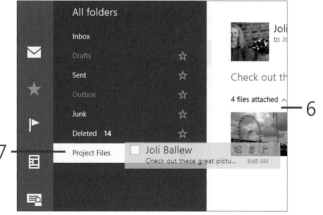

Setting up Skype

Skype is an app available from the Start screen that lets you communicate in real time with others. You can communicate with text, voice, and video, or with a combination of these. To get started, open Skype, and follow the directions for setting it up.

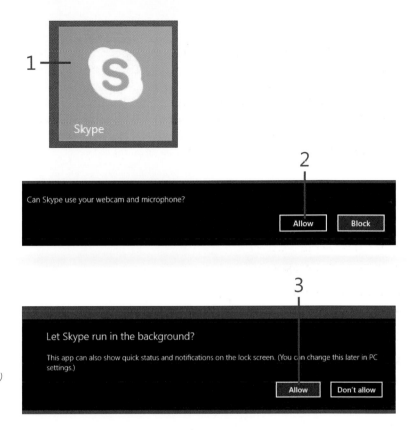

Set up Skype

1 From the Start screen, click Skype.

2 If prompted, click Allow when prompted to let Skype access your webcam and microphone.

3 If prompted, click Allow to let Skype run in the background.

4 If prompted, click one of the following application options:

    a I Have A Skype Account. (You'll have to input account credentials.)

    b I'm New To Skype. (You'll have to agree to terms of service and may be prompted to perform additional tasks.)

(continued on next page)

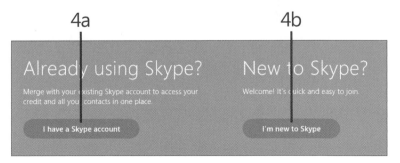

Set up Skype *(continued)*

5 Explore the interface. Scroll right to the People section.

6 Click Echo/Soundtest.

7 Click the phone icon to test Skype.

8 Work through the tutorial by speaking into your microphone as prompted; click the red phone icon when you know Skype is working properly.

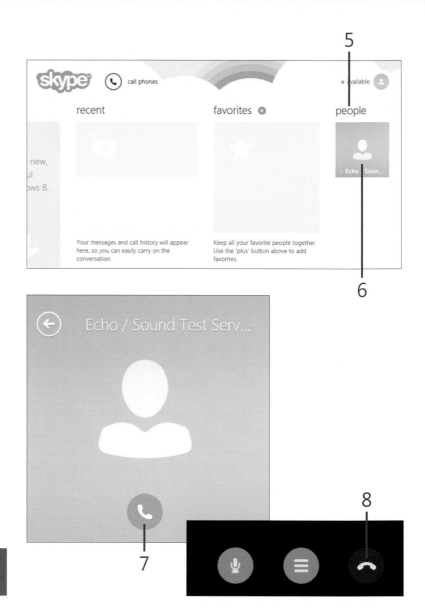

 TIP To return to the Skype home screen, right-click the screen and click Home.

Adding a contact

You will hold Skype conversations, at least initially, with others who also have a Skype account. You might already know people, and those people might already appear in the Skype interface. That's because Skype looks at your contacts and automatically adds those contacts that have a Skype account. You can look for contacts manually from Skype's Home page. You might need to add a contact manually if a Skype contact doesn't appear.

Add a contact

1 With Skype open, right-click an empty area of the screen.

2 Click Add Contact.

3 Type the name of the person to add as a contact in the Search window.

4 Click the Search icon.

5 If you see the person you'd like to add on the screen, click that person's name. If not, click Search Directory.

6 Click the person to add from the resulting list. There might be lots of results.

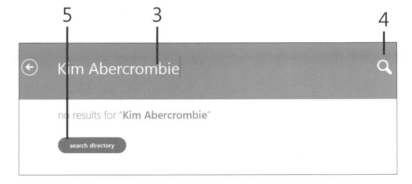

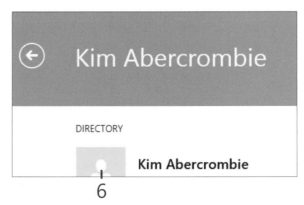

(continued next page)

Add a contact *(continued)*

7 Click Add To Contacts.

8 Type a message, or accept the default message.

9 Click Send.

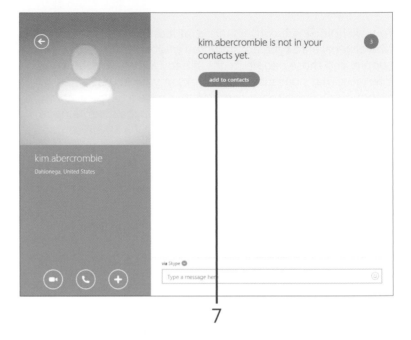

7

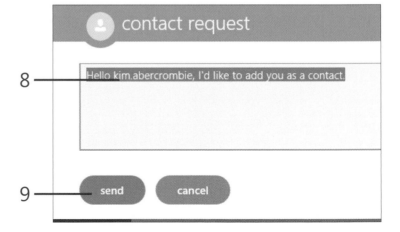

8

9

> **TIP** If you see multiple contacts with the same name as the contact you want to add, look at the city names listed underneath each. You can likely find the desired contact with that information.

Saving a phone number

To make phone calls with Skype, you must have a person's phone number. If the person isn't in your contacts, you'll have to add the number manually.

Save a phone number

1 With Skype open to the Home screen, right-click the screen.

2 Click Save Number.

3 Type a name.

4 Click the arrow beside Mobile.

5 Select a number type.

6 Type a phone number.

7 Click Save.

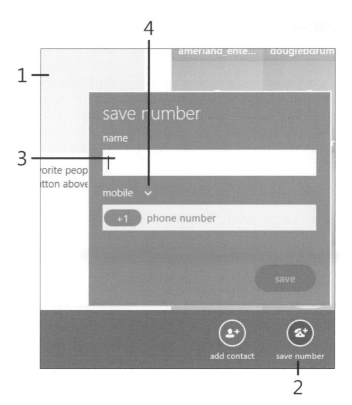

TIP You will have to purchase Skype credit to make calls to mobile phones, land lines, and to other non-Skype entities.

TIP After you perform a task in Skype, including adding a number, adding a contact, and so on, right-click an empty area of the screen and click Home to return to the Home screen.

Messaging with Skype

You can send instant messages to other Skype users for free. You can send text and Short Message Service (SMS) messages for a fee. Instant messages arrive in the recipient's Skype app, because those messages use the Internet for transport. A recipient may have a Skype app on a Windows 8.1 computer, tablet, or phone that they can receive messages on. Text messages are sent to a person's cell phone number and must use cellular towers for transport, which is the reason for the fee.

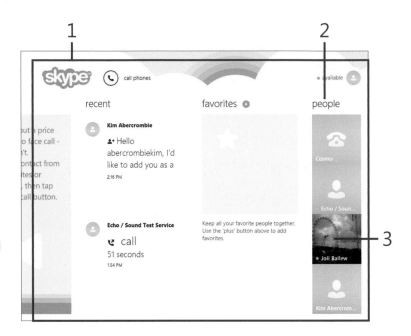

Send a message with Skype

1   With Skype open, access Skype's Home screen by using any method detailed in this section.

2   Scroll right to People.

3   Click a person to send a message to. A green dot means the person is online and available.

4   Verify that Messenger is selected. If it isn't, click the arrow and choose Messenger.

5   Place your cursor in the Type A Message Here box. Type your message.

6   Press Enter on the keyboard.

> **TIP**   If you want to send SMS messages, click SMS Messages in step 3 and then click Buy Skype Credit. After you've purchased the required credits, you can text to others' cell phones from your computer by using Skype.

Making a phone call with Skype

You can make voice calls to other Skype users for free (provide you and they have working microphones). These calls are routed over the Internet and do not use typical phone lines or technologies. However, to make a phone call to a land line or a mobile phone, you'll have to purchase some Skype credit.

Make a phone call to another Skype user

1 With Skype open to the Home page, scroll to locate People.

2 Click a person to call.

3 Click the phone icon.

4 Wait for the other person to answer, and talk as usual; click the red phone icon to end the call.

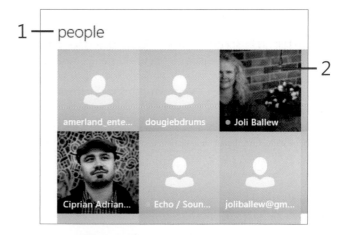

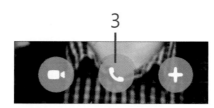

✓ **TIP** From Skype's Home page, you can view your call history under Recent.

✓ **TIP** If the user whom you want to call isn't a contact and you don't see them listed under People in Skype, from the Skype Home page, click the phone icon that is located next to the Skype logo on the far left side of the interface. . You can type the number manually.

Initiating a Skype video call

You can place video calls to other Skype users for free, provided you have a working webcam and microphone. While in the call you can turn off your webcam and/or microphone if you need to, adjust the volume, and even send instant (text) messages.

Initiate a Skype video call

1 With Skype open, scroll to locate People.

2 Click a person to video call.

3 Click the video icon.

4 Wait for the other person to answer, and talk as usual; explore the in-call options.

5 Click the red phone icon to end the call.

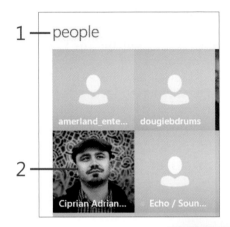

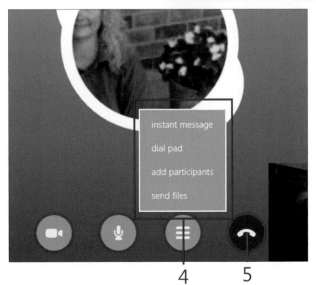

 TIP Skype contacts need to be in your Contacts list to show up in the Skype interface. They need to be online to accept a call.

Buying apps at the Windows Store

11

The Windows Store, available through a tile on the Start screen, offers access to a collection of free and paid apps that let you easily expand the capabilities of Windows 8.1 and personalize your computing experience. You'll find apps there that enable you to do just about anything from tracking your workouts to playing games to watching full episodes of your some of your favorite TV shows.

In this section, you discover how to find the app you need, either searching for it or by browsing different categories in the Windows Store itself. After you know how to find the apps you want, you can download free apps and buy paid ones. You can also discover how to find app reviews, to make sure that you're getting the best app for you, and how to add your own app ratings and reviews to help others find their way.

In this section:

- Searching for apps
- Exploring search options
- Reading app reviews
- Installing free apps
- Viewing your apps in the Windows Store
- Buying an app
- Rating and reviewing an app
- Accessing Windows Store options and syncing app licenses

Searching for apps

If you know the name of the app you want, or have an idea of what it might be called if it were available, you can search for it. You can type just about anything in the search window; you can type the name of your favorite TV channel, your favorite game, or the name of a goal you'd like to achieve (like Healthy Lifestyle).

Find an app

1 From the Start screen, click the Store tile.

2 Right-click an empty area of the screen.

3 Note the available categories (there are more than are shown here).

4 Click Home to return to the home page.

5 Use the scroll bar to access the categories available, including Picks For You, Trending, New & Rising, Top Paid, and Top Free.

6 Click Top Free. (Note what's available.)

(continued on next page)

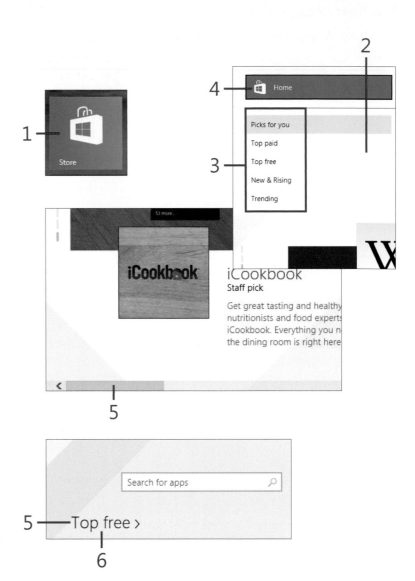

> **TIP** Skype comes preinstalled with Windows 8.1, so if you click Skype in the results you'll see "Installed" on the Details page. However, you can use that page to write a review, see related apps, and to access additional apps created by Skype, like Skype WiFi (which enables you to use Skype at over 1 million public WiFi hotspots worldwide).

Find an app *(continued)*

7 Right-click an empty area of the screen.

8 If you don't see Lifestyle, click the right arrow to move to the right; click Lifestyle. (Note the left arrow appears here in the screenshot to the left of Travel.)

9 Click inside Search For Apps.

10 Type Skype. (Note the options.)

 TIP   In Step 8, you can use your mouse wheel to scroll through the categories to find Lifestyle.

TRY THIS!   From the Windows Store's home page, type inside the Search For Apps window for something generic, such as Weather, and press Enter on the keyboard (or click the search icon in the Search For Apps window). Click the arrow under All Prices, and click Free to cull the results.

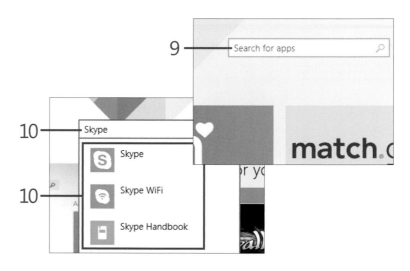

Exploring search options

If you right-click an empty area of the Windows Store's Home page, you have access to the various categories available, including but not limited to Top Paid, Top Free, Photo, News & Weather, and Travel. You can click any of these to view the apps available in that category. After you've clicked something, you can scroll through what's available. However, if you perform a search for a category, say Travel, you have more options than just scrolling through what's available. When you search in this

manner, you can sort the results list for apps by category, price, and other options, such as what is deemed most relevant to your search, what's newest, what has the highest ratings, and what has the highest and lowest price.

Explore search options

1 Click the Store tile.

2 Right-click an empty area of the screen.

3 Click any category to view the results. (We clicked Games.)

4 Type the category name (e.g., Games) in the Search For Apps window.

5 Click the Search icon.

(continued on next page)

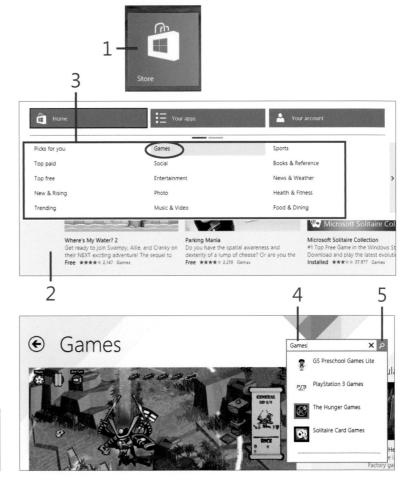

> ✓ **TIP** As you explore the Windows Store, notice the Back arrows that appear. Use the Back arrow to return to a previous screen in the Store.

Explore search options   *(continued)*

6 From the options, select the following:

   a From All Categories: the name of the category you typed.

   b From All Prices: Free And trial.

   c From Sort By Relevance: Sort by highest rating.

7 Scroll through the available apps.

Reading app reviews

Before you buy any app, it's a good idea to see what other people think of it. Even though some apps are free and even though paid apps aren't typically as expensive as desktop software such as Microsoft Office, you still want to make the best choice you can for your needs, saving yourself time and money by getting the right app, right from the start.

Read reviews

1 Using the methods in the previous tasks, locate an app you're interested in.

2 Click the app to display details.

3 Scroll to Ratings And Reviews.

4 Read the reviews.

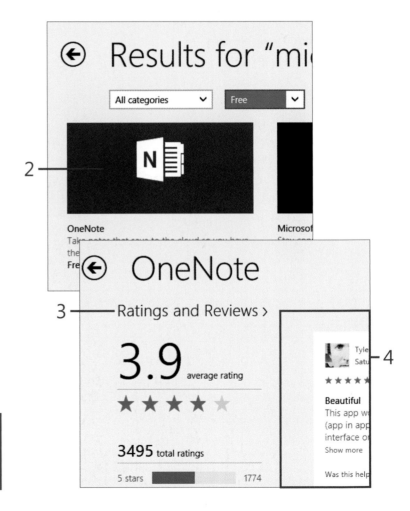

> ✓ **TIP** When you view the details of an app in the Windows Store, you can also view a list of related apps, additional apps available from the same publisher, and more. Make sure to scroll through all of the options while on the details page.

Installing free apps

The best way to learn how to obtain (and ultimately manage) apps is to install a few free apps that pique your interest. After you have these installed, you can learn how to use the apps you acquire, how to uninstall apps you don't like, and how to move from a free version of an app to a paid one, among other things.

Get a free app

1 Locate an app by using any of the methods in the first two tasks of this section.

2 Click the app to display details.

3 Click Try, if prompted.

4 Click Install.

> **✓ TIP** Apps you download from the Windows Store are not pinned to the Start screen; you have to find them in Apps view or search for them using the Search charm. To put a tile for a new app on the Start screen, locate it first, right-click it, and click Pin to Start.

> **✓ TIP** After you click Install, you might find that some apps have a Buy button and a Try button. If you click Try, you can try the app for a while; sometimes this trial is a certain number of hours or a specific number of uses. If you decide you like the app, you can buy it by using the buy option available in the app itself (which will take you to the Windows Store), or you can return to the store.

Viewing your apps in the Windows Store

You can view all the apps that came with Windows 8.1 and all of the apps you've acquired from the Windows Store from Apps view. In that view, you can sort the apps by name, by date installed, by most used, and by category. You can also view the apps you own from inside the Windows Store. You'll do the latter here.

View your apps in the Windows Store

1 Right-click the screen while inside the Windows Store.

2 Click Your Apps.

(continued on next page)

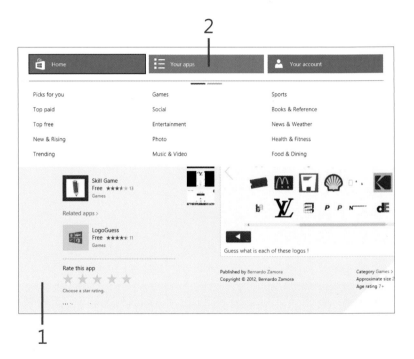

View your apps in the Windows Store *(continued)*

3 Click the arrow in the first window, and select All Apps.

4 Click the arrow in the second window, and click By Name.

5 Click the arrow beside All Apps, and choose a single device, if applicable.

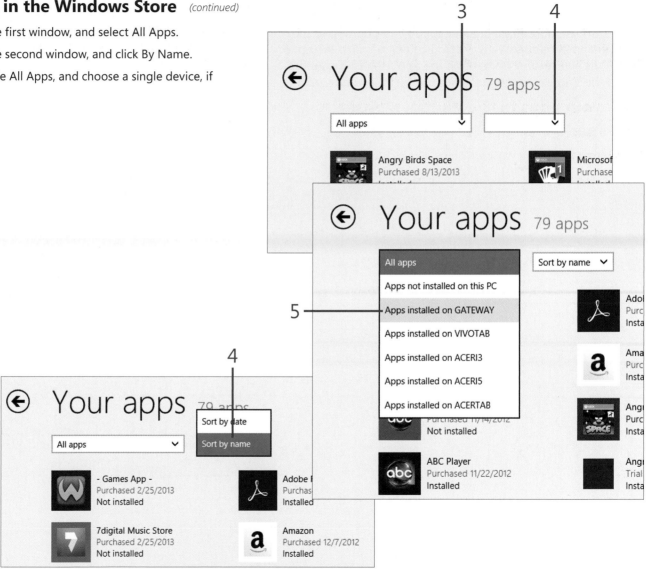

Buying an app

If you installed a free trial of an app, you can upgrade to the paid version in one of two ways. You can either click the option to buy the full version from inside the app itself or locate the app in the Windows Store and click Buy. If you simply want to buy an app that you've located and never tried, click Buy and follow the prompts while inside the Windows Store. Keep in mind that you'll need to configure some way to pay for the app, which you'll have to do only once.

Buy apps

1 Locate an app in the Windows Store, and click it.

2 Click Buy.

(continued on next page)

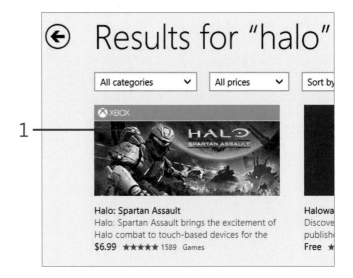

Buy apps *(continued)*

3 Click Confirm.

4 Enter your Microsoft account password.

5 Click OK.

6 Enter payment information, including your billing address. You won't be prompted if you've already entered your information.

7 Click Submit.

✓ **TIP**   App publishers occasionally offer updates. These will be installed automatically unless you specify otherwise. To access the option to turn off automatic updates, while in the Windows Store click the Settings charm. Click App updates. Change the setting for Automatically Update My Apps from Yes to No.

Rating and reviewing an app

Just as you benefit from others' reviews of an app before you invest your time and money in it, other people can benefit from your reviews. You can post a rating for any app that you download from the Windows Store: a one-star rating is low, and a five-star rating is high. You can also submit a written review along with your star rating.

Rate and review an app

1 From the Start screen or Apps view, click a tile to open any app or press Windows logo key+I.

2 Click Rate And Review.

3 Click the star rating.

4 Enter a title.

5 Enter your review.

6 Click Submit.

> **TIP** Your reviews have to comply with Windows Store guidelines, or they can be removed. If you spot a review that's in some way offensive or not in compliance with the rules, you can click the Report This Review link on the review to report the item to Microsoft.

Configuring Windows Store preferences

While in the Windows Store, you can use the Settings charm to configure Windows Store options; there are several to choose from. From the Your Account option, you can change users, enter account information for a user, redeem gift cards, and you can manage the computers you'd like to install your apps on. From the Preferences option, you can configure browsing and recommendation settings for the Windows Store. From the App Updates option, you can opt to automatically update apps (or

not), and you can manually check for app updates. If there's a problem with app licenses, you can sync licenses here too.

In this task, you'll explore how to sync app licenses. This will enable you to fix problems with apps if you aren't seeing up-to-date information for the apps you own (if that ever happens). You'll also see how to access other Windows Store options for future reference.

Access Windows Store options and sync app licenses

1 With the Windows Store open to the Home page, press Windows logo key+I.

2 Note the options, including Your Account and Preferences, and then click App Updates.

3 Click Sync Licenses.

4 Click the Back arrow to return to the Windows Store.

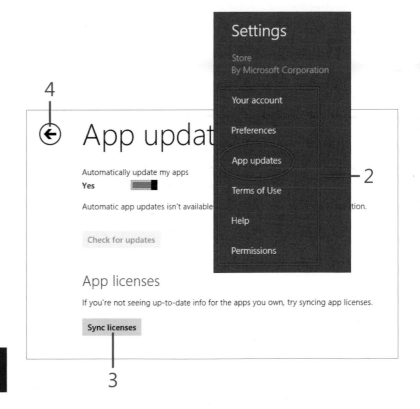

 TRY THIS Repeat the steps here to view what's available from Your Account and Preferences.

Playing music

12

In Windows 8.1, you have two choices for playing and organizing your music: the Music app and Windows Media Player. Both allow you to browse your music collection, play music, and create playlists. When you want to do these things, you can use the app that you feel most comfortable with.

Beyond these similarities, the two apps differ greatly. They do not offer access to all of the same features. For example, if you want to buy music online or listen to Internet radio stations, you need to use the Music app. If you want to burn and rip music CDs, you'll need to use Windows Media Player. If it sounds complicated, don't worry; it isn't. Generally, you'll use the Music app to listen to and purchase music, and you'll use Windows Media Player to manage that music, such as when you burn music CDs, view other types of media (videos and pictures), or sync music to a portable music player.

In this section:

- Navigating the Music app
- Listening to music
- Searching for music
- Creating a playlist in the Music app
- Listening to Radio
- Finding music to purchase by browsing
- Finding music to purchase by searching
- Buying music
- Configuring music in the cloud
- Playing music with Windows Media Player
- Sorting and viewing music
- Creating playlists in Windows Media Player
- Ripping music you own
- Burning music to a CD

Navigating the Music app

The Music app, available from the Start screen, offers access to your personal, local, music collection, to Internet radio stations, and to the Xbox Music store. You can configure the app to also include music stored on external drives and networked computers that share media. This app, like others you might have used, also offers access to related music account settings (including your account name, payment information, and any Xbox memberships you might have) and preferences (which include how you want to manage music in the cloud, downloaded music, and handle media information).

Navigate the Music app

1 From the Start screen, click Music. (If you see any prompts, read them and make choices as applicable.)

2 Click Collection. (You might see that music you own is being added, or you might see other notifications.)

3 While in Collection, click the arrow beside Albums to sort the music in another way, perhaps by Artists.

4 While in Collection, click the arrows beside All Music and By Date Added to further sort the list.

(continued on next page)

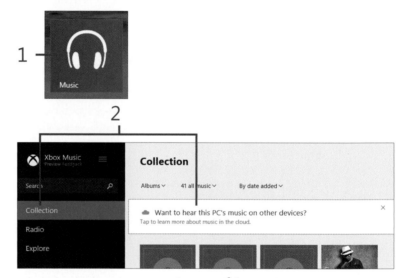

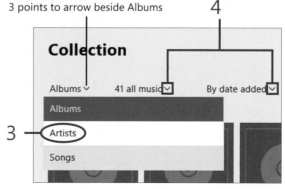

3 points to arrow beside Albums

Navigate the Music app *(continued)*

5 Use the scroll bar on the right side of the screen, if applicable, to view the music available to you.

6 Click Explore to access the Xbox Music store.

7 Use the key combination Windows key+I to open the Settings charm. Note the options, including Account and Preferences.

8 Click outside the Settings charm to hide it.

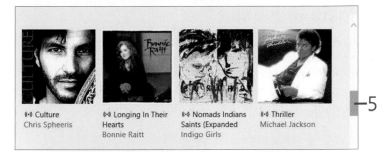

> **SEE ALSO** To work through this section, you'll need to have music on your computer or available from the cloud. If you don't have either, consider skipping to the applicable sections here that show you how to acquire music—specifically, Buying Music and Ripping Music You Own.

> **TRY THIS** You can search directly from the Start screen for music tracks. Just begin typing the name of a song, artist, or album, and press Enter on the keyboard. The results will include the music that matches your search that's available from the Music app.

Listening to music

The Music app is perfect for listening to music. It's easy to sort music by albums, artists, and songs, and by what's stored on your personal PC or music stored in the cloud. You can even sort music by the date it was added, by genre, artist, and other criteria. After a track is playing, controls are available for managing playback.

Play music

1 With the Music app open, click Collection.

2 Click the arrow beside Albums, and click Songs.

3 Click the title of the song you'd like to play.

4 Click the Play button.

(continued on next page)

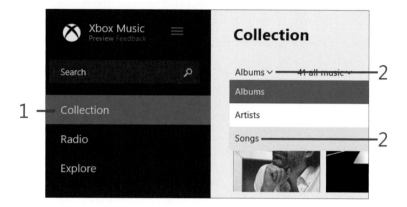

> **TRY THIS** While playing a song, click the album thumbnail that appears along with the playback controls. You'll be able to view additional information about the song and artist.

Play music *(continued)*

5 Click the Volume icon, and use the slider to adjust the volume.

6 Click the back arrow to restart the song.

7 Click the forward arrow to play the next song.

8 Click the Pause button to pause playback.

6   8   7   5   5

> ✓ **TIP** Some songs have icons beside them. A cloud icon means the song is available in the cloud and you can also play it when your device is offline. A Wi-Fi icon means that you can stream the song from the cloud, and you can play it on your device. (If you see a cloud with a rotating arrow on it, the song is syncing to the cloud.) You might see a down arrow with "downloading" showing, meaning the song is currently being downloaded. No icon means that the song is available on your computer only. An exclamation point means there's a problem with the music file or that you downloaded music with a music pass and then canceled your subscription.

Searching for music

If you have a large music collection, one way to find a song or album to play is to search for it inside the Music app. There are two sorting options after performing a search; you can sort the results by In Collection or Full Catalog. Here you'll search inside your personal music collection.

Search for music

1 With the Music app open, click Search.

2 Type something that relates to the track, artist, album, and so on that you'd like to play.

3 Click the item that appears in the results that most closely matches what you're looking for.

4 On the Results page, verify In Collection is selected.

5 Click the desired result.

SEE ALSO If you want to buy music, refer to the sections here titled Finding Music To Purchase By Browsing, Finding Music To Purchase By Searching, and Buying Music.

Creating a playlist in the Music app

A playlist contains songs that you group together yourself, often for a purpose. You might create a playlist for exercising, another for relaxing, and another to listen to while having dinner.

Creating a playlist in the Music app

1 With the Music app open on the Home screen, click New Playlist.

2 Type a name for the new playlist.

3 Click Save.

4 Click Collection.

(continued on next page)

1 —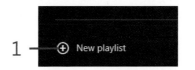

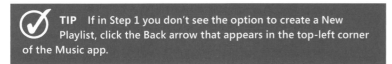

> ✓ **TIP** If in Step 1 you don't see the option to create a New Playlist, click the Back arrow that appears in the top-left corner of the Music app.

Creating a playlist in the Music app *(continued)*

5 Locate a song to add to the playlist, and right-click it.

6 Optionally, repeat step 5, if desired, to select additional songs in the current view.

7 Click Add To.

8 Click the desired playlist.

9 Repeat steps 4-8 as desired.

> **TRY THIS** If you've already created playlists in Windows Media Player, iTunes, or using some other method, you can import those playlists so that you can access them from the Music app. To do this, click Import Playlists, click Import Playlists again, and wait while the Music app updates. (A playlist is just a list of songs; no files are moved to create or import a playlist.)

> **TRY THIS** Click your new playlist in the Music app. Click any song, and click Play to start playback. Playback will continue until the playlist ends. To have the playlist to start over at the first song after it reaches the end, from the Music toolbar (right-click if you don't see it), click the ellipses and move the setting for Repeat from Off to On.

Listening to radio

You can play Internet radio from the Music app, provided that you are online. The Music app chooses the station based on an artist name that you input.

Play music

1 With the Music app open, click Radio.

2 Click Start A Station.

3 Type the name of an artist you like.

4 Make a selection from the results under Radio.

5 Use the controls at the bottom of the screen to control playback.

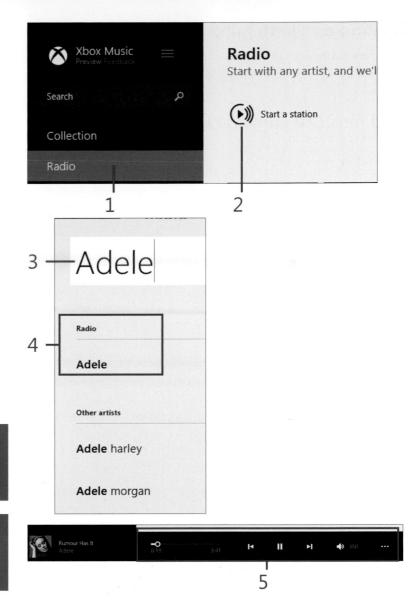

> ✓ **TIP** Click the album art thumbnail available to the left of the playback controls to access a different view that includes album art and a song list. Use the slider (called a scrub bar) that is just to the right of the thumbnail to move through the song quickly.

> ✓ **TIP** Radio stations you create and configure will be available when you click Radio next time. You can then simply double-click the item to play that station; you don't have to start a new station each time.

Finding music to purchase by browsing

There are many ways to find music to buy, but the best ways are to either browse what's new or what's at the top of the charts or to search by name for the track, album, or artist by name you want to find. Here you'll browse the Xbox Music store for new albums.

Find music to purchase by browsing

1 In the Music app, click Explore.

2 Click the View All option by New Albums.

(continued on next page)

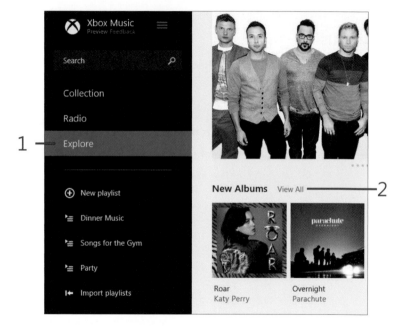

Find music to purchase by browsing *(continued)*

3 Click the arrow beside All Genres.

4 Select a genre.

5 Scroll through the results, and click any album.

6 Click the Back button to return to the previous screen, and browse as desired.

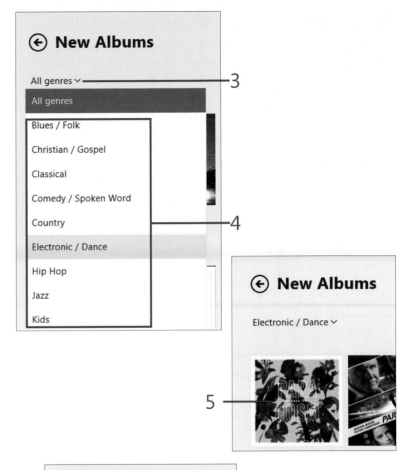

Finding music to purchase by searching

If you know what you want to purchase, you can search for the album or track by name. This is the best way to search if the item you want isn't something brand new or something that has recently hit the top of the charts.

Find music to purchase by searching

1 In the Music app, start typing the name of the artist, album, or song in the Search pane. Notice that it appears in the Search window as you type.

2 Verify that Full Catalog is selected. Click any result.

3 Continue to click and browse as necessary to locate the album or track to purchase.

(continued on next page)

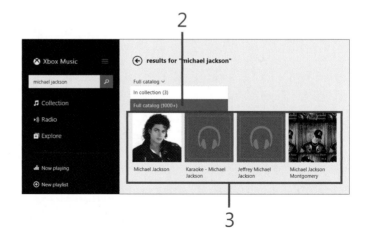

Find music to purchase by searching *(continued)*

4 If you want to preview the music, click Play.

4

Immortal
Michael Jackson, 2011, Pop, EPIC

1   Workin' Day And Night (Immortal Version)

2   The Immortal Intro (Immortal Version)

3   Childhood (Immortal Version)

> **TIP**   If you know the name of the song or album you want to buy, you might also want to try typing it at the Windows 8.1 Start screen and pressing Enter on the keyboard. Look through the results as applicable, and click an entry. The result is that you still end up in the Music app, at the Xbox Music Store, so if you're already in the Music app, using the app's Search window is probably more efficient.

Buying music

If you don't have a subscription for a music pass, you'll have to purchase music. To purchase a song or album, you must have a valid form of payment on file with the Xbox Music store. This payment is associated with your Microsoft account and can be configured in many ways. One way is to access the Settings charm while in the Music app and click Account. You can click Manage Payment Options to get started. However, if you don't have any information on file and want to buy music, simply follow the instructions here and enter information when prompted. These steps assume that you already have payment information on file.

Buy a selection

1 In the Music app, locate a song to buy.

2 Click the Buy button.

3 If prompted, enter your Microsoft account password, and click OK.

4 Click Confirm.

> **TRY THIS** You can enter payment information at *www.microsoftstore.com*. Just log in with your Microsoft account and click Payment. What you enter will be associated with your account and will serve as a valid form of payment at the Xbox Music store, the Xbox Video store, the App store, and any other related entity.

Configuring music in the cloud

When you purchase songs from the Xbox Music store, those songs are stored in the cloud. This means you can access those songs from each Xbox Music device you sign in to. You can also enable Music Match. Music matching lets you listen to the music stored on your PC on other Windows 8-based devices. Any device with Xbox Music is connected to the cloud for free. You configure these options from the Settings charm while in the Music app.

Configure music in the cloud

1 With the Music app open, use the Windows key+C to access the Settings charm. Click it.

2 Click Preferences.

3 Read what is available here regarding your monthly streaming limit (unless you have an Xbox music pass).

4 Verify that the first entry under Music In The Cloud is set to On.

5 To enable music matching, move the slider under Automatically add matched songs on this PC to my music in the cloud from Off to On.

> ✓ **TIP** If you aren't seeing all of the songs in the Music app that you know are saved to your computer, from the Preferences pane shown in step 2, click Choose Where We Look For Music On This PC. Then, click the + sign to navigate to the folder where music is stored. You can add external drives and networked devices here too.

> → **TRY THIS** From Preferences (in step 2), scroll down to locate two additional sections: Downloads and Media Info. Read the description of these and configure as desired.

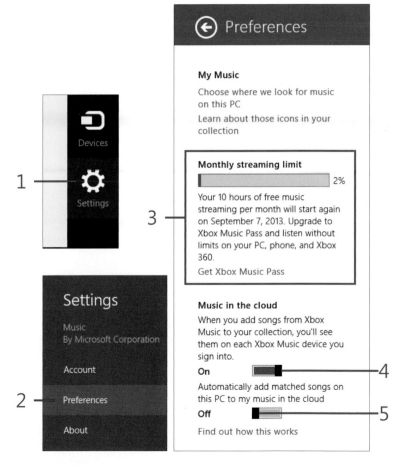

Playing music with Windows Media Player

Windows Media Player offers various ways to organize, access, and view all kinds of media, including music, videos, pictures, recorded TV, playlists, and others, such as audiobooks. However, because this section is about music, music will be the focus here. You can also easily access shared media from other computers on your local network that have been configured to share. That media appears under Other Libraries, and can be accessed and played as if it were on the computer you're sitting in front of. Windows Media Player is a desktop app.

Play music

1 On the Start screen, type **Windows Media Player**.

2 In the search results, click Windows Media Player.

3 To display your music, click Music.

4 To play a selection, double-click it.

5 To go to the next selection, click the Next button.

6 To go to the previous selection, click the Previous button.

7 To play songs in a random way, click the Shuffle button.

8 To repeat a selection while it's playing, click the Turn Repeat On button.

9 To adjust the volume control, click and drag it.

10 To pause playback, click the Pause button.

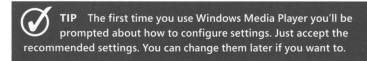

TIP The first time you use Windows Media Player you'll be prompted about how to configure settings. Just accept the recommended settings. You can change them later if you want to.

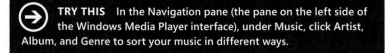

TRY THIS In the Navigation pane (the pane on the left side of the Windows Media Player interface), under Music, click Artist, Album, and Genre to sort your music in different ways.

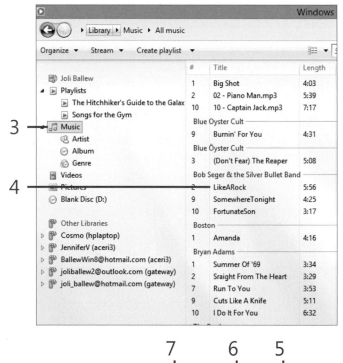

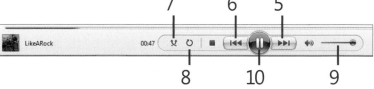

Sorting and viewing music

In Windows Media Player, you can sort items in your music library and playlists by various criteria, such as Title, Artist, Composer, or Length. You can also view music selections by categories such as Artist, Album, and Genre.

Sort and view music

1 With Windows Media Player and the Music library open, click Organize.

2 Click Sort By.

3 Click a criterion to sort by.

4 Click the arrow to the left of Search.

5 Click Icon.

6 Repeat step 4 and click Tile.

7 Repeat step 4 and click Details.

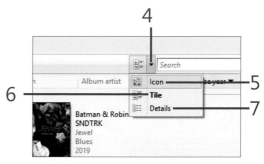

Creating playlists

You can create playlists that contain songs you hand pick and position them in the order you prefer. You can create playlists for all kinds of activities, including exercising, sleeping, eating, and entertaining. Playlists are all about customizing your music experience, and they're easy to create.

Create a playlist

1 With Windows Media Player open, click Create Playlist.

2 Enter a name for the playlist.

3 To save the name, click outside the playlist name field.

4 Click Music (or other option) to search for a song.

5 Browse to a song to add, and right-click it.

6 Click Add To.

7 Click the playlist name to which to add the selection.

8 To add additional selections to the playlist, repeat steps 5 through 7.

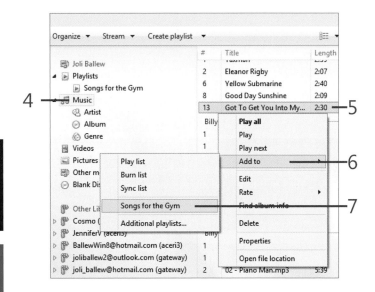

> **TRY THIS** After you've created a playlist, click it in the left pane to show it, and then double-click any song in the list to start playing it. Right-click the playlist, and click Add to, and then click Burn list to burn the playlist to an audio CD. Right-click the playlist, and click Sync list to sync the playlist to a connected, portable music player.

> **TIP** You can select multiple, noncontiguous music tracks by holding down the Ctrl key when making selections. Use the Shift key to select contiguous tracks. (Click the first and last in a list.)

Ripping music you own

If you own music CDs, you can legally copy the songs to your computer (and then share them with other computers on your network or burn them to CDs). This process is called *ripping*.

You can then configure the Music app to use music matching (detailed earlier in this section) so that you can access those songs from other Windows 8-based devices.

Rip music you own

1 With Windows Media Player open, insert a music CD into the CD drive.

2 Deselect any songs that you do not want to copy.

3 Click Rip CD.

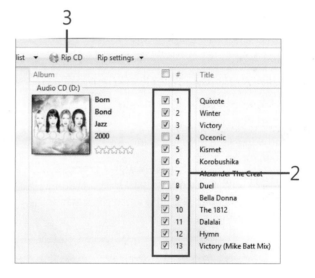

> **TRY THIS** With Windows Media Player open, connect a portable music player. Click the Sync tab. Follow the directions to add songs to the Sync pane to copy to the player.

> **TIP** Click Rip Settings to change the default settings for the ripping process. You can change the audio quality and the format, among other things. One thing you might want to change is Format, especially if you want to sync those songs back to an older MP3 player that doesn't support newer file formats.

Burning music to a CD

You can burn songs you own to CDs so that you can listen to the music in your car's CD player, among other places. However, you can copy only songs that you have the right to copy; you might not be able to copy every track you have on your computer.

Burn music to a CD

1 With Windows Media Player open, insert a blank, recordable CD into the CD drive bay.

2 Click Open The Burn Tab.

3 Browse to a song to add to the Burn list, using any method already introduced in this section.

4 Drag the song to the Burn list.

5 Continue to add songs as desired, and stop when the slider at the top of the Burn tab shows that it's full.

6 Click Start Burn.

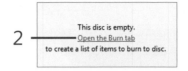

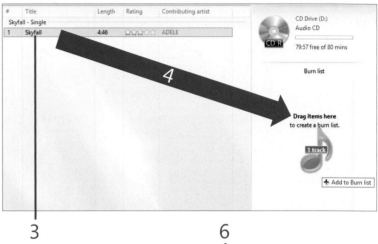

 TIP You can reposition songs in the Burn list by clicking and dragging, and you can right-click to remove songs from the list.

Viewing pictures and video

13

Windows 8.1 comes with three apps for working with visual media. These are the Photos app, Video app, and Camera app, all available from the Start screen. The Photos app lets you access your pictures, create folders for managing those pictures, and edit the pictures you keep. The Video app lets you access your personal videos (perhaps those you've taken with your digital camera), other types of video media you own, and offers access to the Xbox Video store where you can rent or buy movies and TV shows. The Camera app lets you take pictures and video directly from your device (provided that your device includes a camera). Pictures and videos you take with the camera appear in the Pictures folder, and you can view them from the Photos app.

In this section:

- Displaying pictures
- Searching for pictures
- Creating folders for your pictures
- Moving pictures to new folders
- Setting a picture on the Photos tile or lock screen
- Cropping a picture
- Editing a picture
- Playing a slide show
- Exploring the video app
- Playing a personal video
- Buying or renting a video
- Using the camera

Displaying pictures

If you have pictures saved to your computer in the Pictures library or subfolders therein, you'll see them when you open the Photos app. If you've already created subfolders in the Pictures folder to organize your pictures, you'll see those subfolders too. You might see a combination of single pictures and subfolders.

Display a picture

1 From the Start screen, click the Photos tile. The tile might be live and show images on it.

2 Use the scroll bar at the bottom of the screen (move your cursor to see it), to scroll through what's available.

3 Click any single picture to view it in full-screen mode.

4 If there are no single pictures available (but there are subfolders):

   a Click any subfolder to open it.

   b Click any picture to view.

(continued on next page)

1 —

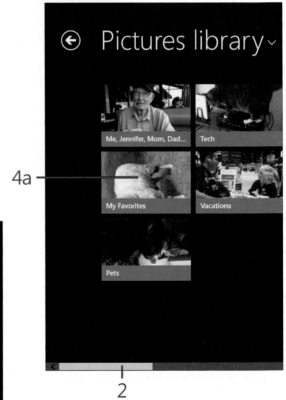

4a

2

4b —

Display a picture *(continued)*

5 Click the screen.

6 Click the Back arrow that appears in the top-left portion of the screen to return to the previous view.

7 Click the Back arrow again if necessary.

⚠ **CAUTION** If you don't have any pictures saved to your computer, you won't be able to view them as outlined in this section. However, you can acquire pictures in many ways; you can import them from a digital camera, take them with a built-in camera if one is included with your device, save pictures from the Internet or an email, or copy them from another computer or drive, among other things.

✓ **TIP** The pictures that you save to your computer are saved, by default, in a folder called Pictures. Generally, after you acquire so many pictures that the Pictures folder becomes unwieldy, you create subfolders. You learn about the Pictures folder and additional folders (Music, Videos, Documents, and so on) in Section 18, "Managing data."

Searching for pictures

If you know the name of the picture you're looking for or a tag associated with it, you can search for it using the Search charm while in the Photos app. When you click on a picture file that is stored in the Pictures library, it will open in the Photos app. (If you click a picture file that isn't located in the Pictures library, currently it opens on the desktop in Paint or your default desktop program.)

Search for photos

1 While inside the Photos app, use the Windows key+S to open the Search bar.

2 Type the name of the file to open.

3 Click the picture file in the results. If the photo is stored in the Pictures library, it will open in the Photos app.

4 Click the screen.

5 Click the Back arrow that appears to return to the Photos app Home page.

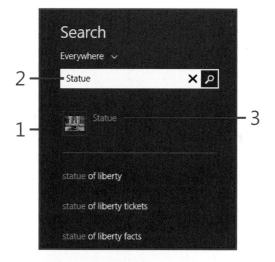

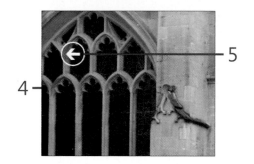

 TIP You can search for a picture file (by name) from the Start screen too. If you see what you want in the results, click it.

TRY THIS Instead of clicking the picture file (step 3) to open it, right-click it. The option Open File Location appears. Click this to open the folder that contains the file. (File Explorer will open on the desktop.)

Creating folders for your pictures

At some point, you'll likely have so many single pictures show-ing in the Photos app that navigating to a specific picture is difficult, if not seemingly impossible. When this happens, you'll need to create subfolders to organize those pictures. Here you'll create subfolders; in the next task, you'll learn how to move pictures to these new folders.

Create folders

1 While in the Photos app, click any Back arrows as applicable to return to the Home page.

2 Right-click the screen, and click New Folder.

3 Type a name for the folder.

4 Click Create.

5 Locate the new folder.

> ✓ **TIP** Create multiple subfolders with names that are represen-tative of the pictures you need to organize, such as Travel, Pets, Friends, Children, and so on. You can then create subfolders inside those folders when desired.

> → **TRY THIS** Right-click the Home screen of the Photos app, and click the Details View icon. The view will switch from Thumb-nails view to Details view. In Details view, you'll be able to see a very small thumbnail alongside the name of the picture file, the date it was taken, and its size. This also enables you to see more items on the screen at one time.

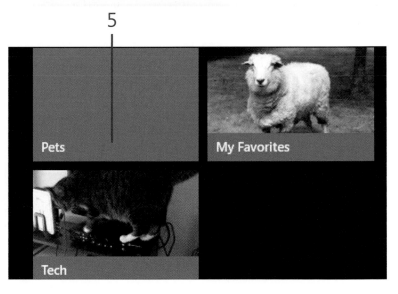

Moving pictures to new folders

If you've expanded the folder system to include subfolders as outlined in the previous task, you can move your pictures into them to organize them. At the present time, you can't drag photos into these folders, so here you'll learn how to cut and paste to move them. However, be careful when cutting pictures; when you cut a picture it is stored temporarily on a virtual "clipboard" and it'll stay there until you opt to paste it elsewhere, which you should do immediately and before you cut or copy something else.

Move pictures

1 Using any technique outlined in this section, locate the picture to move.

2 Right-click the picture to move.

3 Right-click any other pictures to move to the same folder.

4 Click Cut. (Note the other options, including Copy and Delete.)

5 Using the navigation options outlined in this section, locate the folder to move the pictures to and click it to open it.

(continued on next page)

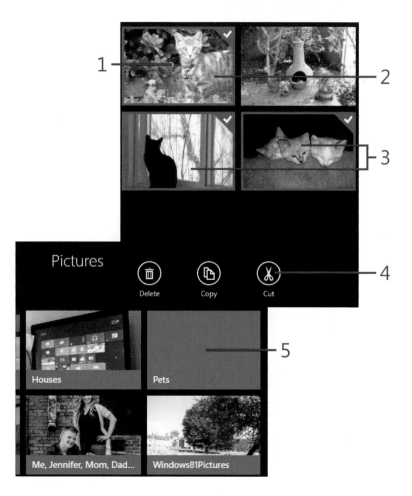

Move pictures *(continued)*

6 Right-click the screen.

7 Click Paste.

8 Note the pictures have been moved.

9 Note the path to the pictures.

10 Click the Back arrow to return to the previous screen.

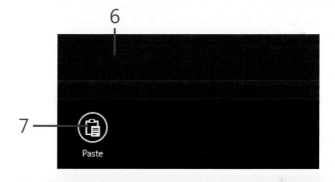

> ⚠️ **CAUTION** Depending on the speed of your computer and other factors, it might take a few seconds for the pictures to be pasted after you click Paste in step 7. Be patient. Also, the folder tile might not show an image on the tile for a while. Closing and reopening the app might speed up this process.

> **TRY THIS** Right-click any folder, and click Rename to rename the folder. You can also rename single pictures this same way.

Setting a picture on the Photos tile or lock screen

The Photos tile is a live tile. This means that pictures will appear on the tile, and they will change regularly. This is a nice feature, unless there are pictures you don't want to see on the Start screen that are also in your Pictures folder! If you'd like a single picture to appear on the Photos tile, you can set one. You can also set a photo to be the picture you see on the lock screen.

Set a picture on the Photos tile or lock screen

1 In the Photos app, browse to a picture to set as the Photo app tile or the lock screen.

2 Click the picture to use to open it in full-screen mode.

3 Right-click the screen.

4 Click Set As.

5 Click Photos Tile or Lock Screen.

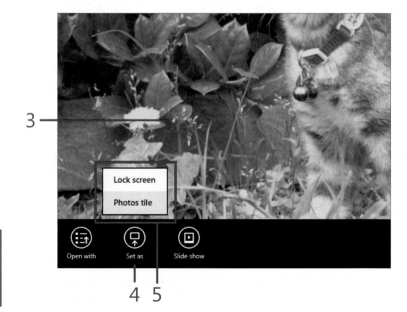

> **TIP** You can share photos via Mail while inside the Photos app. With a picture displayed in full-screen mode, press Windows key+C, click the Share charm, and click the Mail button. Enter an email address, enter a subject, and then click the Send button.

Cropping a picture

You can do some simple editing in the Photos app, including cropping out unwanted parts of pictures. Locate the picture to crop using any method outlined in this section, click it to open it in full screen, and then follow the directions here to crop it.

Crop a picture

1 Open a photo to crop in full-screen mode in the Photos app.

2 Right-click the screen.

3 Click Crop.

4 Drag from each corner to create the desired effect.

5 Click Apply.

6 Click the appropriate option:

   a Save A Copy.

   b Update Original.

   c Undo (and then Cancel, not shown).

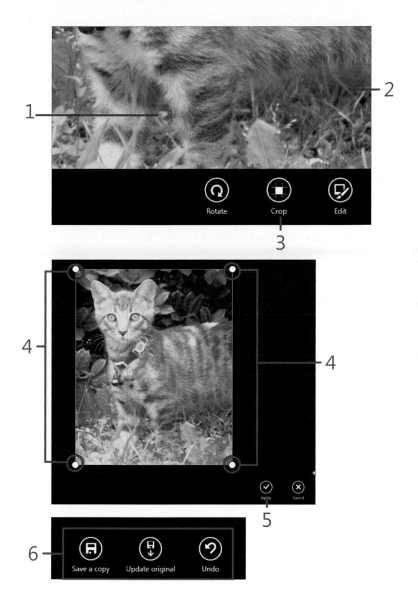

TIP Note in step 3 that Crop is not the only option when you right-click. Rotate and Edit are also options.

TRY THIS To open a picture in another program, right-click the picture while it is in full-screen mode and click Open With. Choose the desired option. You will see Paint and Windows Photo Viewer, but you might also see other options, such as Windows Media Center, Photoshop, or others.

Editing a picture

You can do some simple editing in the Photos app. You can use an automated "Auto Fix" option to let the Photos app fix the image for you. There are thumbnails available to preview what the fix will look like after you apply it. You'll see the Auto Fix option in step 4 here although you won't apply it.

You can also manually apply basic fixes such as rotating, cropping, removing red-eye, and retouching the image; and you can manually manage light, color, and effects. There isn't enough room here to detail each of these options, but you will learn how to apply Light settings, including Brightness, Contrast, Highlights, and Shadows. You'll apply the same techniques to use other editing features.

Edit a picture

1 Using any method outlined thus far, open the picture to edit in full-screen mode.

2 Right-click the screen.

3 Click Edit.

4 Click Light.

(continued on next page)

Edit a picture *(continued)*

5 Note the four options: Brightness, Contrast, Highlights, and Shadows. Click one.

6 Use the wheel to improve the picture as desired.

7 Right-click.

8 Click one of these options:

   a Save A Copy.

   b Update Original.

   c Cancel.

   d Undo (not shown).

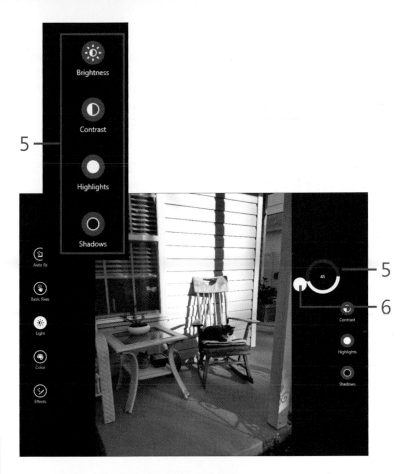

> ✓ **TIP** If the color seems off in a photo, click Color in step 4. There you can manually change the options for Temperature, Tint, Saturation, and you can choose Color Enhance to further refine the color effect..

> → **TRY THIS** To fix red-eye, from the editing options, click Basic Fixes. From there, choose Red Eye. Position the cursor over the red-eye, and click.

Playing a slide show

A slide show of pictures is just what it sounds like: Windows displays one image after another automatically, using the pictures in a folder you select. You can select a set of images to play in a slide show by placing them in a folder, which can be useful for giving sales presentations or sharing personal images with friends.

Play a slide show

1 In the Photos app, navigate to the folder that contains the pictures to use in a slide show.

2 Click to open any picture in the folder.

3 Right-click the image.

4 Click Slide Show.

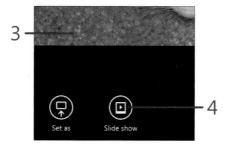

TIP A slide show will run through all the photos in a selected folder and then cycle through them again. There is no way to pause the slide show; you can only start and stop it. To stop a slide show, click the screen.

Exploring the Video app

The Video app offers access to your personal videos, videos you own or have rented, and the Xbox Video store. The Xbox Video store offers recommendations for you based on previous purchases and provides access to new and featured movies and TV shows.

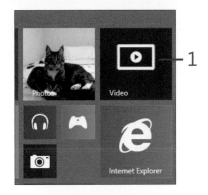

Explore the Video app

1 From the Start screen, click the Video tile.

2 Scroll left to view your personal videos. (You might not have any.)

3 Scroll right to access the Xbox Video store categories.

(continued on next page)

Explore the Video app *(continued)*

4 Locate Featured Movies.

5 Locate New TV shows.

6 Click the Search icon.

7 Type the name of a movie you'd like to locate and press Enter on the keyboard.

8 Continue exploring as desired.

4 and 5

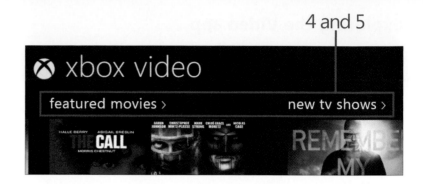

6

7

> ✅ **TIP** If you want to make purchases from the Xbox Video store, you'll have to set up payment options for your Microsoft account. You can do that from the Settings charm, from Account.

> ➔ **TRY THIS** While inside the Video app, open the Settings charm (Windows key+I). Click Preferences to access the app's options. One is Choose Where We Look For Videos On This. If you store videos in places other than the Videos folder, such as an external or network drive, use this to option navigate there to include those areas.

Playing a personal video

There are two things you can do with the Video app: You can view your personal videos, or you can purchase or rent, and then view, professional ones. Here you'll play a personal video. The Video app offers several controls for managing playback after you've started it, including play, pause, stop, fast forward, and rewind. You'll need to have personal videos on your computer in the Videos folder to work through this set of steps.

Play a video

1 In the Video app, scroll left to view your personal videos.

2 Click any video to play.

(continued on next page)

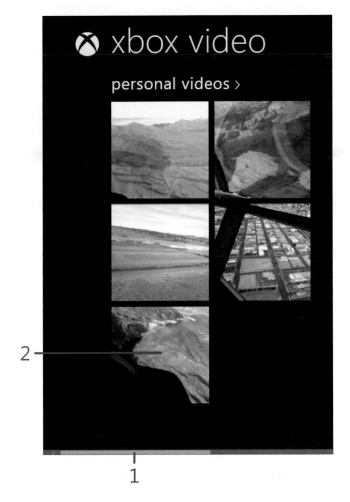

Play a video *(continued)*

3 Right-click the screen to access the playback options.

4 Click Volume.

5 Use the slider to change the volume.

6 Click Pause.

7 Click Play.

8 Click outside these controls to hide them.

9 Move your cursor to access the on-screen controls.

(continued on next page)

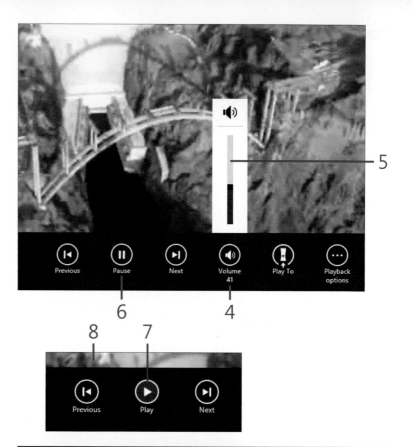

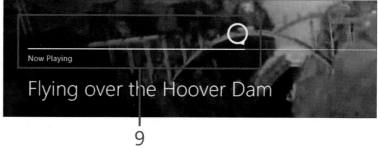

Play a video *(continued)*

10 Drag the circle on the scrub bar to move quickly backward and forward through the video.

11 Click Pause.

12 Click the Back button to return to the previous view.

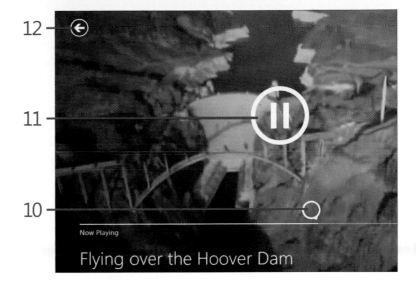

TIP On the toolbar that contains the playback controls (see step 4), click Playback options to turn on closed captions (as applicable) and to turn repeat on or off. Turning repeat on will cause the video to start over when it ends.

TIP You right-click a video to bring up a toolbar at the bottom of the screen, and you can right-click again or click an empty area of the screen to hide it.

Buying or renting a video

To purchase or rent media from the Xbox Video store, you must have a valid form of payment on file. This payment is associated with your Microsoft account and can be configured in many ways. One way is to access the Settings charm while in the Video app and click Account. You can click Manage Payment Options to get started. However, if you don't have any information on file and want to buy media here, simply follow the instructions and enter information when prompted. These steps assume that you already have payment information on file.

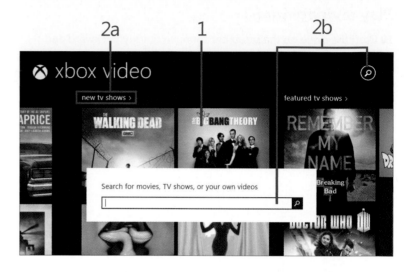

Buy or rent videos

1 In the Video app, locate media to rent or buy on the Home screen.

2 If you don't see what you want on the Home screen you can:

  a Click any title, such as New TV Shows.

  b Click the Search option to type the name of a movie or TV show.

  c Click any result.

(continued on next page)

Buy or rent videos   *(continued)*

3 Click the item you'd like to purchase.

4 Click the Buy button, Buy Season Pass button, or the Rent button as applicable. (You might not see every option.)

5 Type your Microsoft account password.

6 Click OK.

7 Click the Confirm button.

8 Click Done.

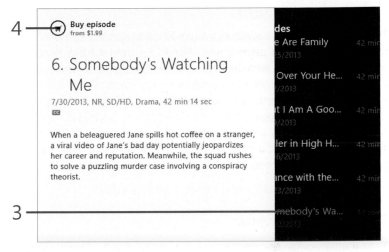

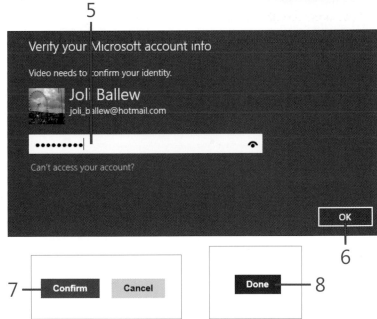

TRY THIS You can enter payment information at *www. microsoftstore.com*. Just log in with your Microsoft account there and click Payment. What you enter there will be associated with your account and will be a valid form of payment at the Xbox Music store.

TIP After you make a media purchase, that media will appear to the far left side of the Video app. You'll see Personal Videos, My TV, and My Movies. The latter two will appear only when you make related purchases.

Using the camera

If your computing device has a built-in camera, you can use that camera to take both photos and videos. Some devices also have a front-facing and a rear-facing camera. The options you see when you open the Camera app will depend on what kind of camera and device you are using.

Use the camera

1 From the Start screen, click the Camera tile.

2 Note the options. Click the digital camera icon to take a picture.

3 Click the video camera icon to start recording video.

4 Click the Stop button to stop recording.

5 Right-click the screen.

6 Note the options, including the following:

    a Camera Roll—to view the images and video you've taken.

    b Timer—to set up a timer.

    c Exposure—to configure exposure settings.

7 Click Exposure.

8 Use the slider to make changes.

(continued on next page)

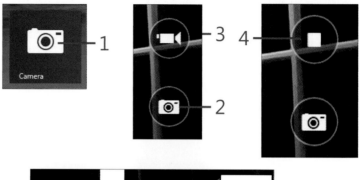

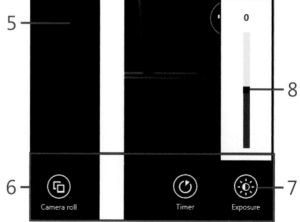

Use the camera   *(continued)*

9 Use Windows key+I to open the Settings charm, and click Options.

10 Configure settings as desired.

11 Use the Windows key to return to the Start screen, and click Photos.

12 Click any applicable back arrows in the top-left corner of the Photos app to get to the Home page (not shown).

13 Click Camera Roll to view the pictures and videos you've taken here.

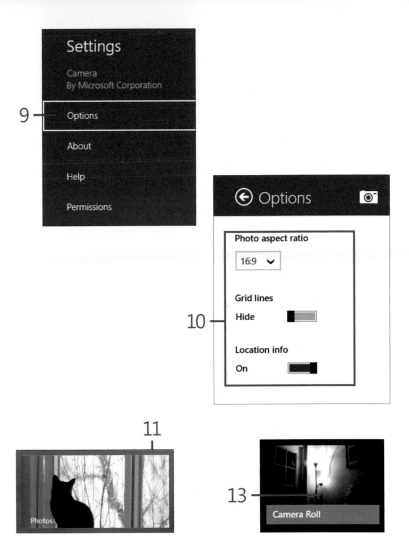

> **TRY THIS**   In step 6, click Camera Roll. Use the back and forward arrows to see what you've captured. Right-click to delete images and videos. Right-click to access Camera to return to the camera app.

> **TIP**   Pictures you take with the camera appear in the Photos app in a folder called Camera Roll. Videos you take appear there too. Both appear in a folder named Camera Roll in File Explorer on the desktop, in the Pictures folder.

> **TIP**   The camera is accessible from the lock screen by using touch. Just flick down from the top to activate it. You can configure the related setting from PC Settings, from PC and Devices, from the lock screen option.

Working with desktop apps

14

Everything today is about the newer, modular apps, those computer applications that are streamlined and that can be used to perform only the tasks you want and need and not much else. With apps, there aren't any traditional interface elements to get in your way, like menus, tabs, ribbons, and on-screen customization and personalization options. These are the apps you've been learning about in the first half of this book.

However, there are still the familiar desktop apps. These are apps that open on the desktop, some of which you might already have experience with. Desktop apps include, but are not limited to, Notepad, WordPad, Paint, Sticky Notes, third-party software that you install from CDs and DVDs, and applications that you download from the Internet. Anything that opens on the desktop is a desktop app.

In this section, you'll learn how to use the most common elements of some of the more familiar desktop apps, including how to use a menu, a ribbon, how to format text, and how to print and save files. You can use what you learn here to work with other desktop apps, all of which will have similar features and can be used in the same manner.

In this section:

- Opening and closing desktop apps
- Using menus
- Using ribbons
- Formatting text
- Using the Clipboard
- Inserting objects
- Printing a document
- Saving a file
- Exploring other desktop apps

Opening and closing desktop apps

Desktop apps open in a window on the desktop. These types of apps typically offer full-featured tools accessible from menus, toolbars, ribbons, and tabs. Almost all desktop apps also offer the ability to save, print, and open documents. You open desktop apps by searching for them, or by clicking the related tile on the Start screen, or from the Apps view. You can have multiple desktop apps open at once, and you can reposition them in many ways. You close desktop apps by clicking the red x in the top-right corner of the app window.

Open and close desktop apps

1 At the Start screen, type **Notepad**.

2 Click Notepad in the results.

3 On the desktop, click the Start button.

4 On the Start screen, begin typing **WordPad**.

5 Click WordPad in the search results.

6 On the desktop, click the Start button.

7 On the Start screen, type **Paint**.

8 Click Paint in the search results.

(continued on next page)

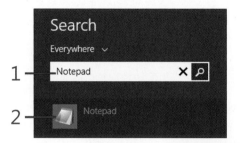

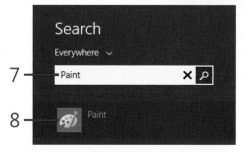

Open and close desktop apps *(continued)*

9 Drag from any corner or the top edge of any of the three open apps to resize them.

10 Drag from the title bar of any of the three open apps to move them.

11 Click the x in each of the three app windows to close them.

Alternatively, you could leave them open if you plan to work through the rest of the exercises in this section.

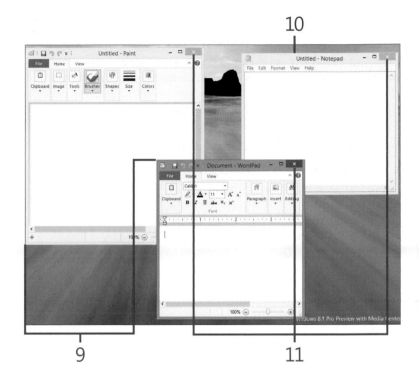

TIP Click the − sign in the top-right corner of any window to minimize the window to the taskbar. Click its icon on the taskbar to restore it. Click the single square (or, if maximized, the double-square) to maximize and restore a window.

TIP Click the down arrow on the Start screen (which appears when you move the cursor), to access Apps view. This view shows all of the available apps and desktop apps. You can then use the scroll bar at the bottom of the screen to locate the app you want to open.

Using menus

Menus have been part of desktop applications for a long time. You click a menu, and a list of commands appears. Click a command, and something else happens: a dialog box might be displayed offering a group of settings; a submenu might be displayed offering additional commands, or the applications might take an action, such as opening a new, blank document.

Use the File menu in Notepad

1 On the Start screen, type **Notepad**.

2 Click Notepad in the search results.

3 Click File.

4 Click commands to open a new document (New), open an existing document (Open), save a file (Save and Save As), and so forth.

5 Note the keyboard shortcuts. Ctrl+N opens a new documents; Ctrl+O opens an existing document, and so on.

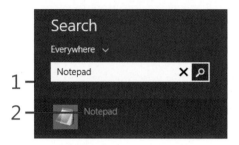

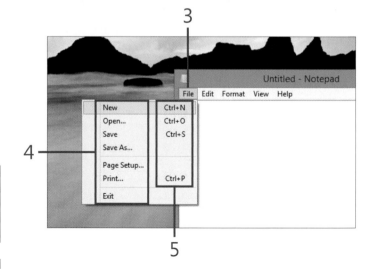

 TIP Some desktop apps that have a menu bar have entries in their menus that include an arrow beside the menu option. This means that when you click that option in the menu, more options will appear. To continue, you'll need to choose the option you want.

TIP To hide a menu without selecting an option, click outside the menu or press the Escape key.

Using ribbons

Many robust desktop applications provide a graphical interface that groups like items together. Instead of a simple menu,
tools are arranged on various tabs on a *ribbon*. For example,
the ribbon generally includes a File tab that displays commands
for working with files, such as Open, Save, and Print. There is
usually a Home tab that offers the most commonly used editing
tools, including Cut, Copy, Paste, Resize, Select, and so on, as
applicable to the program. Most desktop applications that use
a ribbon also offer a View tab on which you can use available
tools to zoom, show rulers, view full screen, and so forth.

Explore the ribbon in Paint

1 From the Start screen, type **Paint**.

2 Click Paint in the results.

3 Click the File tab.

4 Move the cursor over Save As.

5 Note the options to save a file.

6 Click outside the options to hide them.

(continued on next page)

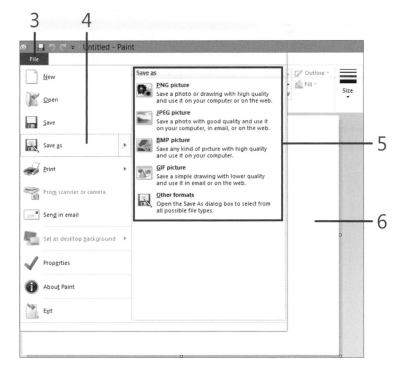

Explore the ribbon in Paint *(continued)*

7 Click the Home tab and view the options.

8 Click the arrow under Brushes to see options.

9 Click the View tab.

10 Click Rulers.

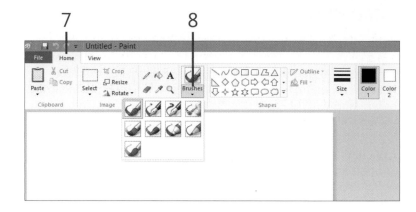

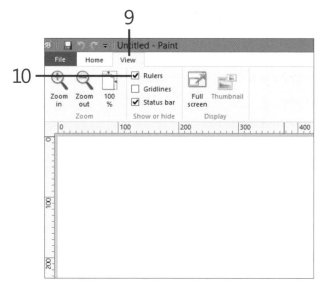

✓ **TIP** In some programs, such as those in the Microsoft Office Suite, groups of tools, such as Font on the Home tab, include an additional symbol in the lower-right corner of the tab group. Clicking this opens a dialog box with additional options.

Formatting text

In most desktop apps you use, including Notepad and Word-Pad, you'll need to enter text. After you enter text, tools are often available to format the text with color or by applying bold, italic, or underline effects, among others. Most formatting options are on a ribbon's Home tab.

Format text in WordPad

1 On the Start screen, type **WordPad**.

2 Click WordPad in the results.

3 Verify that the Home tab is active.

4 Type a few words.

5 Click and hold the left mouse button, and then drag the mouse across some of the text.

6 Click Bold.

7 Click Italic.

8 Click outside the selected text to deselect it.

(continued on next page)

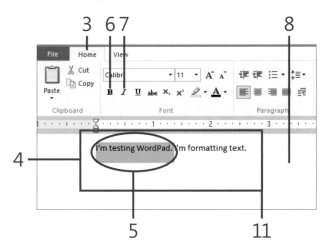

Format text in WordPad *(continued)*

9 Position your cursor in the line of text.

10 Click the Center option in the Paragraph group.

11 Click and drag to select all of the text again (shown on previous page).

12 Click the arrow beside the font size.

13 Click 72.

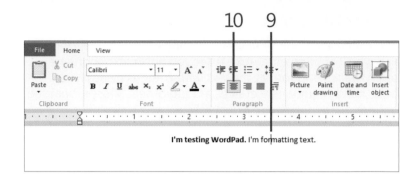

TIP While on the Home tab, select some text and experiment with the different fonts available from the Font list in the Font group. Also, experiment with changing the font color.

Using the Clipboard

When you want to copy or move a piece of text, an object such as clip art, or something else, perhaps a picture from one location to another, you'll use the Clipboard. This is a virtual holding area for text and objects that you cut (remove) or copy from a document. An item stays on the Clipboard until you paste it somewhere else. By default, the Clipboard holds only one item at a time, the last item you cut or copied. If you cut or copy several items, only the last item will be available for pasting.

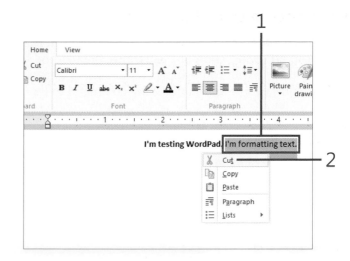

Use Notepad with the Clipboard

1 With WordPad open and text entered, select some text.

2 Right-click and select Cut.

3 Click the Start button.

4 On the Start screen, type **Notepad**.

5 Click Notepad in the results.

6 In Notepad, right-click inside the document and select Paste.

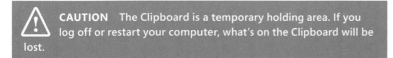

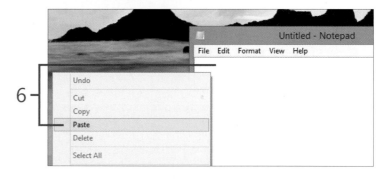

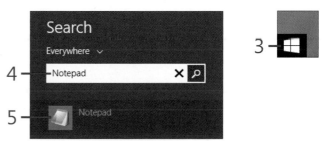

> ⚠ **CAUTION** The Clipboard is a temporary holding area. If you log off or restart your computer, what's on the Clipboard will be lost.

> ➔ **TRY THIS** Select and then cut some text. Then, use the key combination Ctrl+Z to "undo" the cut and put the text back. (The cut data will still be available on the Windows Clipboard.)

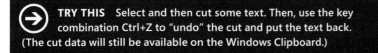

Inserting objects

In many applications, you can insert a graphic element like a photo or clip art (a collection of illustrations, photos, and animations that come with some applications, such as Microsoft Word). In highly robust applications, the command to do this might be on an Insert tab on the ribbon, and you might be able to insert additional items too, like tables, shapes, different types of word art, graphs, and so on. In WordPad, you can insert only a few things, and the options to do so are on the Home tab.

Insert a picture in WordPad

1 With WordPad open, click the Home tab.

2 Click Picture.

3 Click a picture to add. (You might have to double-click a subfolder to locate the one you want.)

4 Click Open.

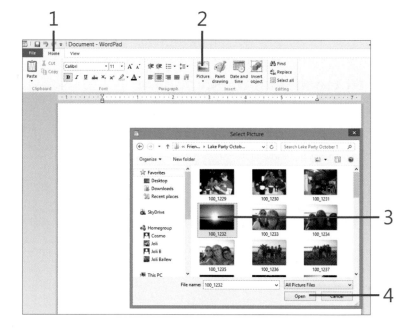

✓ **TIP** In WordPad, you can also insert a drawing you've created in Paint, the date and time, and other WordPad documents, among other things.

Printing a document

You can access the Print command in almost all desktop applications. Most of the time, the command is available from the File menu or the File tab, as is the case with Notepad and WordPad. In some applications, you can select text and then right-click that selection to have the option to print in a drop-down menu, as you'll see here in Internet Explorer. Finally, some applications also offer a Print Preview option so that you can see what the printout will look like before you actually print it. You'll see Print Preview in WordPad and Paint, among other desktop apps. To print, you must have a printer installed and turned on.

Print a file from the Internet Explorer desktop app

1 From the desktop, locate the taskbar.

2 Click Internet Explorer.

3 Click inside the Address bar.

4 Type *www.microsoft.com,* and press Enter on the keyboard. (You might see results under the Address bar.)

5 Right-click any picture.

6 To print the picture, click Print Picture.

7 To print a webpage, right-click and empty area of the page and click Print.

> **→** **TRY THIS** In WordPad, type a few words. Click the File tab, point to Print, and note the three options: Print, Quick Print, Print Preview. Repeat with Notepad, and click File to access the one option: Print. Finally, open Paint. From the File tab, point to Print. Note the three options: Print, Page Setup, and Print Preview. Experiment as desired.

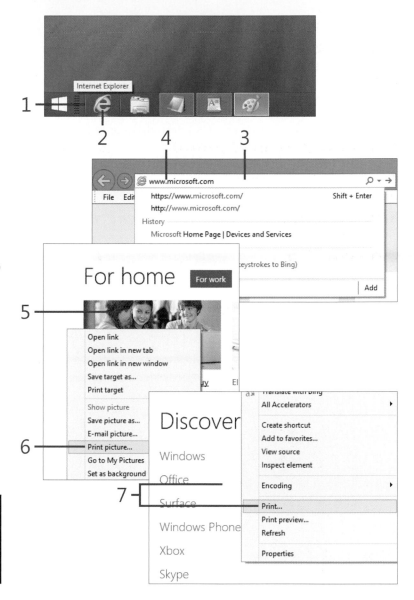

Saving a file

After you have entered some content in a document, created a graphic in an image editing program, created slides for a presentation, or otherwise generated some type of file, it's a good idea to save the file on a regular basis so that you don't lose your work. You can save a file to your computer's hard disk or to external storage such as a USB flash drive or networked computer. When saving for the first time, you can give the file a name, choose a place to save the file, and choose a file format.

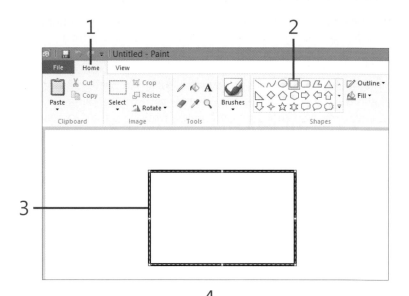

Save a file with Paint

1 With Paint open, click the Home tab.

2 In the Shapes group, click any shape shown.

3 Click and drag to draw the shape using your mouse.

4 Click Brushes.

5 Draw a design with the brush.

(continued on next page)

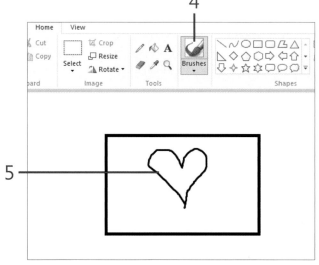

Save a file with Paint   *(continued)*

6 Click File.

7 Point to Save As.

8 Click GIF Picture.

9 Note where the file will be saved by default. You can select another folder or subfolder if desired.

10 Enter a document name. Untitled is the default name.

11 Note that GIF is listed in the Save As Type box. You can select a different file type if desired.

12 Click Save.

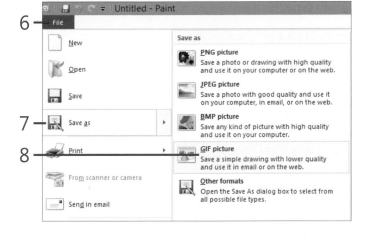

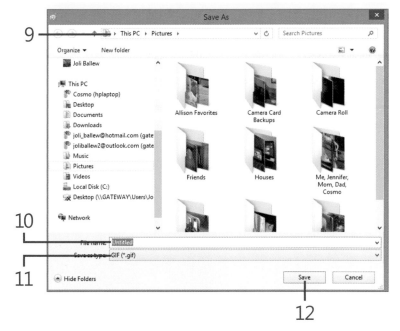

TIP You can save a file to a computer on your network if you have the proper permissions to do so. Click Network in step 9 to locate a folder to save to.

Exploring other desktop apps

There are many desktop apps available in Windows 8.1. You can find them from Apps view, available from the Start screen. Each time you open a new desktop app that you've yet to experience, you'll see familiar features, including menus and ribbons.

Explore other desktop apps

1 From the Start screen, click the down arrow to access the Apps view.

2 Click the arrow beside Apps.

3 Click By Category.

(continued on next page)

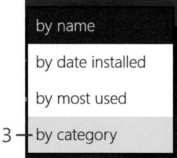

Explore other desktop apps *(continued)*

4 Locate the category Windows Accessories.

5 Click Calculator.

6 Note the three menus, and click each: View, Edit, Help.

7 Repeat steps 1, 2, and 4, and click Snipping Tool.

8 Click the arrow beside New.

9 Click Full-Screen Snip. (A *snip* is a screen capture.) You can minimize, close, or save the snip, as desired.

(continued on next page)

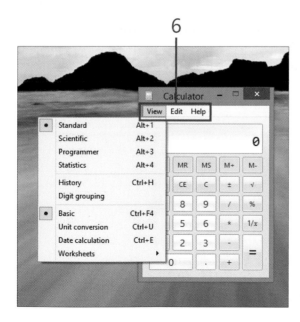

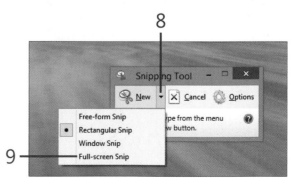

Explore other desktop apps (continued)

10 Note the resulting menu options: File, Edit, Tools, and Help. Explore as desired.

11 Repeat steps 1 and 2. Under Windows System, click This PC.

12 File Explorer opens. Note the ribbon's tabs: File, Computer, and View. Explore as desired.

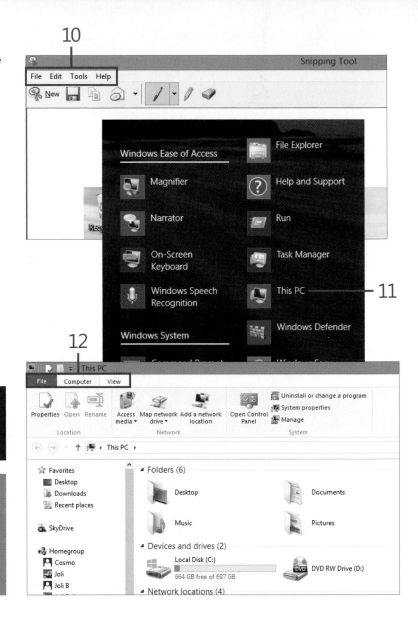

TRY THIS From the Apps view screen, open Control Panel, Math Input Panel, and Windows Defender. If you decide you prefer the Apps view over the Start screen, set it as the default in Taskbar Properties on the Navigation tab.

CAUTION You won't be able to see all of the menu options or the ribbon options in all cases and in all views. If you feel you're missing out on something, maximize the window of the application. Also, look for a small arrow to the left of the blue question mark in the top-right corner of some desktop applications to maximize (or unhide) the ribbon. Finally, note that you'll see additional ribbon options when you select specific things, such as pictures, documents, and so on.

Working with devices and networks

15

Hardware devices, such as printers, scanners, cameras, and so on, must be connected to your computer before they can be used. The first time you connect a device, a device driver is installed to let the hardware communicate with the computer and vice versa. Windows 8.1 makes installation of these device drivers easy, because it has a library of drivers available, and if Windows can't find the right one for your device, it'll go online to find it. Usually, all you have to do is connect the device, plug it in, and turn it on. Installation is automatic.

In addition to connecting to other devices, you can connect your computer to other computers to network them. You can connect to both wired and wireless networks, and to private and public ones. If you have a home network, you can join it to share printers, files, an Internet connection, media, and more. If you have access to a free, public network, you can use it to connect to the Internet.

In this section:

- Adding a device
- Troubleshooting device installations
- Connecting to a Bluetooth device
- Connecting to a private network
- Sharing with a homegroup
- Troubleshooting network connectivity
- Connecting to a public network
- Changing network settings
- Using Airplane Mode

Adding a device

If you have a device, perhaps a printer or camera, that you want to use with your computer, you first need to establish a connection between the two. Generally, you'll use a USB cable or, in rarer situations, a FireWire cable. Follow the directions included with the device to make the physical connection, and plug the device into a wall outlet if applicable (or install fresh or charged batteries) before you continue here. If the device also came with an installation CD, put that CD in the CD drive bay.

Add a device

1 With the device physically connected to the computer and plugged into a wall outlet, turn on the device.

2 Wait to see whether the device installs on its own.

3 On the Start screen, type **view devices and printers**.

4 In the results, click View Devices And Printers.

5 Verify that the device installed properly. (It should not have an exclamation point beside it.)

> ✓ **TIP** If the device's icon has an exclamation point beside it in step 5, refer to the next section, "Troubleshooting device installations," to apply a fix.

> ⚠ **CAUTION** If a device is grayed out in the Devices And Printers window (see step 5), the device is unavailable. Usually, this is because the device has been turned off or has been physically disconnected.

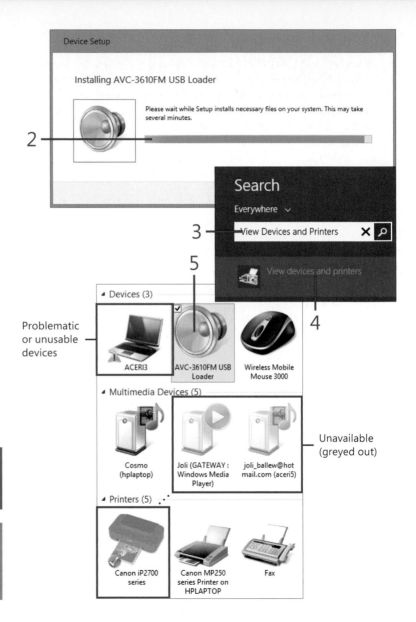

Troubleshooting device installations

If a device doesn't install properly, it's almost always because a compatible device driver could not be found for it. A device driver enables the computer to communicate with the device and vice versa. To fix installation problems (and to fix problems that occur after a successful installation), you'll want to work through the available troubleshooting wizards. If the wizard can't solve the problem, you'll have to visit the website of the device manufacturer and search for a device driver that will (and install it using the instructions you'll find there).

Troubleshoot device installations

1 On the Start screen, type **view devices and printers**.

2 In the results, click View Devices And Printers.

3 Click the problematic device's icon. (If installation was unsuccessful, the device name might not be correct.)

4 Click Troubleshoot.

5 Wait while the wizard offers a solution; click Apply This Fix if applicable.

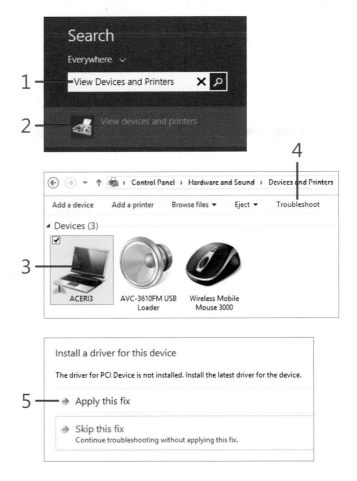

> ✓ **TIP** Control Panel offers an entire section named Hardware And Sound. There you can troubleshoot and configure all kinds of devices, including monitors and displays, pen and touch settings, power options, sound devices, and more.

> ⚠ **CAUTION** If you work through the troubleshooting wizard and apply a fix but the problem persists, you'll have to get a compatible device driver from the manufacturer's website. Make sure that you know the exact make and model of your device, and that you get a driver created for Windows 8-based computers. If there is not driver for Windows 8, try a driver that is compatible with Windows 7.

Connecting to a Bluetooth device

Bluetooth is a technology that allows you to connect two compatible Bluetooth-enabled devices wirelessly. Making a Bluetooth connection is called *pairing*. Bluetooth technology is used for short-range communications between the two compatible devices, such as when you connect a tablet to a Bluetooth keyboard or mouse or connect a desktop PC to wireless speakers. To connect to a Bluetooth device, Bluetooth must be enabled on your computer or tablet and the device itself must be turned on and "discoverable". (Not all computers and devices come with built-in Bluetooth technology.)

Make your computer discoverable

1 At the Start screen, type **Bluetooth**.

2 Click Bluetooth Settings in the results.

3 If applicable, move the slider for Bluetooth from Off to On.

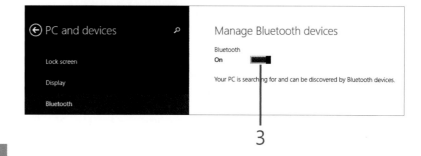

⚠️ **CAUTION** When you don't need to connect to a Bluetooth device, it's a good idea to turn Bluetooth off, especially if you're using a tablet or laptop. Your device will deplete its battery reserves more quickly if Bluetooth is left enabled, because it'll always be looking for a device to pair with. Also, there's a risk that someone might use a device like a tablet or phone to tap into your computer's contents or settings.

Connect to Bluetooth devices

To connect your computer to your Bluetooth device, the Bluetooth device (a keyboard, mouse, sound device, and so on) must be turned on. Most devices also require you to press a "pair" button to make the device itself discoverable. Because devices differ from manufacturer to manufacturer, you'll have to refer to your specific device documentation to find out how to do this. When you've enabled your Bluetooth device and readied it for pairing, the two devices should be ready to pair. (You might be prompted to input a pairing code: again, this depends on the device, the manufacturer, and the device type.)

1 At the Start screen, type **Bluetooth**.

2 Click Bluetooth Settings in the results.

3 Click Ready To Pair.

4 Click Pair. (If prompted, type the pairing code and perform any other required tasks.)

5 To disconnect at any time, click the Bluetooth device that is connected and click Remove Device.

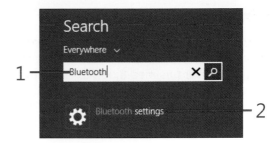

> **TIP** Generally you use a Bluetooth device the same way you use a device that's physically connected to your computer. For example, if it's a wireless speaker, you can use the volume and playback controls in the Music app just as you would with connected speakers.

Connecting to a private network

A private network is one that you trust. It's a network that includes computers you want to share files, media, and devices with, and can include various media devices, such as an Xbox 360. Most of the time, a private network is your home network, although it can also be a network at your place of business.

However, it is not a network that you find in a coffee shop or library; that's a public network. In this example, you'll connect to a personal wireless network.

Connect to a private network

1 Click the Windows logo key+I to open the Settings charm; click the Network button.

2 If necessary, move the slider under Wi-Fi from Off to On.

3 Click the network name.

4 If desired, click Connect Automatically.

5 Click Connect.

(continued on next page)

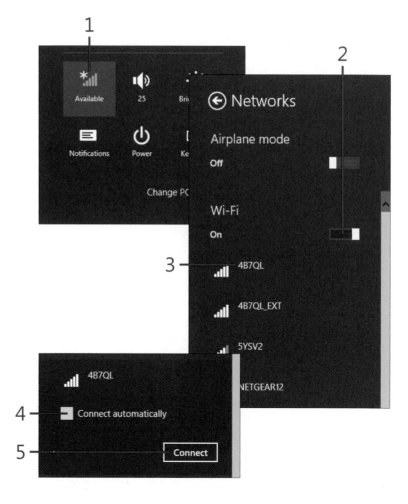

> **TIP** If prompted, choose the appropriate network type during the connection process and choose to share (private) or not share (public) data on the desired network.

Connect to a private network *(continued)*

6 If prompted, type the network security key, press an applicable WPS button, or perform any other required task, and click Next.

7 Note that you are connected.

6 ─

7 ─

> **TIP** Homegroups are networks of computers that are Windows 7 -based and Windows 8-based, of which the purpose is to make sharing resources easier than manually configuring sharing. If you connect a private network that has previously been configured as a homegroup, you will likely be prompted to join that homegroup to have sharing configured automatically. If you don't yet have a home-group set up and are prompted to create one, you can work through the wizard that appears to do so.

> **TIP** If you opt use Ethernet to connect to a device such as a router, switch, or hub, you won't need to enable Wi-Fi and join the network as outlined in these steps. Usually, you'll just be con-nected. However, you will likely be prompted regarding what to share or if you want to join a homegroup, so continue to the next section if that's the case.

Sharing with a homegroup

The first time you connect to any network, you are prompted regarding what you'd like to share, if anything. If it's a private network you trust, like one in your home, you'll probably want to share your music, photos, documents, printers, and so on. (You won't want to share anything on a public network.) You might be able to complete this part of sharing without much effort at the time you make the network connection.

However, the best way to configure sharing for the long term is to create or join a homegroup. A homegroup automatically shares what you want shared, and keeps private what you want

private. When you create a homegroup, other computers and people who are authorized to use your network can join it. Here, you'll learn to create a homegroup; however, if during this process you find there is already a homegroup to join, do that instead.

Although there are lots of ways to share data, the easiest is to create or join a homegroup. If, as you work through the steps here, you find that you can join a homegroup that already exists, do that instead.

Create a homegroup

1 On the Start screen, type **homegroup**.

2 Click HomeGroup Settings.

(continued on next page)

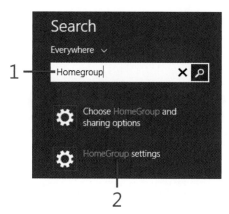

Create a homegroup *(continued)*

3 For each of the following options, perform the described action:

   a **Join**—Click Join, and follow the prompts as instructed to join an existing homegroup.

   b **Leave**—Review what you are currently sharing, and make changes as applicable (see step 4).

   c **Create**—Click Create.

4 Move the sliders for the various options for sharing from Off to On, as desired.

5 Write down the password; type the password when prompted when you want to join other computers to the homegroup.

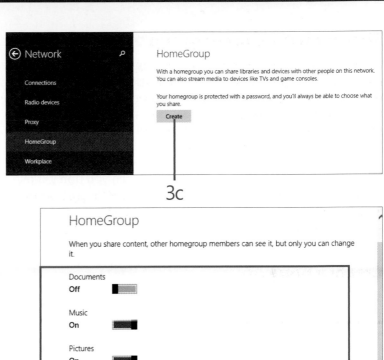

3c

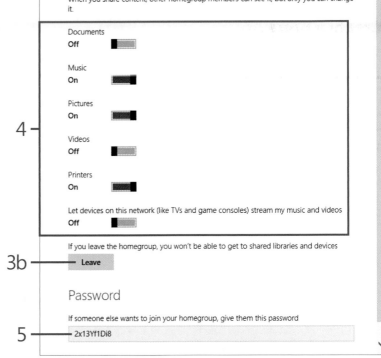

> ⚠️ **CAUTION** If you can't set up a homegroup and you need to share files and folders with a legacy machine—for example, one with Windows XP installed—you'll have to right-click the item to share and click the Sharing option. Then, you'll have to set up sharing manually.

> ✓ **TIP** If you opt to join an existing homegroup, you'll need the homegroup password. To find it, log on to a computer that is part of the homegroup already, and search for "homegroup password". You'll find it in Control Panel, in the Network And Sharing section.

Troubleshooting network connectivity

Sometimes (and often for no obvious reason), you'll lose network connectivity. A lot of things can cause this, including but not limited to a network address conflict, a bad physical connection, a disconnected or damaged Ethernet cable, a disabled device like a router or gateway, or even a network outage from your Internet service provider. Sometimes it's because the Wi-Fi feature of your device has been turned off. It's difficult to troubleshoot these types of problems when you don't know where to start. That's where the troubleshooting wizards come in handy.

Troubleshoot network connectivity

1 On the Start screen, type **network and sharing**.

2 Click Find And Fix Networking And Connection Problems.

3 Click Next to start the troubleshooting wizard.

4 Let the troubleshooter run, and make choices when presented with them.

(continued on next page)

> ⚠ **CAUTION** If the troubleshooter prompts you to restart your network, turn every network device off, including modems routers, and gateways. Then, turn them back on in the following order, giving each item time to completely initialize before turning on the next: Cable or satellite modems or routers, gateways, networked computers.

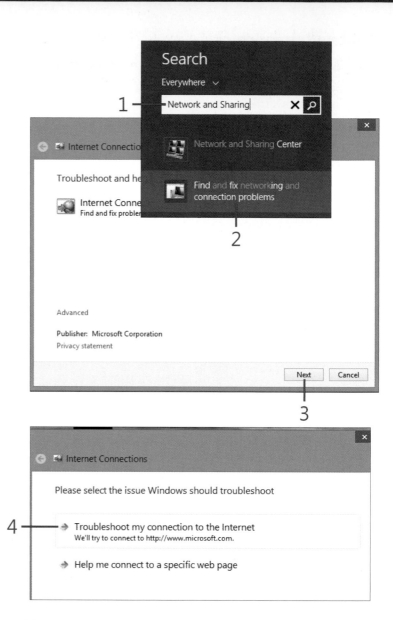

Troubleshoot network connectivity *(continued)*

5 Apply the solution if you think it's a valid one. (In this scenario, you might not use an Ethernet cable to connect to your network, making it an invalid option.)

6 Click Check To See If The Problem Is Fixed, if you applied the fix.

7 If the solution isn't valid, click Skip This Step.

(continued on next page)

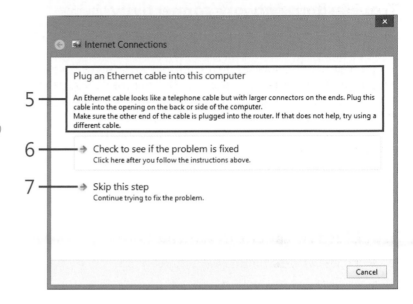

Troubleshoot network connectivity *(continued)*

8 If a valid solution is presented, opt to try the repairs.

9 Click Close when the problem is resolved.

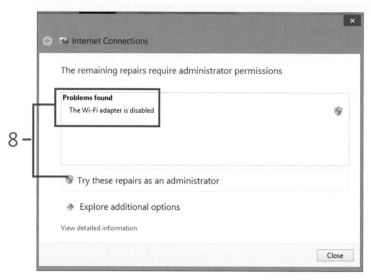

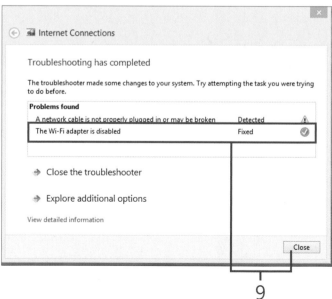

Connecting to a public network

A public network is one that you find in a coffee shop, library, hotel lobby, and so on. You connect to these networks as you would to any other, from the Network icon in the Settings charm. Usually, you don't have to input a network security key, although you might have to purchase a cup of coffee or sign up for a library card.

Connect to a public network

1 Click the Windows logo key+I to open the Settings charm; click the Network button.

2 Click the network name.

3 If desired, click Connect Automatically.

4 Click Connect.

1 —

.ıll	◀))	☼
4B7QL	25	Brightness
▤	⏻	⌨
Notifications	Power	Keyboard

Change PC settings

2 — .ıll NETGEAR12

3 — ☑ Connect automatically

4 — Connect

✓ **TIP** If you opt to connect automatically in step 3 and are signed in with your Microsoft account, the next time you are within range of the network and logged in with your Microsoft account on any device, you'll be connected to the network automatically. You won't be prompted again.

⚠ **CAUTION** If you are prompted to share (or not to share) after connecting to a public network, opt not to share. You don't want other people to see your computer and possibly try to connect to it.

Changing network settings

After you're connected to a network, you might decide to change the network settings. One common change is to reconfigure initial settings, such as whether to share or not to share while connected to it. Another is to mark a connection as a metered connection and to show estimated data usage, which is useful if you're connecting to the Internet via a cellular connection that has a monthly data limit.

Change network settings

1 Use the Windows key+I to open the Settings charm, and click Change PC Settings.

2 If you see a Back arrow, click it.

3 Click Network.

4 Click the connection to manage.

(continued on next page)

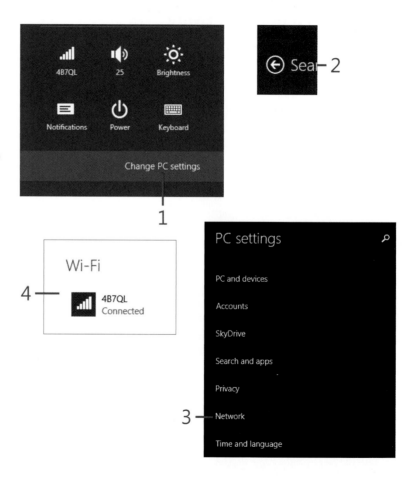

Change network settings *(continued)*

5 To mark the network you're connected to as private, configure Find Devices And Content to Off. To mark the network you're connected to as public, configure Find Devices And Content to On.

6 To mark the network connection as a metered connection, such as one you'd subscribe to with a cellular data plan, under Set As Metered Connection, move the setting from Off to On.

7 To show estimated data usage in the Networks list (from the Settings tab), under Show My Estimated Data Usage In The Networks List, move the setting from Off to On.

⊘ **TIP** If you need to be connected to the Internet even when there's no private or public Wi-Fi or local Ethernet network to connect to, your device will have to have the appropriate 3G/4G hardware installed and you'll have to sign up for a data plan from an Internet service provider, or, you'll have to be able to tether your phone to your device using a cell phone and plan that you already own and pay for. Additionally, your phone and/or laptop or tablet must support such a connection.

⊖ 4B7QL

Find devices and content

Find PCs, devices and content on this network and automatically connect to devices like printers and TVs. Turn this off for public networks to help keep your stuff safe.

5 On

Data usage

Show my estimated data use in the Networks list

7 Off

Set as a metered connection

6 Off

Using Airplane Mode

If you've flown anywhere in the past five years, you've probably heard the pilot or flight attendant tell you to turn off all electronic devices. However, they usually tell you later that it's okay to turn your devices back on, provided you disable all network functionality. When this is the case, you enable Airplane Mode.

Use Airplane Mode

1 Use the Windows key+I to open the Settings charm, and click Network.

2 Move the slider for Airplane Mode from Off to On.

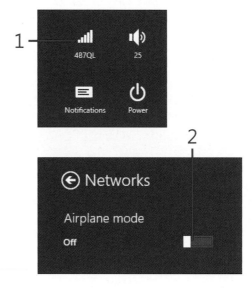

TIP   To disable Airplane Mode, repeat these steps, but move the slider from On to Off.

Working with users and privacy

16

Windows 8.1 offers a lot of features to help keep you, your children, your computer, and your data safe. Some of these features keep intruders, hackers, and malware at bay while you are connected to the Internet; others keep unwanted users from accessing your personal data if they ever gain physical access to your computer. Still other features can help keep your kids safe by restricting what they can and can't do while using the computer. When you enable and incorporate all of the security features outlined in this section, and if you make sure to lock your computer when you aren't using it, you can rest assured that your computer and its data will be as safe and secure as possible.

Enabling Windows Firewall

Windows Firewall protects your computer several ways. Succinctly, Windows Firewall looks at all of the data going in and out of your device and blocks transmissions deemed harmful or transmissions that you don't explicitly approve (such as a person who wants to access and control your computer from a remote location). Windows Firewall is enabled by default, but it's best to verify this and to explore the firewall's basic settings.

Enable Windows Firewall

1 On the Start screen, begin to type **Windows Firewall**.

2 In the results, click Windows Firewall.

3 Verify that the firewall is turned on.

4 If the firewall is not enabled and you know you have not installed a third-party firewall, do the following:

    a Click Turn Windows Firewall On Or Off.

    b Select the Turn On Windows Firewall option under Private Network Settings and Public Network Settings.

    c Click OK.

> ✓ **TIP** When you want to use an app that is blocked by default by Windows Firewall, you'll be prompted to allow it (make an exception for it). This will happen when you want to enable certain apps, or when you want to use Windows features such as Connect To A Network Projector or Windows Media Player Network Sharing Service.

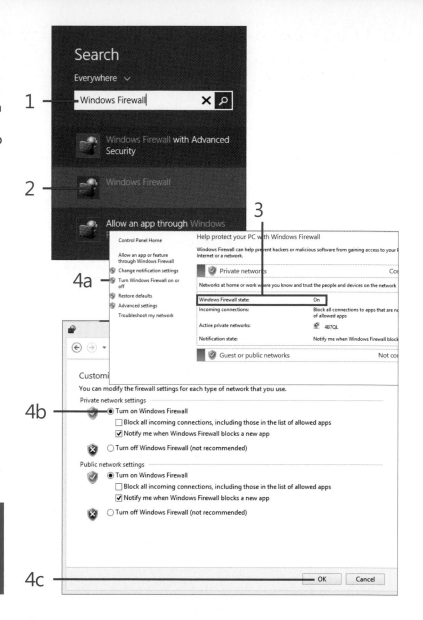

Allowing apps to access your personal information or location

You can use privacy settings in Windows 8.1 to allow apps to access your physical location or your name and account picture. There are times where you will need this to be enabled—for example, when using Maps to get directions from your current location to another (without having to type your current location in manually). There are times when offering access isn't necessary too, such as when an app asks for personal information and doesn't need it (like a dictionary app).

Allow access to your personal information or location

1 Press Windows logo key+I to open the Settings charm.

2 Click Change PC Settings.

3 If you see a Back arrow, click it.

4 Click Privacy.

5 From the General tab, use the slider to configure the desired settings, taking specific note of Let Apps Access My Name, Picture, And Other Account Info.

(continued on next page)

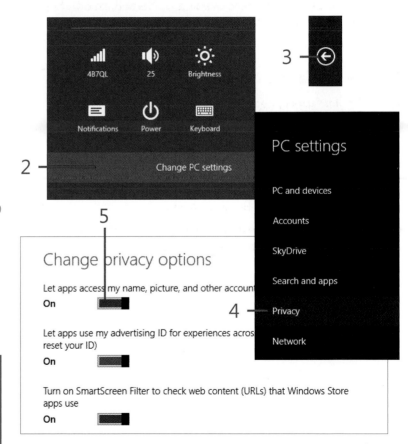

✓ **TIP** There is some danger associated with allowing access to your location. If you or your children are concerned that an individual might want to know where you are at any point in time, you are more at risk if you carry a laptop or tablet device with you, and you might consider blocking this access. However, for most people, this feature simply adds convenience when using certain applications.

Allow access to your personal information or location *(continued)*

6 Click Location.

7 To disable all apps from learning your location, move the slider under Location from On to Off.

8 To disable specific apps from learning your location, move the slider for each of those apps from On to Off.

SEE ALSO Network security can help you control who has access to your files and data. When you create a network, you establish your network security type. See Section 15, "Working with devices and networks," for more about network security settings.

Using Windows Defender

Windows 8.1 provides built-in protection against viruses and spyware with a feature called Windows Defender. Integrated with Internet Explorer, Windows Defender scans files you download from the Internet to detect threats. When turned on, the program automatically provides real-time protection against multiple types of threats, stopping malware from being downloaded. You can also run manual scans any time you like, if you feel your computer has been compromised.

Use Window Defender

1 On the Start screen, begin to type **Windows Defender**.

2 Click Windows Defender in the results.

3 Click the Settings tab.

4 Make sure the Turn On Real-Time Protection check box is selected.

(continued on next page)

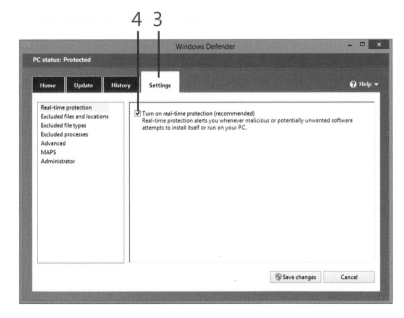

Use Window Defender *(continued)*

5 If applicable, click Save Changes.

6 Click the Home tab.

7 If desired, click Scan Now.

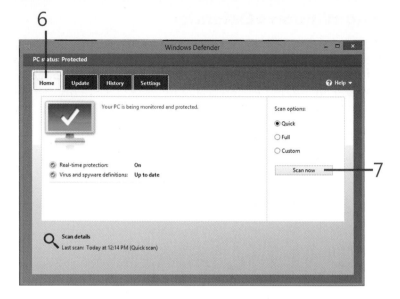

TIP Updates are performed automatically when real-time protection is turned on. These updates happen at least twice a day, provided your computer is connected to the Internet and turned on. To run a manual update at any time, click the Update tab of Windows Defender and then click the Update button.

TRY THIS! You can customize a Windows Defender scan. Follow the steps in this task, but at step 7, click the Custom option. When you click the Scan Now button, you can select check boxes for the drives you want to scan. For example, you can scan only your hard disk, any DVD or removable/external drive attached to your computer, or all drives. Click OK to run the scan.

Creating new users

When you set up your computer for the first time, you created and logged in with your own user account. Ideally, that was a Microsoft account. This first account was automatically assigned to be an Administrator account, which means that you, as the administrator, have complete control over the computer.

If anyone else is going to use the computer, they should have an account too. It should also be a Microsoft account, provided the user is a teenager or adult. Because you are the computer administrator, you can create the account. By default, that account won't be another Administrator account, but will instead be a Standard account. Standard users can't make administrative changes to the computer like administrators can, and thus are limited in the damage they can do. (Alternatively, you can create a child account, which is a local account and is not associated with a Microsoft account.)

Create a new user

1 Press Windows logo key+I to open the Settings charm.

2 Click Change PC Settings.

3 If you see a Back arrow, click it.

4 Click Accounts.

(continued on next page)

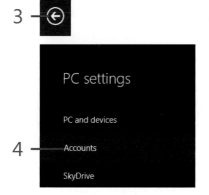

Create a new user *(continued)*

5 Click Other Accounts.

6 Click Add An Account.

7 Type the user's Microsoft Account. (You can also sign up for a new email address or opt to add a child's local account.)

8 Click Next.

9 Click Finish.

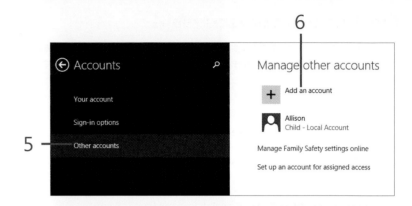

> ✓ **TIP** You won't know the password associated with the Microsoft account you've created in these steps. To fully activate the account, have the new user log on to the computer with it.

> ✓ **TIP** If you opt to create a child's account in step 7 or sign up for a new Microsoft account, the remaining steps will differ from what is offered here.

Creating a picture password

If typing your password is cumbersome (which it can be on a touch screen device), you can create a picture password for logging in. You get to pick the picture and create three unique on-screen gestures to associate with it, which you repeat to log on.

Create a picture password

1 On the Start screen, type **Picture Password**.

2 In the results, click Set Up Picture Password.

3 Under Picture Password, click Add.

4 Enter your password.

5 Click OK.

(continued on next page)

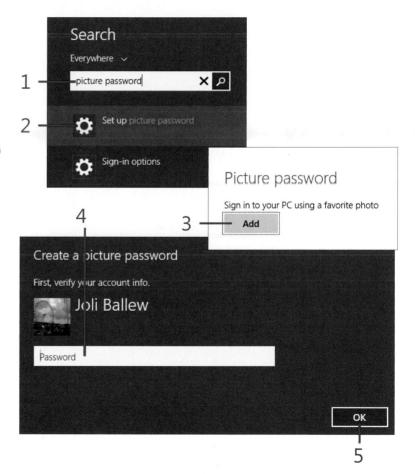

Create a picture password (continued)

6 Click Choose Picture.

7 Navigate to a picture to use.

8 Click the picture to use.

9 Click Open.

(continued on next page)

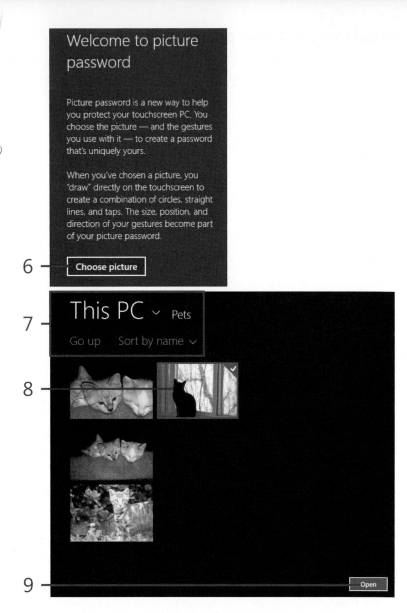

Create a picture password *(continued)*

10 Click Use This Picture.

11 Apply the gestures as instructed.

12 Click Finish.

10 — Use this picture

12 — Finish

How's this look?

Drag your picture to position it the way you want.

Use this picture

Choose new picture

Set up your gestures

Draw three gestures on your picture. You can use any combination of circles, straight lines, and taps.

11 — Remember, the size, position, and direction of your gestures — and the order in which you make them — become part of your picture password.

1 2 3

Start over   Cancel

SEE ALSO   To learn how to navigate to a file as instructed in step 7, refer to Section 18, "Managing data."

Creating a PIN

Entering an email address and password might require that you type 20 or 30 characters, which takes a bit of time. It can be cumbersome too, especially if you use a touch screen. If you'd rather, you can create a PIN, a password that consists of only four numbers.

Create a PIN

1 On the Start screen, type **Set up PIN**.

2 Click Set Up PIN Sign-In in the results.

3 Under PIN, click Add.

4 Enter your password.

5 Click OK.

6 Enter a PIN and then confirm it.

7 Click Finish.

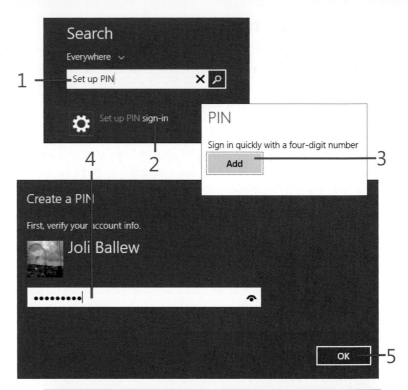

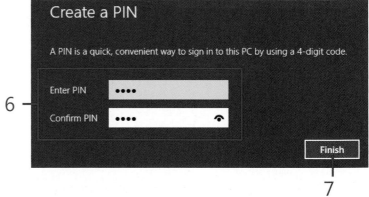

> **TIP**   Just as with a password, make your PIN hard to guess, even though the characters are limited in number. For example, don't use part of your phone number, street address, or date of birth, because these pieces of information are often publicly available. If you need something that's not totally random to help you remember it, use a number that represents a date or year that has special meaning known only to you, or part of a phone number from 10 years ago.

Switching among user accounts

After you've set up multiple user accounts on your Windows 8.1-based computer, you'll want each user to log in with that account when they want to use the computer, and then log out, lock, or shut down the computer when they're finished. You change to a different account from the lock screen.

Log in as a different user

1 If the previous user did not lock the computer, click Windows logo key+I to lock it.

2 Drag the screen upward to reveal the user logon screen, if applicable.

3 Click the applicable user picture.

4 Enter the user password, and press Enter on the keyboard, or enter the PIN.

> **TIP** If you have administrative privileges on your Windows 8.1-based device, you can manage the accounts you've created. You can set up Family Safety for each account, change the account type, delete accounts, and more.

> **TIP** When you are ready to end a computing session, you should return the computer to its lock screen. You can do this in various ways. One way is to click your user account picture on the Start screen and then click either Lock or Sign Out. (They keyboard combination Windows key+I works too.) If you lock the computer, the next time you log in things are just as you left them; your apps and data are exactly where they were before. If you sign out, you'll need to save your work, close all open desktop applications, and end your computing session. When you log back in, you'll start a new session.

Managing User Account Control settings

You can use the User Account Control Settings dialog box to set up, by user, how Windows notifies you before programs are installed on your computer or when there are attempts to make changes to your Windows settings. You can choose a level of protection that works best for each user. If only one user on the computer has administrative level permissions, it can be useful to set up the Always Notify level of account control for that person so that she knows when other users try to make changes.

Change User Account Control settings

1 Right-click the Start button.

2 Click Control Panel.

3 Click System And Security.

4 Under Action Center, click Change User Account Control Settings.

5 Drag the slider to the setting you prefer, with Always Notify being the most secure and Never Notify being the least secure.

6 Click OK.

⚠ **CAUTION** You should not disable UAC. UAC protects against all kinds of malware. If you disable it, you are opening several holes for hackers, viruses, and other evils.

🔍 **SEE ALSO** For more information about making settings for individual users, see "Create a new user," earlier in this section.

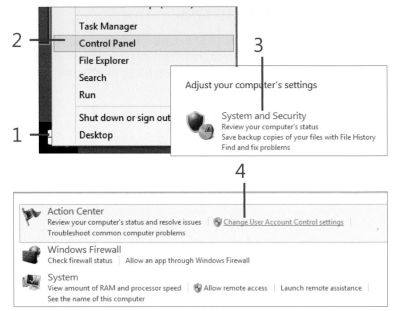

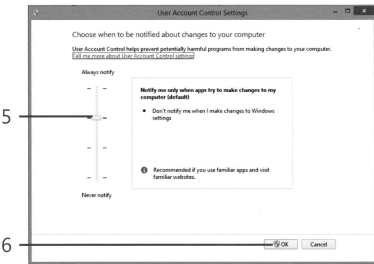

Turning on Family Safety

If children use your computer, consider setting up Family Safety controls through their user accounts. These controls allow you to configure different settings for each child. For example, you might want to limit the time a teen spends online, or block a younger child from using certain programs on your computer.

Turn on Family Safety

1 Right-click the Start button.

2 Click Control Panel.

3 Click Set Up Family Safety For Any User.

4 If applicable, work through the wizard to create a child account. Click the first instance of Accounts to get started.

(continued on next page)

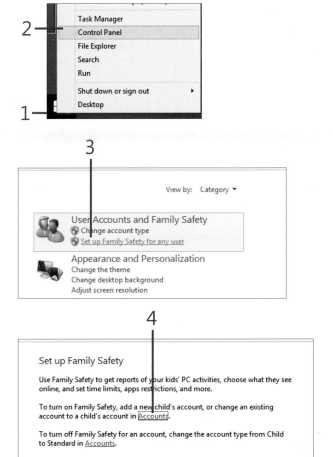

Turn on Family Safety *(continued)*

5 In PC Settings from the Other User tab from Accounts, click Add An Account.

  a Click Add A Child's Account.

  b Choose to add a child's account with or without email, or sign up for a new email address.

  c Work through the required process depending on what you selected in step 5b, and then create a user name and password.

5

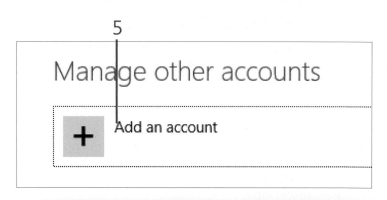

5a

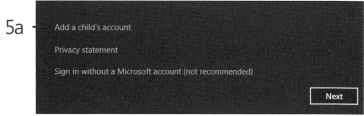

5b

5c

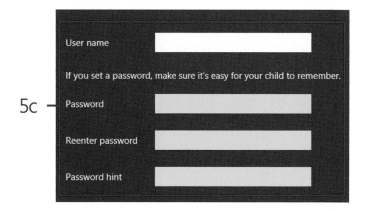

> **SEE ALSO** See the next task for managing individual Family Safety control settings after you've enabled and/or created a child's account.

Working with Family Safety settings

With Family Safety settings, you can set time limits so that you can control the amount of time and the time periods for which your child can use the computer. You can choose which games children can access by rating, content, or title. Finally, you can block specific programs from being used by your child on your computer. Ideally, you should configure Family Safety settings online and manage them there. This set of steps outlines how to do this. (Note that you can also set up an account for "assigned access", where you choose an account to have access to only one Windows Store app.)

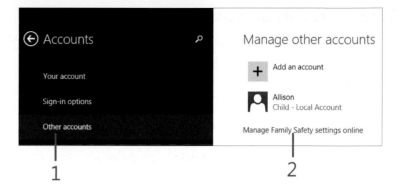

Work with Family Safety settings (set a time allowance)

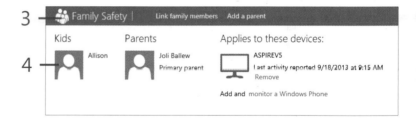

1 Return to PC Settings, Accounts, Other Accounts, where you created the child account in the previous set of steps.

2 Click Manage Family Safety Settings Online.

3 If prompted, input your user name and password to access the Family Safety web page, shown here.

4 Click your child's account.

5 Note the options in the right pane; click Time Limits.

(continued on next page)

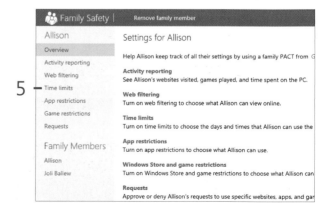

Work with Family Safety settings (set a time allowance) *(continued)*

6 Move the slider for Time allowance from Off to On.

7 If desired, set how many hours the child can use the computer weekdays and weekends, using the drop down lists. If you'd rather select specific times of the day, change these to Varies and skip to step 7.

8 Click Curfew.

9 Move the slider for Curfew hours from off to On. .

10 Click and drag with the mouse to block off periods of time when the child cannot use the computer.

11 Continue in the same manner to configure additional options including Activity Reporting, Web filtering, App Restrictions, Game Restrictions, and Requests.

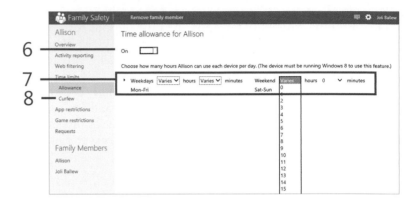

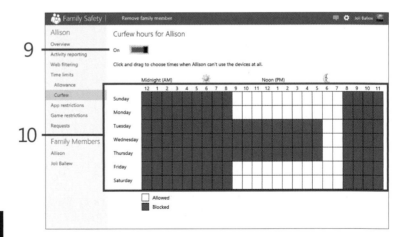

TRY THIS Make a list of the types of content that make sense for each of your children so that you can access and review those choices periodically as they grow up. For example, you might choose to change settings for the junior high student to appropriate settings for a high school student when the time comes to help him "graduate" to a more mature phase.

Sharing settings and files in the cloud

17

Windows 8.1 provides two useful ways to connect your computing devices and content together in the cloud. First, you can sync your personal computer settings so that those settings will be applied no matter what computer you log on to (provided you use you Microsoft account). Settings can include your Start screen configuration and app data, among other things.

Second, you can share files with yourself and others by saving them to the cloud. SkyDrive lets you upload, access, and share all kinds of data on the Internet, including music, video, pictures, and documents. If you commit to saving all of your data to SkyDrive, you can essentially make all the content on your computer available when you log on securely from other computers through your Microsoft account.

In this section, you'll learn lots of ways to store data in the cloud, including uploading files using Internet Explorer, saving to the cloud from both apps and desktop apps, and creating new folders for SkyDrive using File Explorer. You'll learn about the SkyDrive app too, which offers an easy way to access your files, create folders, and add content to SkyDrive.

In this section:

- Choosing settings to sync to SkyDrive
- Choosing files to save to SkyDrive
- Saving files to SkyDrive
- Creating a new folder in SkyDrive
- Adding files to a folder
- Sharing a folder
- Managing SkyDrive storage
- Creating a folder and adding data to it from the SkyDrive app

Choosing settings to sync to SkyDrive

Syncing settings across the Windows 8-based devices you log in to with your Microsoft account is enabled by default. Settings that are already configured to sync include the layout of your Start screen, app data, web browser favorites, and settings for your languages, Ease of Access configuration, and more. You can change what is currently being synced from the SkyDrive tab of PC Settings.

Choose settings to sync

1 Press Windows logo key+I to access the Settings charm.

2 Click Change PC Settings.

3 If you see a Back arrow, click it.

4 Click SkyDrive.

5 Click Sync Settings.

6 Click the On/Off buttons, as preferred, for the available sync settings.

7 Scroll to see more sync settings.

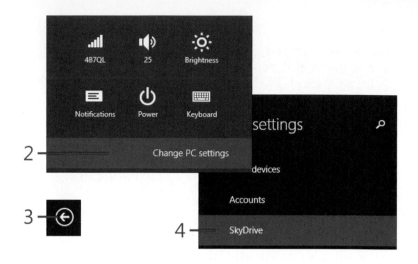

> **TIP** If you don't want items to sync when you're being charged for connection time, In the SkyDrive options, click Metered Connections. Configure how you want to use SkyDrive while using metered connections.

Choosing files to save to SkyDrive

SkyDrive is a storage area on the Internet that you can use to save files to, and, depending on when you obtained your Microsoft account, you have either 7 GB or 25 GB of free storage space available to you (and you can buy more if that isn't enough). If you have an Office 365 subscription, you'll have more than that. When you opt to save files to SkyDrive, you can access them from any device you can log in to with that account. This serves as both a backup and a convenience, because your files can be accessed from almost anywhere.

You can also choose to automatically upload photos and videos from your Camera Roll folder to SkyDrive. (These are pictures you take with your device, provided it has a camera.) Again, this serves as a backup and also enables you to access that media from any computer or device that you can log into your Microsoft account with.

Choose files to save to SkyDrive

1 Press Windows logo key+I to access the Settings charm.

2 Click Change PC Settings.

3 If you see a Back arrow, click it.

4 Click SkyDrive.

(continued on next page)

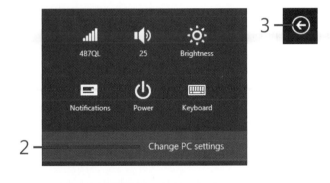

Choose files to save to SkyDrive *(continued)*

5 Click File Storage.

6 Verify Save documents to SkyDrive by default is set to On.

7 Click Camera Roll.

8 Configure the desired options for uploading photos and videos.

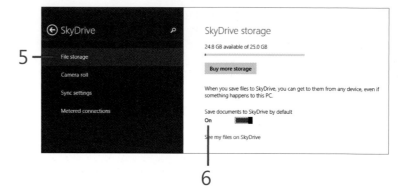

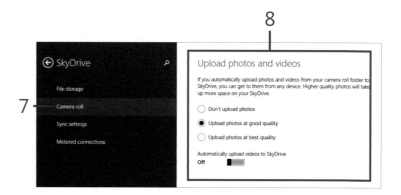

TIP Video files are generally quite large. You might not want to opt to automatically upload videos to SkyDrive if you only have 7 GB of space available.

Saving files to SkyDrive

You can save files to SkyDrive using various methods. One is to use File Explorer on the desktop to drag files there to copy or move them. Another is to save directly from a compatible desktop application, such as Paint and WordPad. You can save to SkyDrive from certain apps, too, including Mail.

In the following steps you'll learn how to save a file to SkyDrive from WordPad. You'll apply the same technique to save data in virtually all other desktop apps. In the next set of steps, you'll save an attachment in an email (in Mail) to SkyDrive. You'll apply this technique to save data in virtually all other apps.

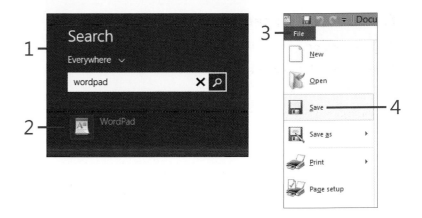

Save to SkyDrive from WordPad

1 On the Start screen, type **WordPad**.

2 Click WordPad in the results.

3 Click File.

4 Click Save.

5 In the Save As dialog box, click SkyDrive in the Navigation pane.

6 If desired, click a subfolder in the Content pane.

7 Type a file name.

8 Click Save.

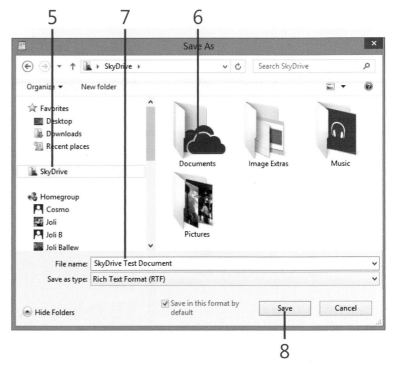

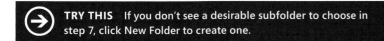

TRY THIS If you don't see a desirable subfolder to choose in step 7, click New Folder to create one.

Save to SkyDrive from Mail

1 From the Start screen, click Mail.

2 Locate an email that contains an attachment you've already down-loaded (or download it if needed).

3 Right-click any attachment in the email.

4 Click Save.

5 Click the arrow beside This PC.

6 Click SkyDrive.

7 If desired, rename the file.

8 If desired, change the file type.

9 If desired, click a subfolder.

10 Click Save.

Creating a new folder in SkyDrive

You can add folders to SkyDrive to organize the data you store there. You can also share those folders with others. There are several ways to create a folder. You can create one from inside the SkyDrive app. (Just right-click and choose New Folder.) You can create one while logged on to the SkyDrive website using Internet Explorer. You can add a folder from File Explorer. And you can create a folder while saving from a desktop app's Save As dialog box. Here you'll learn how to create a new folder using File Explorer.

Create a new folder using File Explorer

1 Use the keyboard shortcut Windows key+D to access the desktop.

2 On the taskbar, click File Explorer.

3 Click SkyDrive in the Navigation pane.

4 Click the Home tab of the File Explorer ribbon.

5 Click New Folder.

6 Enter a name for the folder.

7 Click anywhere outside of the folder to save the name.

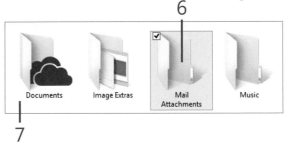

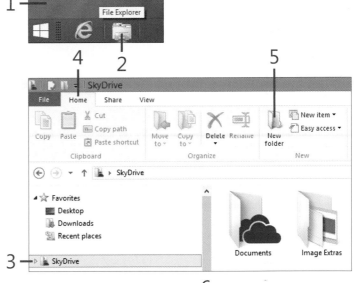

> 🔍 **SEE ALSO** See "Create a folder and add data to it from the SkyDrive app," at the end of this section.

> ➡️ **TRY THIS** On the Home screen, click the SkyDrive tile. Right-click the screen, and note that one of the options is New Folder. You can create new folders here too.

Adding files to a folder

After you have created a folder in SkyDrive, you can upload files to that folder using the SkyDrive website. You can also drag files by using File Explorer. You can opt to navigate to the desired SkyDrive folder when you're ready to save a file. In the following steps, you'll add a file to a folder by uploading it using the SkyDrive website. (As with many other tasks detailed in this section, you can also add files using the SkyDrive app.) You need to learn this technique because it's the technique you'll use when you want to add files to a SkyDrive folder from a non-Windows 8-based machine.

Add files to SkyDrive with Internet Explorer

1   From the Start screen, click the Internet Explorer tile.

2   Right-click anywhere to display the address bar.

3   Type **skydrive.live.com** in the address bar, and press Enter on the keyboard.

4   If desired, click a folder to open it.

5   Click Upload.

(continued on next page)

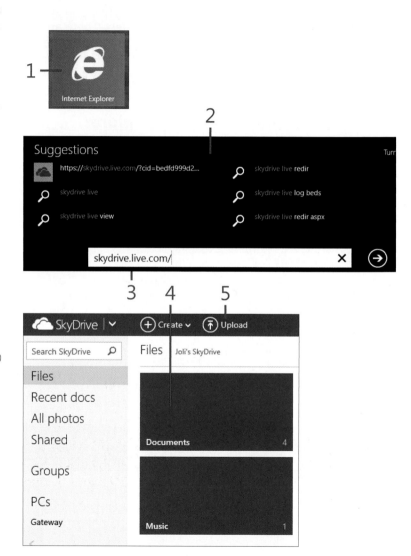

Add files to SkyDrive with Internet Explorer

(continued)

6 Click the arrow beside SkyDrive.

7 Click This PC to navigate to the file (or other applicable option).

8 Click a file. (You can click multiple files.)

9 Click Open.

TRY THIS Open the SkyDrive app from the Start screen. Right-click and choose Add Items to upload files using the app.

SEE ALSO See "Create a folder and add data to it from the SkyDrive app," at the end of this section.

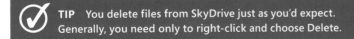

TIP You delete files from SkyDrive just as you'd expect. Generally, you need only to right-click and choose Delete.

Sharing a folder

One of the main functions of a file sharing site such as SkyDrive is to share content with yourself (when you're away from your own computer) and others. However, if you want to share with others, you'll need to specifically configure it as so. One way to share a folder is to share it from the SkyDrive website you accessed in the previous task.

Share a folder

1 Use Internet Explorer to open the SkyDrive website as outlined in the previous task.

2 With SkyDrive open, click Files to display the Files list.

3 Right-click a file or folder.

4 Click Sharing.

5 Verify that Send Email is selected in the left pane.

6 Enter an email address.

7 Enter a note (optional).

8 If you don't want the person to edit files, clear the Recipients Can Edit check box.

9 Click Share.

10 Click Close.

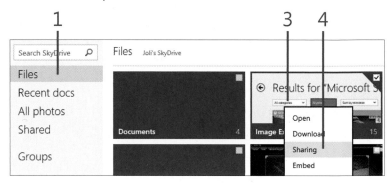

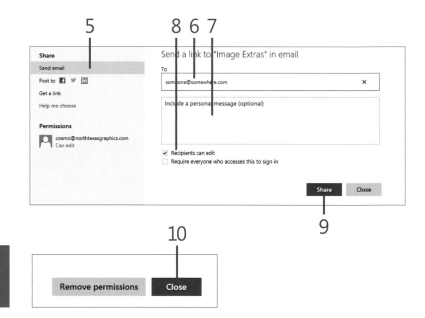

TIP Instead of sending an email in step 5, you can post a link to the folder to various social networking sites or get a link that you can share in other ways.

Managing SkyDrive storage

You get a specific amount of storage space to use on SkyDrive; it can be 7 GB or 25 GB, depending on when you obtained your Microsoft account (and you'll have more if you have a subscription to Office 365). Although that's a lot of space, it is possible run out. If you do, you can purchase additional space as needed, for a yearly fee. To see how much storage space you have left and to buy more, access the appropriate options in PC Settings.

Manage SkyDrive storage

1 Press Windows logo key+I to access the Settings charm.

2 Click Change PC Settings.

3 If you see a Back arrow, click it.

4 Click SkyDrive.

5 Click File Storage.

6 If desired, click Buy More Storage and perform the related tasks.

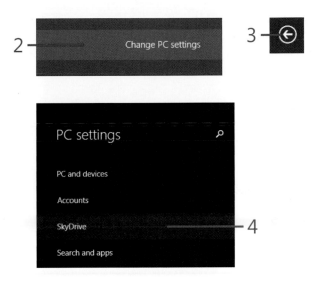

TIP Currently you can purchase up to 100 GB for about $50 (US) a year.

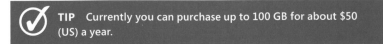

Creating a folder and adding data to it from the SkyDrive app

You can perform some tasks with SkyDrive from within the SkyDrive app. You can select files to open, create new folders, and add items to your SkyDrive storage space. You access these features with a right-click.

Create a folder and add data to it from the SkyDrive app

1 From the Start screen, click SkyDrive.

2 Note the folders and files already there.

3 Right-click an empty part of the screen.

4 Click New Folder.

5 Type a name for the folder.

6 Click Create.

7 Click Add Files.

(continued on next page)

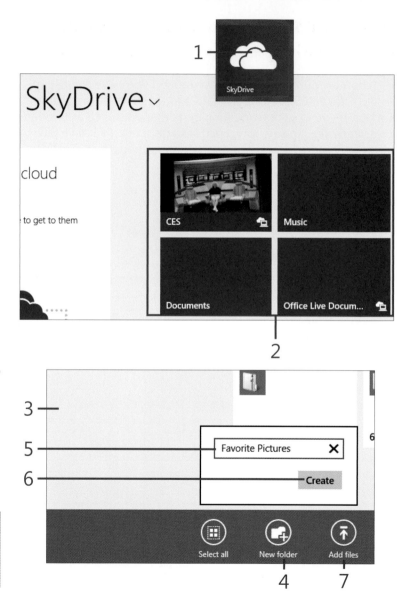

> **⚠ CAUTION** It is extremely important that you know how to create folders and upload data from Internet Explorer, because Windows XP, Windows Vista, Windows 7, and other non-Windows 8 operating systems won't have a SkyDrive app that you can use.

Create a folder and add data to it from the SkyDrive app *(continued)*

8 Click the arrow beside SkyDrive.

9 Click This PC.

10 Navigate to an item to add, and click it.

11 Click Copy To SkyDrive.

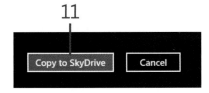

Managing data

18

Windows 8.1 comes with a built-in file structure; it already has folders to hold your data. There are folders named Desktop, Documents, Downloads, Music, Pictures, and Videos, and there are public counterparts. Whenever you save a file, you're prompted to save it to the folder that Windows 8.1 thinks it should be saved to. For example, if you're saving a .jpg file, you'll be presented with the Pictures folder. If it's a .doc file, you'll be presented with the Documents folder.

Windows 8.1 also offers various ways to manage the files you save. You can rename, move, copy, and delete files. You can compress a group of files so that they take up less storage space, you can back up files, and you can share files with a homegroup or specific people. You can work with folders too; you can create your own, move or copy data into them, and share them, among other things. You can do all of these things in File Explorer on the desktop. Finally, there are many ways to back up your data. You can use SkyDrive, but there's also File History and various options for backing up files manually.

In this section:

- Using the File Explorer ribbon
- Navigating File Explorer
- Locating files in File Explorer
- Changing views in File Explorer
- Creating folders
- Renaming files and folders
- Moving and copying files
- Creating and extracting compressed files
- Sharing content
- Using File History
- Backing up data manually
- Deleting files and folders
- Working with the Recycle Bin

Using the File Explorer ribbon

File Explorer opens in a window. That window has a navigation pane, a content pane, and a ribbon. When you select an item in the navigation pane or the content pane, what is offered on the ribbon changes to offer the tools that you'll likely need for the item you've selected. Thus, at any given time, you might see various tabs on the ribbon, each offering different tools that you will need to perform desired tasks.

Ribbon

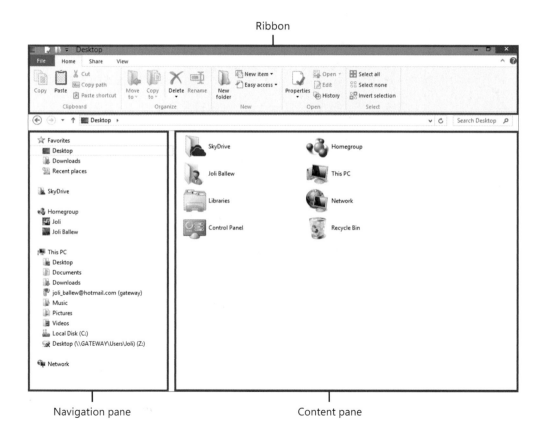

Navigation pane

Content pane

The tabs you'll see most often while working in File Explorer include the following:

- **File**   To open a new File Explorer window, to get help, and to view places on the computer you frequent.

- **Home**   To perform tasks on selected files and folders such as cut, copy, paste, rename, move, select, and so on. You can also opt to create new folders here. If you look closely, there are five groups on the File tab shown here: Clipboard, Organize, New, Open, and Select. You won't see Home (and some of the other tabs listed here) if you have selected Homegroup, This PC, or Network in the Navigation pane.

- **Share**   To share selected files and folders using various techniques including to print, fax, burn to disc, share with a homegroup, and so on. Note the two groups here: Send and Share With.

The File tab

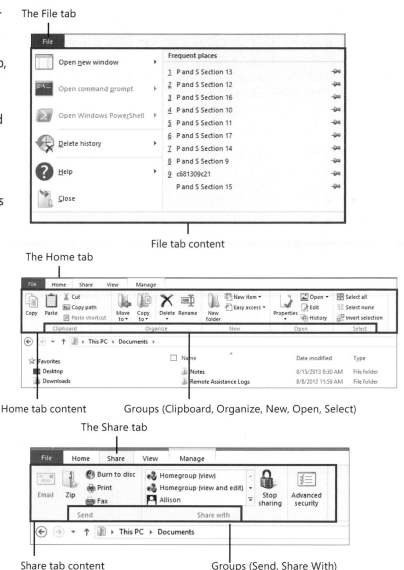

File tab content

The Home tab

Home tab content   Groups (Clipboard, Organize, New, Open, Select)

The Share tab

Share tab content   Groups (Send, Share With)

- **View**   To change how data appears in the content pane, to sort data, to hide items, and to change the File Explorer interface by showing additional panes. Note the four groups shown here: Panes, Layout, Current View, Show/Hide. There are two screen shots associated with the View menu shown here (the top two); the first is maximized, and the second is not. Note in the latter that the groups are condensed.

- **Computer**   To map network drives, add a network location, access media servers, open Control Panel, view system properties, and otherwise manage what you see when This PC is selected in the navigation pane. Note the three groups shown here: Location, Network, System.

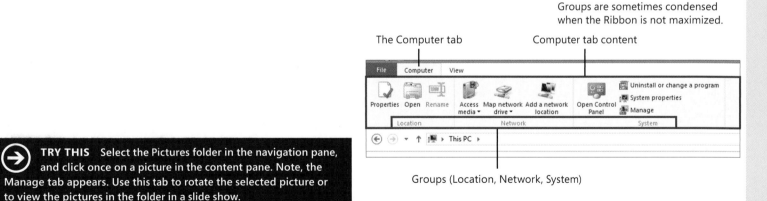

The View tab   View tab content

Groups (Panes, Layout, Current View, Show/Hide)

Groups are sometimes condensed when the Ribbon is not maximized.

The Computer tab   Computer tab content

Groups (Location, Network, System)

> **TRY THIS**   Select the Pictures folder in the navigation pane, and click once on a picture in the content pane. Note, the Manage tab appears. Use this tab to rotate the selected picture or to view the pictures in the folder in a slide show.

> **TIP**   Content-specific tabs, such as Music Tools, Video Tools, and Picture Tools, appear when you have selected compatible content.

Navigating File Explorer

File Explorer offers access to various areas of your computer in the navigation pane. Some of these areas are actually folders, such as Downloads, Documents, Pictures, and so on. File Explorer also offers access to locations on your network, your homegroup, and SkyDrive. These areas are generally located somewhere other than your computer. You can open these folders and access these locations to get to the data you've organized and saved there. As you do, and then as you continue to open related folders and subfolders, you navigate deeper into the folder structure itself. There are several ways to get back to where you started or where you were previously; there is a back arrow, an up arrow, and the navigation pane.

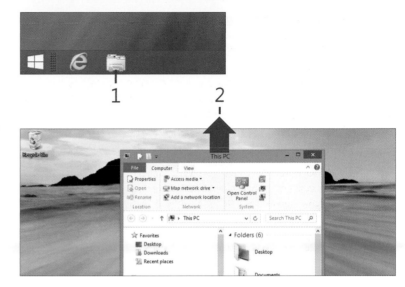

Navigate File Explorer

1 On the Windows desktop, click the File Explorer icon.

2 If the File Explorer window does not take up the entire screen, drag the window, from the title bar, up to the top of the screen to maximize it.

3 Click This PC. If nothing is listed under This PC, click the arrow available beside it. You can click here to return to this view anytime. Note the other available locations:

   a Default folders for saving files.

   b Access to SkyDrive.

   c Homegroup participants.

4 Double-click Pictures to open the Pictures folder.

(continued on next page)

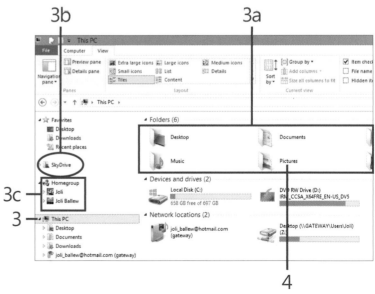

Navigate File Explorer *(continued)*

5 Under This PC, click Documents to open the Documents folder.

6 Click the up arrow to the left of the address bar to go up one level in the file/folder hierarchy.

7 Click the back arrow to display the Documents folder contents again.

8 Click the drop-down arrow to the right of the Forward button.

9 Note the list of items you've recently viewed in File Explorer.

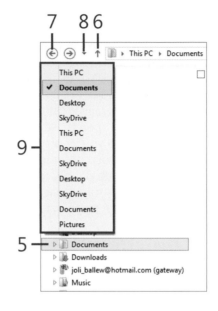

> ✓ **TIP** With a folder open in File Explorer, you can click Properties on the Home tab. The window that appears will give you information about the folder, such as how many files and subfolders it contains, the date it was created, and whether the folder is shared with others.

Locating files with File Explorer

File Explorer has default folders that you can use to save related files. You save documents in the Documents folder, pictures in the Pictures folder, and so on. Because you will likely create subfolders to hold data and because sometimes you might save a file to the wrong folder, a file might be difficult to navigate to manually. While you could methodically work through the hierarchy until you find the file you want, an easier way is to simply search for it.

Search for a file

1 In File Explorer, click This PC in the navigation pane.

2 Click in the Search This PC box.

(continued on next page)

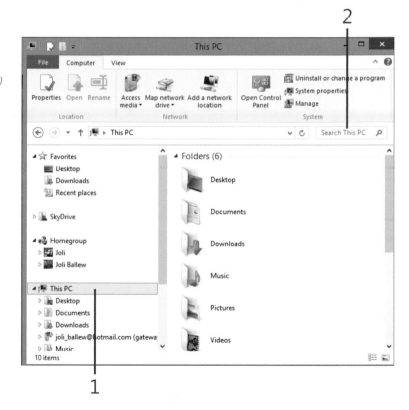

Search for a file (continued)

3 Type your first name, and press Enter on the keyboard.

4 Note that the results come from all areas of your hard drive.

5 In the navigation pane, click Pictures.

6 Click inside the Search Pictures box.

(continued on next page)

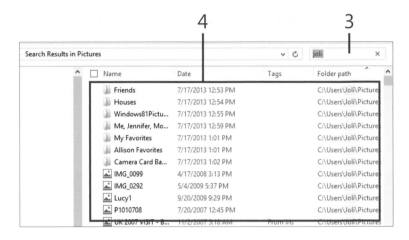

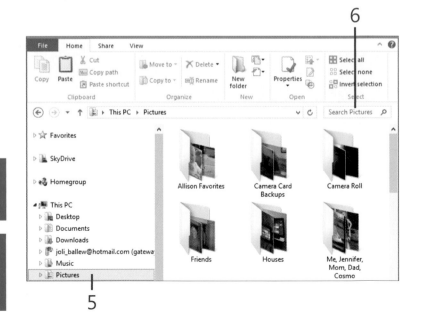

> ✓ **TIP** If you know that you recently worked on a file and you want to find it again, click the File tab. It might be listed under Frequent Places.

> ✓ **TIP** You can search for files by using other search terms, beyond names of files and files you've created. You can search by metadata associated with the file, such as the location a picture was taken, tags you've created to describe the files, and so on.

Search for a file *(continued)*

7 Type your name, and press Enter on the keyboard.

8 Note that the results come only from the Pictures folder.

9 Repeat these steps using other folders (perhaps Videos), and type names of actual files you have created and saved.

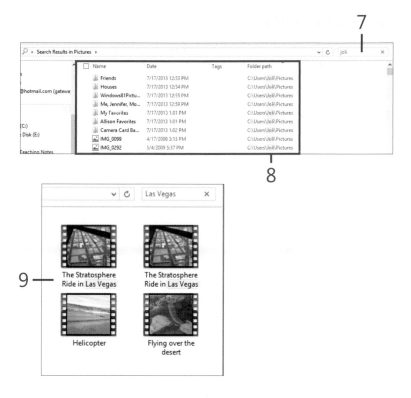

> → **TRY THIS** From the View tab, in the Layout group, choose the desired option for viewing the results. You can choose from Extra large icons, Large icons, Medium icons, Small icons, List, and Details.

> ✓ **TIP** You can show the Preview pane on the right side of File Explorer. When the Preview pane is enabled, you can click any file one time in the content pane, and for many files, a preview will be displayed in the new Preview pane. To enable this, from the View tab, click Preview Pane.

Changing views in File Explorer

File Explorer's View tab lets you change how you view data in the content pane. For example, you might choose to view picture files as large icons, which enables you to see what the picture looks like without opening the actual file. You might want to organize documents in a detailed list that includes the file names, the date they were last modified, and size so that they can be easily sorted.

Use View tab tools

1 In File Explorer's navigation pane, click Pictures.

2 Click the View tab.

3 In the Layout group, click Large Icons.

4 In the Current View group, click Group By and then click Date Taken.

5 In the Current View group, click Group By and click None. (None will appear in the list after you click Date Taken.)

6 In the Layout group, click Details.

> ✓ **TIP** To hide an item, such as a file or folder, in File Explorer, click to select it, and then on the View tab, use the Hide Selected Items button to hide it from view. Select the Hidden Items check box to display hidden files again.

> ✓ **TIP** The Manage tab becomes available on the ribbon when you select certain items in File Explorer, such as a picture, song, or video. You can use the tools on the Manage tab for functions specific to the type of content. For example, if you've selected a picture file, you can run a slide show of all pictures or rotate the picture right or left.

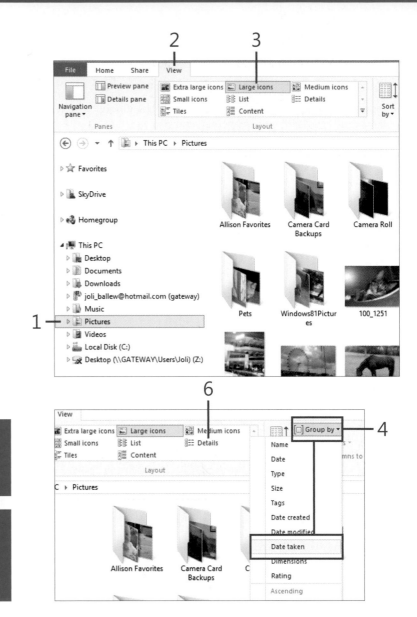

Creating folders

The default folders in Windows 8.1 provide the basics for organizing files, but as time passes, you might need a larger folder structure. For example, as you create documents, you might need to group those documents into subfolders, perhaps named Taxes, Letters to the Editor, CVs, and so on. As you acquire pictures, you might need to group those as well, perhaps into subfolders named Pets, Children, Friends, Weddings, and Me.

Create a new folder

1 With File Explorer open, navigate to the folder that needs a subfolder. You can click SkyDrive if you want.

2 Click the Home tab.

3 Click the New Folder button.

4 Enter a name for the folder, and press Enter.

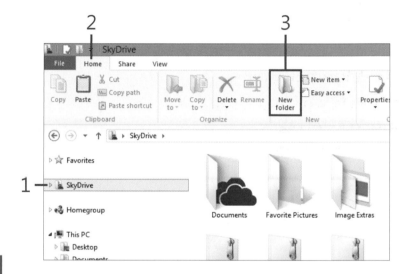

> ✅ **TIP** If you upgraded to Windows 8.1 from Windows 7, you will still see the old format for libraries, meaning you'll have access to both the personal and public folders if you opt to show Libraries in the Navigation pane. However, if you upgraded from Windows 8, or if you installed Windows 8.1 clean, you won't.

> ✅ **TIP** From the View tab, click Navigation Pane. You can opt to show (or hide) various parts of the navigation pane here. One thing you can show is Libraries. If you used Libraries in Windows 7, you might want to use them still. Note that Libraries have changed; they no longer offer access to any Public folders by default.

Renaming files and folders

Sometimes it's useful to change the name of a file or folder. For example, you might have named a folder Taxes, but later decided that Taxes 2013 would be a better choice because you'll have multiple tax folders as the years pass. You might also need to change the name of a folder from Granddaughter to

Grandkids! Beyond folders, files can be named inappropriately too; this is especially common after you've imported pictures from a digital camera. You might have 40 pictures that are named DSCN001, DSCN002, DSCN003, and so on, all of which need to be renamed.

Rename a file or folder

1 With File Explorer open, locate the file or folder that you want to rename and click to select it.

2 Click the Home tab.

3 Click the Rename button.

4 Enter a new name for the file or folder, and press Enter.

TIP You cannot give two files or two folders (that are located in the same folder or library) the same name, so when you rename a file or folder, make the new name unique. However, even in instances where you could create a subfolder with the same name as an existing one located somewhere else on the computer, you should not.

Moving and copying files

When you create subfolders to expand the current folder structure, purchase external backup drives, or connect portable USB drives, it's generally because you want to move or copy data to them. There are lots of ways to copy and move data. One way is to hold down the right-mouse button while you drag the data to its desired location, and then choose Move or Copy from the pop-up window that appears. Another way is to right-click to cut or copy the data, and then right-click at the desired location to paste it. Here you'll learn how to use the ribbon to move and copy data to new locations.

Move or copy a file to another folder

1 In File Explorer, click a file or folder to move or copy.

2 Click the Home tab.

3 Click either Move To or Copy To.

4 If the location you want to move or copy the data to is listed in the resulting list, click it.

5 If the location you want to move or copy the data to is not listed, click Choose Location. Then do the following:

   a Navigate to the desired location.

   b Click Move or Copy as applicable.

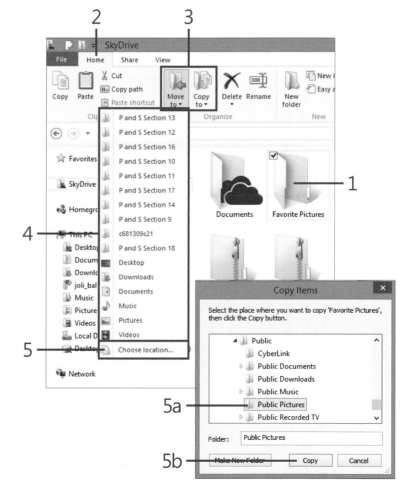

> ⚠ **CAUTION** If you are organizing your files with subfolders, don't copy the data; move it. You want to put the data in the proper location, and you don't want a copy of it left where it shouldn't be. If you are backing up data, don't move the data; copy it. You want to create a copy of the data for safekeeping and you want the original files to remain accessible from your hard drive.

Creating and extracting compressed files

If you want to save space on your drive or take several files and squeeze them together into a file that is smaller than the combined file sizes so that you can send them as an email attachment, you can compress the files. The compressed, or *zipped*, files that you create are perfect for archiving sets of documents or sending content more quickly across the Internet. The easiest way to create a compressed file is to select files already contained in the same folder. When you want to view the files again, you extract them.

Create a compressed file

1 Navigate to the files you want to compress by using File Explorer.

2 Click the first file.

3 Press and hold Shift, and then click the last file in a sequence of adjacent files (or press and hold Ctrl and then click non-adjacent files, one by one).

4 Click the Share tab.

5 Click Zip.

(continued on next page)

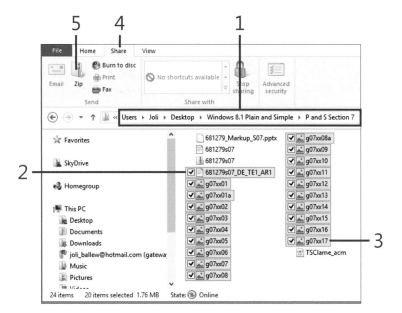

Create a compressed file *(continued)*

6 If desired, type a new name for the zipped folder.

7 Double-click any compressed file to open it (extract the files from it).

8 If the folder doesn't open on its own, click Extract All.

9 If applicable, click Browse to locate a place to save the files to.

10 If applicable, click Extract.

7 ——

6 ——

| 681279_Markup_S07.pptx |
| 681279s07 |
| 681279s07 |
| 681279s07_DE_TE1_AR1 |
| 681279s07_DE_TE1_AR1 |
| g07xx01 |
| g07xx01a |
| g07xx02 |
| g07xx03 |

View   Extract

S Section 12	P and S Section 16
S Section 11	P and S Section 17
S Section 9	c681309c21

Extract all —— 8

tract To

9

□ ×

◄ 🗒 Extract Compressed (Zipped) Folders

Select a Destination and Extract Files

Files will be extracted to this folder:

Desktop\Windows 8.1 Plain and Simple\P and S Section 7\681279s07_DE_TE1_AR1   Browse...

☑ Show extracted files when complete

Extract   Cancel

10

✓ **TIP** You attach a compressed folder to an email just as you would any file, by using your email program's attachments feature. The person receiving the email double-clicks the file to decompress it.

Sharing content

Often you will want to share the documents, pictures, and other files on your computer with others. You can share with a homegroup or homegroup member; you can share with specific people on your local network. You can burn the data to a writable disk, and you can print or email the data too. Here you'll learn how to share content with your homegroup, and then, how to share with a specific person.

Share content

1 With File Explorer open, click an item that is saved to your hard drive that you want to share with your homegroup.

   a Click the Share tab.

   b In the Share With group, click either Homegroup (View) or Homegroup (View and Edit).

2 With File Explorer open, click an item that is saved to your hard drive that you want to share with a specific person.

   a Click the arrow in the Share With group that enables you to see all of your sharing options.

   b Click the person that you want to share with.

> **TIP**   To stop sharing a selected item with a group or individual, click the item to select it, and then on the File Explorer Share tab, click the group or individual on the list and then click the Stop Sharing button.

> **TIP**   You can also use the Send group on the Share tab to share content by emailing, printing, or faxing a copy of your file to another person.

Using File History

It's good practice to save your work and back it up. You can use a few methods to do this. You can turn on the File History feature, which saves default folders, contacts, and favorites to a hard disk on a regular basis, behind the scenes. You can let File History run using default settings, or, you can configure File History to exclude specific folders that you name. You can also choose how often you want to save copies of your files, and how long to keep saved versions, among other things.

Enable File History

1 Insert a USB stick, or attach an external hard disk to your computer.

2 From the Start screen, type **File History**.

3 Click Save Backup Copies Of Your Files With File History.

4 Click Turn On.

5 Leave this window open if you want to configure File History in the next task.

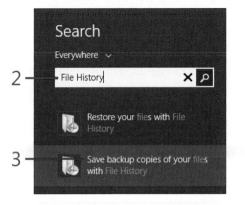

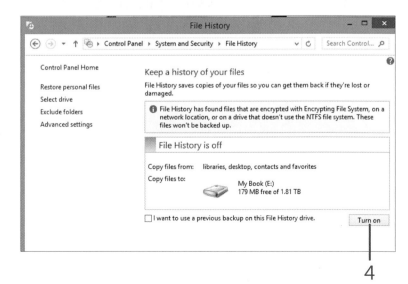

Configure File History

1 In the File History window, in the left pane, click Advanced Settings.

2 Note the options; optionally, make changes to do the following:

   a Save copies of files–to change how often to backup files.

   b Size of offline cache–to change how much of the computer's hard disk is reserved backups that are replicated on your hard drive.

   c Keep saved versions – to configure how long to keep saved versions (consider changing Forever to Until Space Is Needed.

3 In the Advanced Settings window, click Save Changes.

4 In the File History window, click Exclude Folders.

(continued on next page)

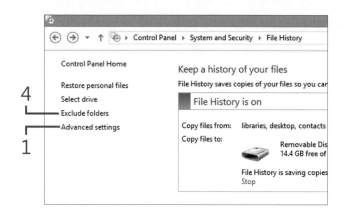

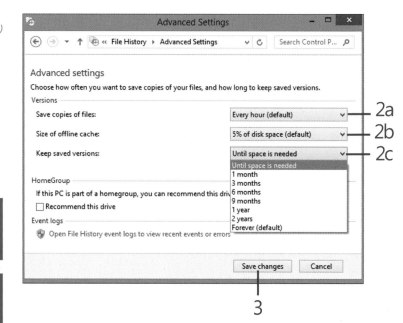

> ✓ **TIP** If you want to change the drive File Explorer saves to, in the File Explorer window, click Select Drive. Then, click the desired drive in the list and click OK.

> ✓ **TIP** To restore files from File History backups, return to the File History window and click Restore Personal Files. Follow the prompts to choose what to restore. It is possible to restore a previous version of a file that was backed up with File History, if the file was backed up hourly while you were working on it.

Configure File History (continued)

5 Click Add.

6 Browse to the folder to exclude, and click it once.

7 Click Select Folder.

8 Click Save Changes.

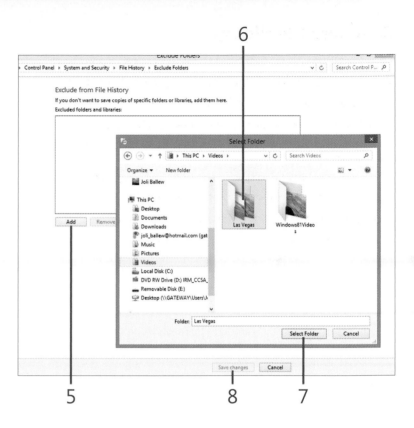

> ⚠ **CAUTION** Make sure to take note of any pop-up windows that you see on the desktop regarding File History. After a while, your drive might get full. This happens when File History is configured to keep the data "forever." You'll be prompted to change this setting if this is the case.

> ⚠ **CAUTION** When you insert a USB stick to use for File History, if File History states that it doesn't recognize the drive, you'll have to format it. To do this, locate the device in File Explorer, right-click it, and click Format. It's okay to perform a quick format.

Backing up data manually

It's a good idea to back up data manually, even if you have a backup program in place. You can back up important files, pictures, family videos, and so on to CDs, DVDs, USB drives, memory cards, and external and network drives, to name a few options. Here you'll learn to save data to either a network drive or an external drive. If the data is extremely important to you, you can perform the task twice and store one of these drives in a safe deposit box or some other offsite location. (Remember, you can also use SkyDrive as a backup option!)

Save to a network or external drive

1 Insert a USB stick, connect an external drive, or, have access to a networked drive.

2 Click the File Explorer icon on the desktop's taskbar.

3 Using techniques you learned in this section, select the data to save.

4 Click the Home tab.

5 Click Copy To.

6 Click Choose Location.

7 Select the drive.

8 Click Copy.

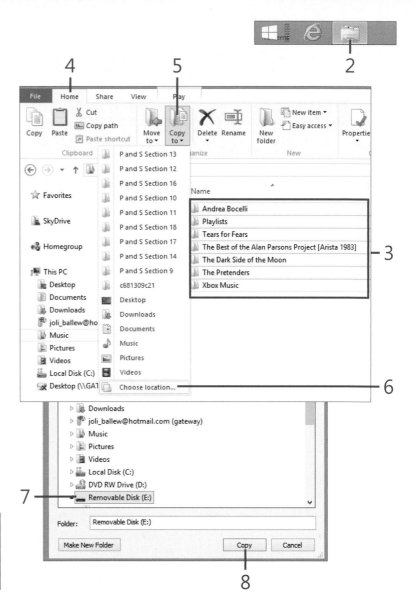

> ✓ **TIP** You can copy files to another drive by using the Copy and Paste buttons on the Home tab of File Explorer or by clicking and dragging selected files and folders between two File Explorer windows.

Deleting files and folders

An important part of managing files on your computer is to know when to get rid of files that you no longer need. Deleting unwanted files gets rid of clutter, frees up disk space, and makes it easier to find what you want. If you delete a file and then decide that you need it back, you do have a window of time in which you can retrieve deleted files from the Recycle Bin. (That window is determined by how much content the Recycle Bin can hold, when it fills up, how and when older files are deleted, and whether you manually delete the files.) Here you'll learn how to delete files.

Delete files

1 In File Explorer, click the file or folder you want to delete.

2 Click the Home tab.

3 Click the Delete button.

> **TIP** If you're trying to recover disk space, consider deleting unwanted video files and audiobooks. Delete any data that you've downloaded from the Xbox Video store too. Video files are generally the largest files on your computer. (Don't forget to delete unwanted data from SkyDrive too.)

> **TIP** There are many more ways than this to delete files. You can drag files directly to the Recycle Bin, and you can right-click a file and click Delete on the resulting menu. You can select entire folders and delete them too.

Working with the Recycle Bin

The Recycle Bin holds deleted files and folders for a period of time. That period of time depends on how much space the Recycle Bin is configured to use to hold deleted files. However, if you right-click the Recycle Bin icon on the desktop and click Empty Recycle Bin, those files are gone, no matter what settings are configured.

Here you'll learn how to restore files from the Recycle Bin (provided you haven't recently emptied it). You'll also learn how to increase the amount of space that the Recycle Bin can use, if you want to use it to provide a safety net for deleted files and folders.

Restore a file or folder from the Recycle Bin

1 On the desktop, double-click the Recycle Bin.

2 Locate the file or folder that you want to restore, and then click to select it.

3 Click the Restore The Selected Items button.

4 Click the Close button.

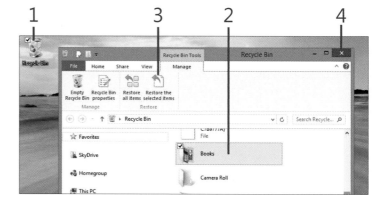

TIP To permanently delete files from your computer, you can use the Empty Recycle Bin button in the Recycle Bin to remove all contents. However, remember that although files might be gone from the Recycle Bin and unavailable to you, they might still be on your hard disk (if the person looking for them is knowledgeable in such matters). If you are giving away or selling your computer, consider restoring your computer to its original state.

TIP If you want to restore the entire contents of the Recycle Bin to the folders from which you deleted them, with the Recycle Bin open, click the Restore All Items button.

Change how much space the Recycle Bin uses to hold deleted files

1 On the desktop, right-click the Recycle Bin.

2 Click Properties.

3 In the Custom Size box, type the desired number of MB to use (1000 MB is approximately 1 GB).

4 Click OK.

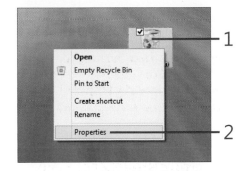

⚠️ **CAUTION** In the Recycle Bin's Properties dialog box, you can see how large your hard drive is—in this case, 697 GB. However, this does not represent the amount of free space that's available. To see how much free space is available, click This PC in File Explorer.

✅ **TIP** If you need to use the Recycle Bin as a safety net for deleted files, consider moving files that you no longer need to a backup device, such as an external drive. You could also save those files to CDs and DVDs.

Working with Accessibility settings

19

In this section:

- Switching from a right-handed to left-handed mouse
- Adjusting double-click speed and indicator motion
- Adjusting keyboard settings
- Enabling High Contrast
- Letting Windows suggest Ease Of Access settings
- Using Magnifier
- Using Narrator
- Working with speech recognition

To provide input to your computer, you use a mouse, touchpad, keyboard, or your fingers on a touchscreen. You can make input easier if you have minor hearing, vision, or dexterity challenges by reconfiguring a variety of settings in Windows 8.1. These options are universal to virtually all computing devices and have been addressed elsewhere in this book; you can almost always turn up the volume, change the screen resolution, and make tiles on the Start screen larger so that they're easier to tap or click, among other things.

There are additional options available in Windows 8.1 that you might not find on other devices; they are located in various places including PC Settings, Control Panel, and the Ease Of Access Center. You can change how the mouse works and looks on the screen, enable high contrast for your display, and use tools such as Magnifier, Narrator, and Speech Recognition, among others to make your computer easier to use.

Switching from a right-handed to left-handed mouse

If you are left-handed (or if your right hand is injured), you will want to reverse the default settings for the mouse buttons. You might also want to switch from right-handed to left-handed use on a regular basis (say weekly) to avoid repetitive use injuries, like carpal tunnel syndrome.

Switch from right-hand to left-hand clicking

1 From the Start screen, type **Mouse**.

2 In the results, click Change Your Mouse Settings.

3 Click the arrow under Select Your Primary Button, and select Right instead of Left.

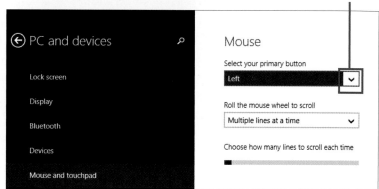

> **➔ TRY THIS** If the size of the pointer is difficult for you to see on the screen, repeat step 1, but in the results in step 2, click Ease Of Access Mouse Settings. There you can change the pointer size, pointer color, and more.

> **✓ TIP** If you use a laptop's touchpad to move the cursor on the screen and you want to change settings for it, on the Start screen, type Touchpad. You'll find settings for changing touchpad settings in PC Settings, under PC and Devices, in Mouse and Touchpad. You might also turn off the touchpad if you use a mouse (and often inadvertently touch the touchpad while working).

Adjusting double-click speed and indicator motion

If double-clicking presents a challenge because you have trouble clicking fast enough, you can adjust the speed at which the mouse responds to a double-click. You can also modify how fast the mouse indicator moves across your screen so that you can follow its path more easily.

Change double-click speed and motion settings

1 Right-click the Start button, and click **Control Panel.**

2 Type Mouse in the Search window.

3 Click Change Mouse Click Settings.

(continued on next page)

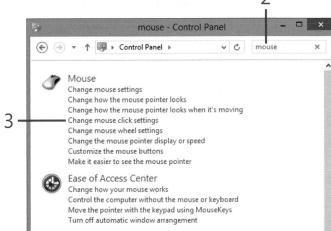

Change double-click speed and motion
settings *(continued)*

4 On the Buttons tab, drag the slider in the Double-Click Speed category to set the speed at which you want to double-click your mouse to initiate an action.

5 Double-click the folder icon to test the setting.

6 Click the Pointer Options tab.

7 Drag the slider in the Motion setting section to adjust how fast or slow the pointer moves on your screen in response to mouse movements.

8 Click OK.

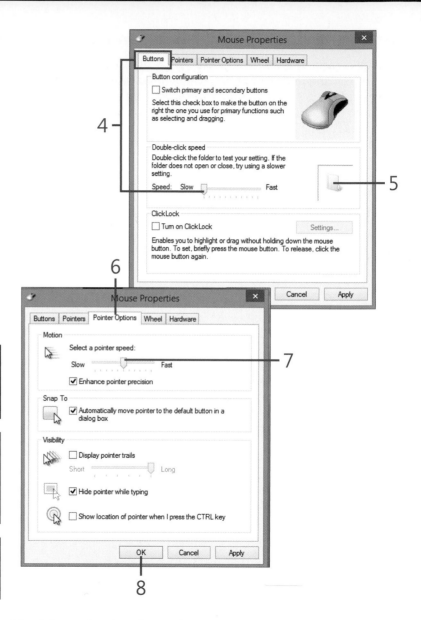

> **→ TRY THIS** You can change how fast or slow you must double-tap on a touch screen to make something happen. Search for Pen And Touch from the Start screen, and click Pen And Touch in the results to access the settings.

> **✓ TIP** You'll find different mouse schemes on the Pointers tab in the Mouse Properties dialog box. Windows Default (System Scheme) is selected, but you can choose another. If you have trouble seeing the mouse, try Windows Standard (Extra Large) (System Scheme).

> **→ TRY THIS** Before you click OK in step 8, see what's available from the other tabs: Pointers, Wheel, and Hardware. You might find other options that you want to change.

Adjusting keyboard settings

You can change how your keyboard works, to make it easier to use if you have dexterity issues. The best place to access the keyboard settings is Control Panel. Among other things, there you can change how fast the cursor blinks on the screen; configure the keyboard so that the numeric keyboard can be used to move the cursor around on the screen (Mouse Keys); configure the keyboard so that keyboard shortcuts that require you hold down more than one key at a time can be performed with only one finger (Sticky Keys); and configure the keyboard to ignore brief repeated keystrokes when you have trouble getting your hands off the keys fast enough (Filter Keys).

Adjust keyboard settings

1 Right-click the Start button, and click **Control Panel.**

2 Type Keyboard in the Search window.

3 Click Change How Your Keyboard Works.

(continued on next page)

> **TIP** You can change what happens when you type on a keyboard. You can change whether or not Windows will autocorrect misspelled words; will show text suggestions as you type; will add a period when you double-tap the Spacebar; and more. Beyond that, you can configure what happens when you use the Touch Keyboard, including whether to hear sounds as you type, capitalize the first letters of each sentence, and so on. You access these options in PC Settings, PC and Devices, Typing.

Adjust keyboard settings (continued)

4 Read all of the options, and select the options to enable.

5 Click OK.

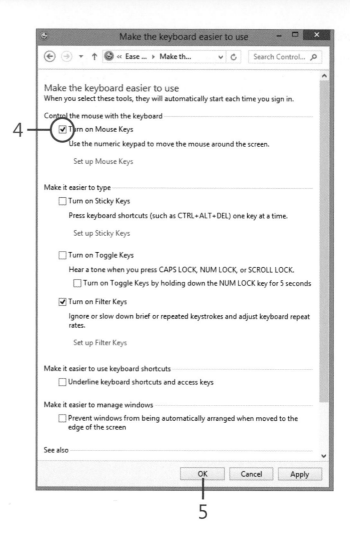

TIP In PC Settings, in Ease Of Access, and just underneath High Contrast, note the Keyboard option. You can quickly enable or disable Sticky Keys, Toggle Keys, and Filter Keys there.

TIP If the charms open when you don't need them, because you regularly and inadvertently move the cursor into an active hot corner, turn off corner navigation. Access these settings in PC Settings, PC and Devices, Corners and Edges.

Enabling High Contrast

If you have difficulty seeing items on your screen, especially because of its color or contrast settings, you will want to try the available high-contrast options. These options change the background color of the screen as well as the screen elements. Try it; seeing is believing!

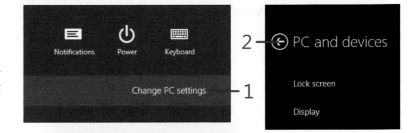

Enable High Contrast

1 Press Windows logo key+I, and click Change PC Settings.

2 If you see a back arrow, click it.

3 Click Ease Of Access.

4 Click High Contrast.

5 Click the arrow by None.

(continued on next page)

Enable High Contrast *(continued)*

6 Select High Contrast #2.

7 If you like what you see, click Apply. (If not, repeat steps 5–6 to select another option.)

8 To turn off High Contrast , do the following:

a Click the arrow by the selected theme (not shown), and click None.

b Click Apply.

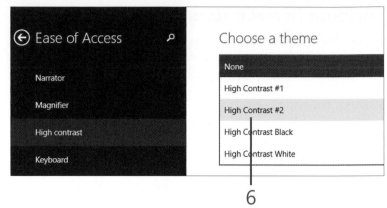

6

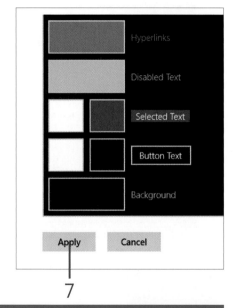

7

8a

8b

> ✓ **TIP** If you're still having trouble seeing what's on the screen or if enabling High Contrast didn't work as you'd like, try increasing the size of the items on the screen. Right-click the desktop, click Screen Resolution, and opt to make text and other items larger or smaller.

Letting Windows suggest Ease Of Access settings

There are many options to make it easier to use your computer if you have a disability. In fact, there are too many to detail in this section. There are options that can help you if you get distracted easily, if you are blind, if you are deaf, or if you are dyslexic, among other things. Windows offers a tool that can offer recommendations based on answers that you give to five questions, to tell you what accessibility options might work best for you.

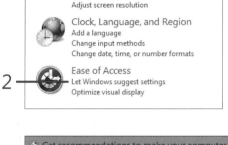

Let Windows suggest Ease Of Access settings

1 Right-click the Start button, and click Control Panel (not shown).

2 Under Ease Of Access, click Let Windows Suggest Settings.

3 For the first question, check applicable answers.

4 Click Next.

5 Repeat steps 3 and 4 to answer the other four questions.

(continued on next page)

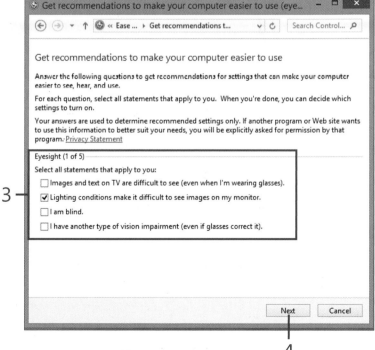

> **TIP** Learn more about specific Ease Of Access options in the remaining tasks in this section: Using Magnifier, Using Narrator, and Using Speech Recognition.

Let Windows suggest Ease Of Access settings

(continued)

6 Review the results, and select any item to enable.

7 Read the Caution shown on this book page, and then, if desired, click OK.

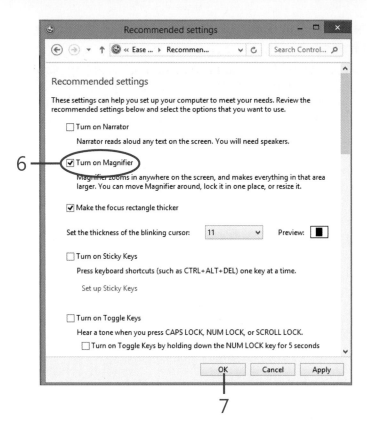

⚠️ **CAUTION** In step 6, if you enable features such as Magnifier and Narrator and then click OK in step 7, those features will immediately start. This might come as a surprise if the screen is suddenly magnified and a voice starts talking to you. Consider reading about how to use these features before you click OK.

Using Magnifier

Magnifier magnifies what's on the screen. You can configure what part of the screen is magnified and how much it's magnified after it's running. There are many ways to start Magnifier, including from the Ease Of Access Center, and from PC Settings, Ease Of Access, and Magnifier. After it's running, it's important to know three keyboard shortcuts for managing it:

- **Stop Magnifier**   Windows+Esc.

- **Zoom in or out**   Windows+Plus sign or Windows + Minus sign, respectively.

- **Restart Magnifier when stopped**   Windows+Plus sign.

Use Magnifier

1 From the Start screen, press Windows and the ı key. The screen is magnified (provided you haven't used it yet and changed the settings to 100%).

2 Move the cursor over one of the following:

a Magnifier window if it's available. (This will change to a magnifying glass in a couple of seconds.)

b Magnifying glass if it's available. To show the Magnifier window, click the double arrows that appear.

(continued on next page)

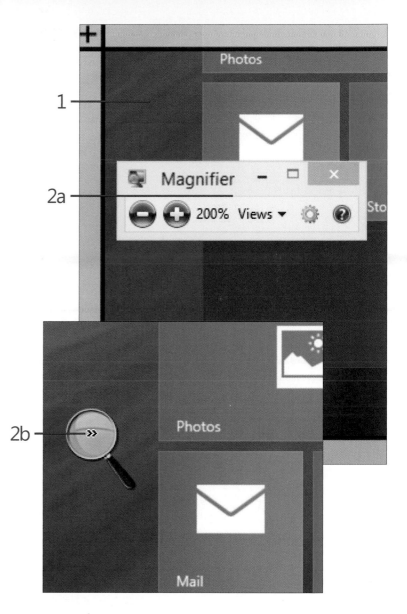

Use Magnifier *(continued)*

3 With the Magnifier window open, click the – and + signs to zoom out and in.

4 Click Views to explore other views; try Lens. (Docked isn't available on the Start screen.)

5 Press Windows+Esc to exit Magnifier, or, click the X in the Magnifier window.

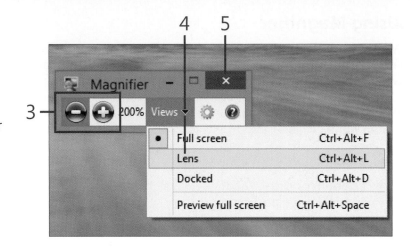

Using Narrator

Narrator tells you what is happening on the screen in real time. It lets you know when you've opened a dialog box, navigated to a webpage, or opened or closed an app. It doesn't detail the content in a file (like what's on a PowerPoint slide or what a picture looks like), although it will tell you when you've opened and closed files. It can also read what you type. Narrator can sometimes read items that you select in apps, too. For example, it will say aloud the month or day you select from a list when configuring an event in Calendar.

Start Narrator and configure settings

1 From the Start screen, type **Narrator**.

2 Click Narrator Settings in the results. (To start Narrator later, click Narrator in the results.)

3 Move the slider for Narrator from Off to On. (If you don't hear Narrator start, turn up the volume on your computer.)

4 If desired, change additional settings, such as Speed and Pitch (move the sliders).

5 Click the arrow beside Microsoft David, and click Microsoft Hazel.

(continued on next page)

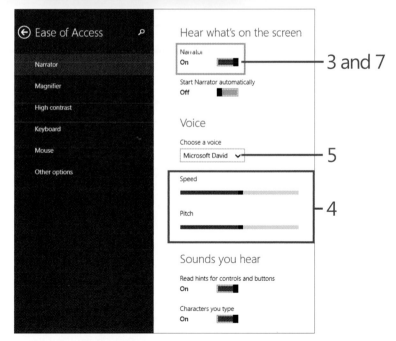

Start Narrator and configure settings *(continued)*

6 Scroll to see additional settings; configure as desired.

7 Scroll back up, and move the slider for Narrator from On to Off (shown on the previous page).

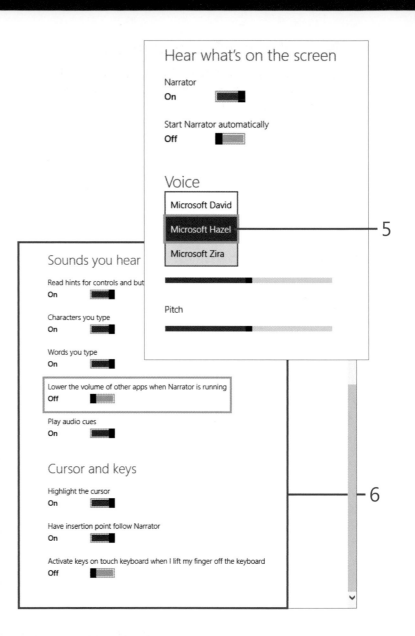

> ✓ **TIP** There are a lot of keyboard shortcuts that you can use with Narrator. Caps Lock+Esc will turn it off, and Ctrl can be used to make Narrator stop reading.

> ✓ **TIP** Narrator's capabilities are constantly being expanded. Although Narrator will never be able to tell you what a picture looks like, by the time you read this, it might be able to do things it currently can't, like read the content of webpages, Excel and Power-Point entries, and PDF files.

Working with speech recognition

Speech recognition has been around for many years, and the technology has made great progress in its ability to recognize voices and accents and deliver accurate results. Windows 8.1 comes with its own speech recognition program, you can use to give oral commands like Click File, Click Start, Double-Click Recycle Bin, Scroll Up, Scroll Down, New Paragraph, Select Word, and so on. However, you have to turn it on first, configure it, and train it. After you've worked through the setup tasks, you can start using it.

Start Speech Recognition and configure your microphone

1 From the Start screen, begin to type **Speech Recognition**.

2 Click Speech Recognition in the results. (Do not click Windows Speech Recognition.)

3 Click Set Up Microphone.

4 Choose your microphone type, click Next, and work through the setup wizard as instructed.

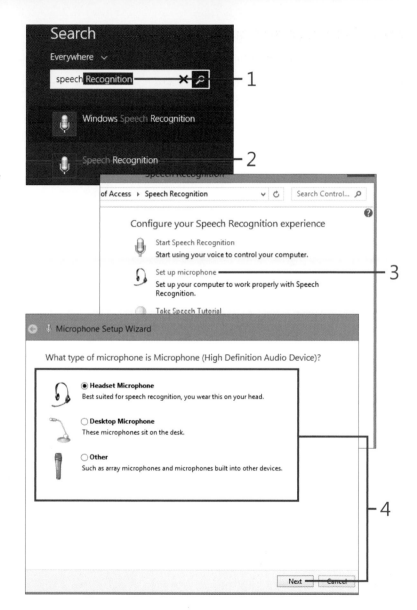

Work through the speech tutorial

1 In Control Panel, in Speech Recognition, click Take Speech Tutorial.

2 Click Next.

3 Work through the speech tutorial as prompted, speaking (and clicking Next) as applicable.

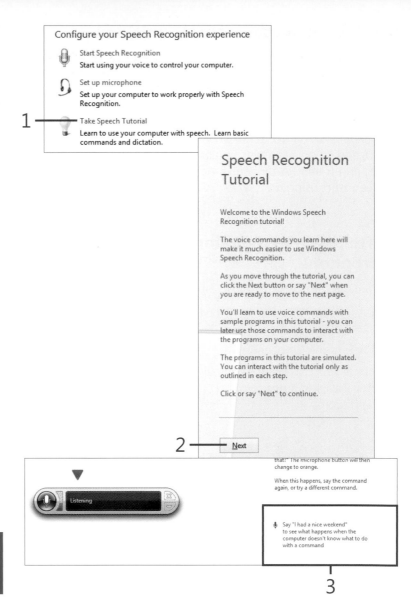

Configure your Speech Recognition experience

Start Speech Recognition
Start using your voice to control your computer.

Set up microphone
Set up your computer to work properly with Speech Recognition.

1 —— Take Speech Tutorial
Learn to use your computer with speech. Learn basic commands and dictation.

Speech Recognition Tutorial

Welcome to the Windows Speech Recognition tutorial!

The voice commands you learn here will make it much easier to use Windows Speech Recognition.

As you move through the tutorial, you can click the Next button or say "Next" when you are ready to move to the next page.

You'll learn to use voice commands with sample programs in this tutorial - you can later use those commands to interact with the programs on your computer.

The programs in this tutorial are simulated. You can interact with the tutorial only as outlined in each step.

Click or say "Next" to continue.

2 —— Next

that?" The microphone button will then change to orange.

When this happens, say the command again, or try a different command.

Listening

Say "I had a nice weekend" to see what happens when the computer doesn't know what to do with a command

3

> **TIP** It takes a long time to work through the speech tutorial, but it's worth it. If you plan to use speech recognition regularly, make time to work through the tutorial completely.

Use Speech Recognition

After you have set up Speech Recognition, you can try it out. You can start Speech Recognition from Control Panel's Speech Recognition window, or you can search for Speech Recognition from the Start screen.

1 From the Start screen, begin to type **Speech Recognition**.

2 Click Windows Speech Recognition in the results.

3 If the Speech Recognition controls shows Off (or anything other than Listening), click the Microphone button on the Speech Recognition controls.

4 Verify that the Speech Recognition controls show Listening.

5 Speak the following into your microphone: "Open WordPad." WordPad opens.

6 Begin to speak a sentence. Note the words that appear in WordPad.

7 Say "Close WordPad."

8 Click the Don't Save button.

(continued on next page)

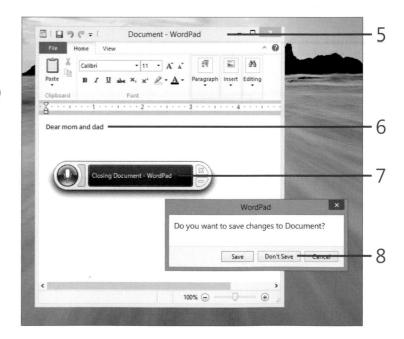

Use Speech Recognition *(continued)*

9 Say "What can I say?" and then silently read the information about the commands you can use with Speech Recognition.

10 Click the X in the Speech Recognition controls to exit the application.

11 Say "Stop listening."

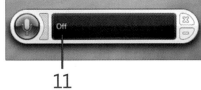

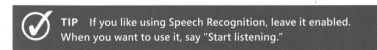

TIP If you like using Speech Recognition, leave it enabled. When you want to use it, say "Start listening."

Maintaining and troubleshooting your computer

20

Windows 8.1 has several built-in features to help you keep your computer running at its best, improve performance when needed, guide you through troubleshooting tasks, and help you restore your computer when you experience a problem that you can't resolve by using other methods. In this section you'll learn about many of these features, including but not limited to creating a recovery drive, using ReadyBoost, configuring Windows Update, resolving problems by using Action Center and various troubleshooting wizards, using Advanced Startup Options to perform automated checks and fixes, and refreshing and resetting your PC when all else fails.

Creating a recovery drive

A recovery drive can help you repair your computer even if the computer won't start. When you create this drive, you can also copy a manufacturer's recovery partition if your computer came with one (and if the drive you're saving to is large enough to hold it). It's best to create this drive before a problem occurs, versus wishing you had after the fact. The best way to start is to purchase and then connect an empty USB disk (or thumb drive) that is at least 256 MB, although you can also use a DVD.

Create a recovery drive

1 Insert the USB stick into an available USB port on your computer.

2 From the the Start screen type **Recovery**.

3 Click Create A Recovery Drive in the results.

4 If applicable, select Copy The Recovery Partition From The PC To The Recovery Drive. Click Next.

(continued on next page)

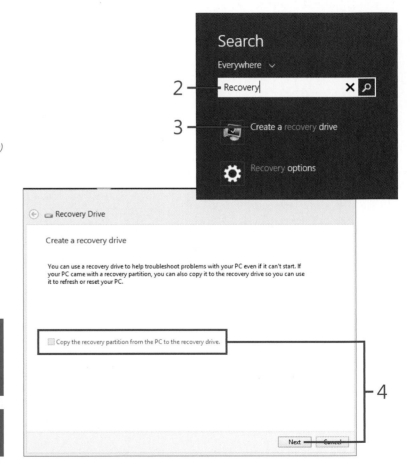

 TIP   You can rename the USB drive in File Explorer under This PC. You might want to name it Recovery so that you don't accidentally write over it later. In File Explorer, right-click the drive and click Rename.

 TIP   Store the recovery drive you create in a safe, dry, climate-controlled area like a drawer or filing cabinet.

Create a recovery drive *(continued)*

5 Select the USB drive in the list. The name of the drive is the name given by the manufacturer.

6 Click Next.

7 Click Create.

8 Click Finish when prompted.

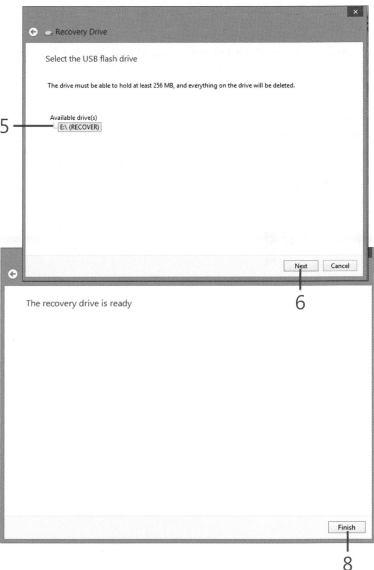

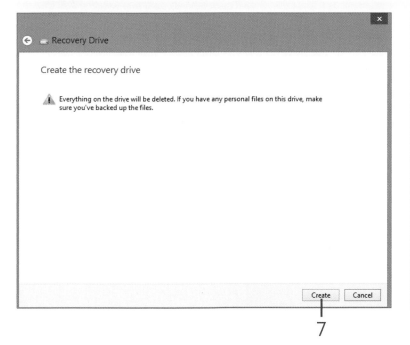

Using ReadyBoost

Computers store data that is needed only temporarily in physical random access memory (RAM) located inside your device. Temporary data can be information being sent to a printer, or it can be data needed to perform calculations; it isn't generally data you'd save to your hard drive. In general, the more RAM a computer has, the faster it will perform.

Unfortunately, it's often difficult to add more RAM to a device. When it is an option, it's invasive and can be expensive. If you want more RAM but don't want to go this route, you can use a technology called ReadyBoost to improve performance. ReadyBoost acts like RAM and serves the same purpose, but it requires only a USB stick or compatible memory card.

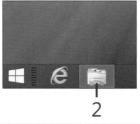

2

Use ReadyBoost

1 Connect a compatible USB drive or memory card.

2 If File Explorer does not open, click the File Explorer icon on the desktop taskbar.

3 Right-click the drive, and click Properties. (We've named our drive ReadyBoost; yours will be named differently.)

(continued on next page)

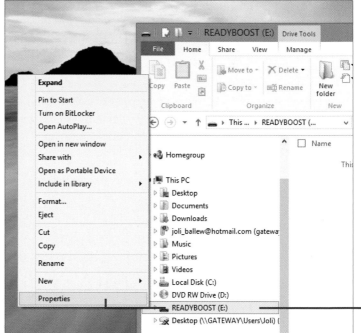

3

Use ReadyBoost *(continued)*

4 Click the ReadyBoost tab.

5 Click Use This Device. (Alternatively, you can opt to dedicate the device to ReadyBoost.)

6 Move the slider to select a value greater than 1000 MB (which is approximately 1 GB).

7 Click OK.

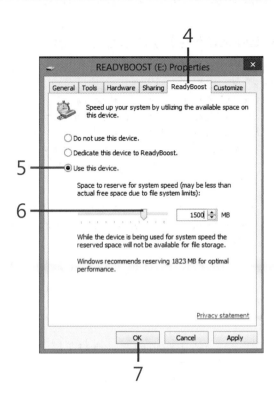

> ✓ **TIP** There are some requirements for the USB stick or memory card you use to serve as ReadyBoost, but you'll be informed if it doesn't meet those requirements. Microsoft recommends that you choose a disk that is greater than 1 GB, but 2-4 GB will give better results.

> ⚠ **CAUTION** If your computer has a hard disk that uses solid-state drive (SSD) technology, you might not see an option to speed up your computer with ReadyBoost when you plug in a USB flash drive or flash memory card. Instead, you might receive the following message: "ReadyBoost is not enabled on this computer because the system disk is fast enough that ReadyBoost is unlikely to provide any additional benefit." This is because some SSD drives are so fast that they're unlikely to benefit from ReadyBoost.

Configuring Windows Update

Periodically, Microsoft sends out updates to its operating system to make improvements or fix problems that have surfaced. They also address security issues. These updates can apply features changes too. You can set how you want Windows 8.1 to download and install these updates, although the recommended settings are best in most cases.

Update Windows automatically

1 From the Start screen, begin to type **Windows Update**.

2 Click Choose Whether To Automatically Install Windows Updates.

3 The best setting is Install Updates Automatically (Recommended), with Give Me Recommended Updates The Same Way I Receive Important Updates selected. Click the arrow beside the former to see other options.

(continued on next page)

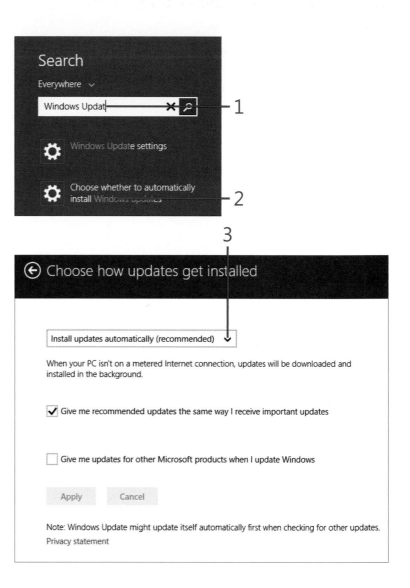

Update Windows automatically *(continued)*

4 If desired, select another option.

5 If you'd like, select Give Me Updates For Other Microsoft Products When I Update Windows.

6 Click Apply.

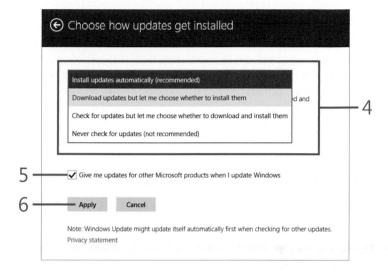

TRY THIS Note the back arrow next to Choose How Updates Get Installed in step 2. In the resulting screen, you'll see an option to check for updates manually, at any time (you can also opt to view your update history). If you'd like, click Check Now to see how this process works. (If you don't see this option, it's because updates have recently been installed and you need to restart, as prompted.)

Exploring the Action Center

The Action Center keeps track of problems you encounter, looks for solutions, and if solutions are found, notifies you of the fix. It also monitors your computer to make sure that it's doing all it is configured to do, and it lets you know whether there are

any problems. For example, if you have File History enabled and your drive becomes full or is disconnected, the Action Center will notify you. If your antivirus program is out of date and can't be updated on its own, it'll tell you about that too.

Explore the Action Center

1 On the desktop's taskbar, click the white flag in the notification area. If you don't see the flag, click the up arrow in the Notification center to find it.

2 Click Open Action Center.

3 If you see issues, they'll be marked as red (important) or yellow (needs attention).

4 Click the option available to resolve the problem.

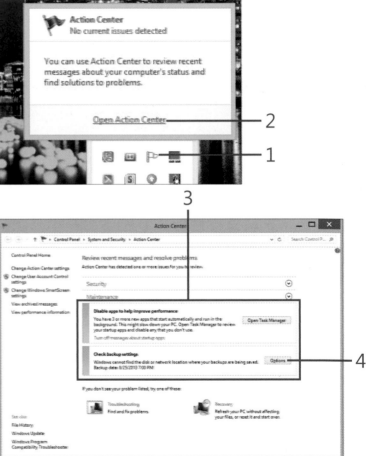

TIP Ideally, you don't want any color at all in the Action Center window (nothing red, nothing yellow). Resolve all issues as they arise.

TRY THIS In Action Center, in the left pane, select Change Action Center Settings. From the resulting window, you can turn off messages about specific issues, although this isn't recommended. Some of the messages you can turn off include those you'll see regarding Windows Update, Virus Protection, File History, HomeGroup, and Automatic Maintenance.

Running Disk Cleanup

When you save data and apps to your hard disk or view or download temporary Internet files, those bits of data can be stored at various locations across your hard disk. Over time, the out-of-date bits of data can cause your computer performance to slow down. Disk Cleanup allows you to erase stray data (among other things) to improve your computer's performance.

Run Disk Cleanup

1 From the Start screen, begin to type **Disk Cleanup**.

2 Click Disk Cleanup in the results.

3 Note the items that you can clean up. Leave the selected items selected, and if desired, select more (perhaps to empty the Recycle Bin).

4 Click OK.

5 Click Delete Files.

> ✓ **TIP** If your computer has more than one drive that contains data, you might be prompted to select a drive in step 3. Select the primary drive if this happens.

> ✓ **TIP** Disk Defragmenter is another tool that you can use to clean up a disk drive. This tool looks for files that are not stored together; intead they are fragmented across the drive. Consolidating fragmented files helps those files open faster. However, this tool runs on its own and on a schedule, so it probably isn't necessary to ever run it manually. If you use this feature on an SSD drive, it'll happen very quickly, relatively speaking, if you're used to it taking quite a bit of time on a traditional hard drive.

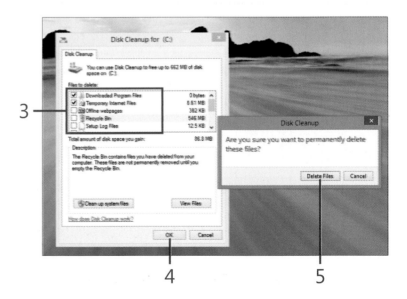

Restarting your computer

Sometimes you will need to restart your computer. It might be frozen, the display might be distorted, or you might be asked by a software application to restart the computer to apply changes.

There are many ways to restart your computer, including accessing the Power icon by using Ctrl+Alt+Del or from the Settings charm. The easiest way is to right-click the Start button.

Restart your computer

1 Right-click the Start button.

2 Click or point to Shut Down or sign out.

3 Click Restart.

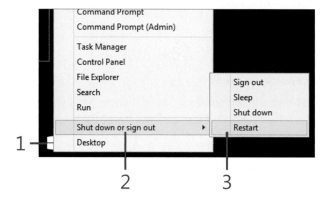

⚠️ **CAUTION** Don't ever press and hold the Power button on a traditional laptop or desktop PC to shut it down or turn it off. Likewise, never unplug a desktop PC from the wall unless there simply isn't any other way to power it down. Always look for a valid Shut Down or Restart option. In a worst case scenario, use Ctrl+Alt+Del to access the Power icon. Click it to shut down or restart.

✓ **TIP** After some actions (like installing updates for a desktop application), you are prompted to restart your computer to finalize the update process. However, if you don't need those updates immediately, you generally don't have to restart your computer right then. The next time you turn off and then turn on the computer, the process will be completed.

Using troubleshooting wizards

Windows 8.1 comes with several built-in troubleshooting wizards. If you know what type of problem you're having, you can use one of these wizards to try to resolve the problem. Troubleshooting wizards are available in the following categories: Programs, Hardware and Sound, Network and Internet, and System and Security.

What happens in a wizard differs depending on the one you select, but the process is the same. You select the type of problem you're having, and the wizard prompts you to try various fixes until the problem is resolved.

Select and start a troubleshooting wizard

1 From the Start screen, type **Find and Fix Problems.**

2 Select Find And Fix Problems in the results.

3 Click the entry that most closely represents the problem that you are having, such as Use A Printer.

4 Click Next to start the wizard.

(continued on next page)

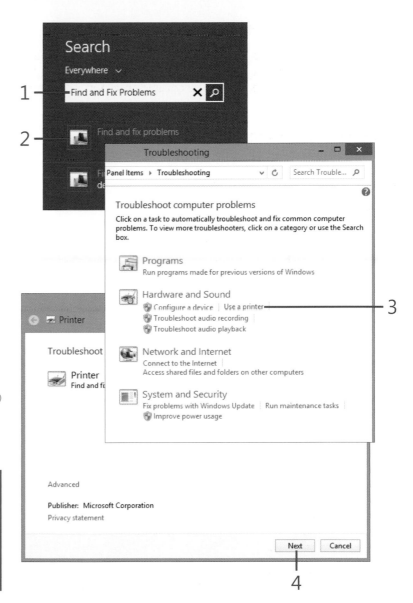

> ✓ **TIP** In Step 3, if you click a heading instead of an entry—for example, you click the heading Hardware And Sound instead of the entry under it, Use A Printer—additional options will appear. These options will offer the general ones you already saw, such as fixing problems with printing, and audio recording and playback, but you'll also see options that address other hardware components, such as network adapters.

Select and start a troubleshooting wizard

(continued)

5 On the resulting screen and those thereafter, answer prompts, make selections, and try solutions, clicking Next where applicable.

6 If a fix is found, click Apply This Fix.

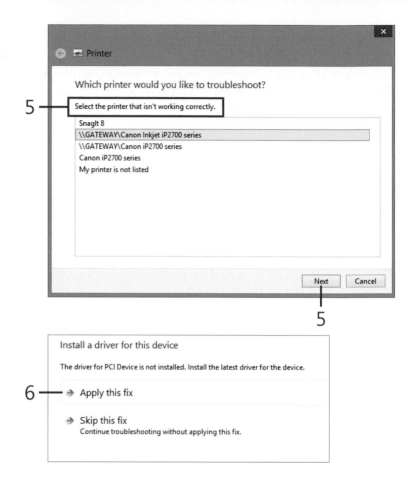

Using Microsoft Fix It

Microsoft Fix It is an online troubleshooting tool. If you're having a problem that is common to a lot of users, you might be able to find an entry for the issue you're having, as well as an automated fix for it. If you find the solution that you need, you can give Microsoft Fix It permission to run the automated solution for you. You don't have to have a problem to explore Microsoft Fix it, so work through the steps here so that you'll know what to do when a problem arises.

Use Microsoft Fix It

1 Use Internet Explorer to browse to *http://fixitcenter.support.microsoft. com/Portal.*

2 Click Try It Now.

3 Click Run.

(continued on next page)

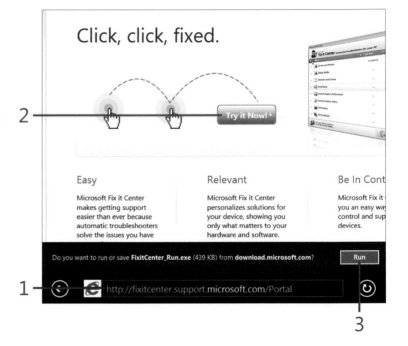

Using Microsoft Fix It: Use Microsoft Fix It   **311**

Use Microsoft Fix It *(continued)*

4 Wait while setup completes, and then click a problem area.

5 Under What Are You Trying To Do, select an issue.

6 Make a selection to refine the issue.

7 Find the solution to try.

8 Click Run Now.

9 Click Run.

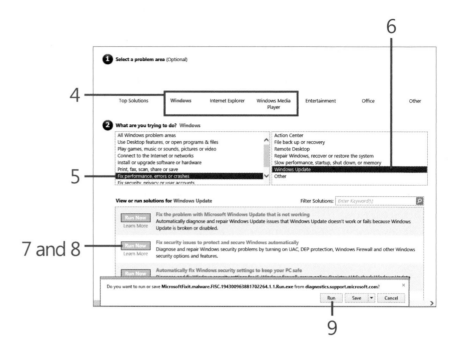

SEE ALSO To learn how to use Internet Explorer, refer to Section 8, "Going online with Internet Explorer 11."

CAUTION The first time that you run Microsoft Fix It, you might be prompted to install various things, such as Microsoft .Net Framework. If you want to use Microsoft Fix It, you'll have to perform the required installations. However, you'll only have to do it once; the next time that you use Microsoft Fix It, your computer will be ready.

Asking for Windows Remote Assistance

Remote Assistance lets you ask a person you know to help you resolve a problem over the Internet or a local network. You send an invitation (generally via email), the person accepts the invitation and connects to your computer, and then you give that person permission to fix your computer for you by taking control of it and resolving the problem themselves.

Get remote help

1 Open Control Panel, and in the Search box, type **Remote Assistance**.

2 Click Invite Someone To Connect To Your PC And Help You, Or Offer To Help Someone Else.

3 Click Invite Someone You Trust To Help You.

(continued on next page)

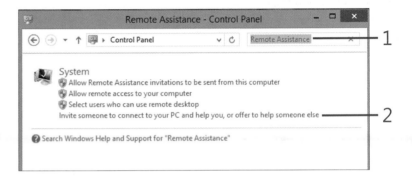

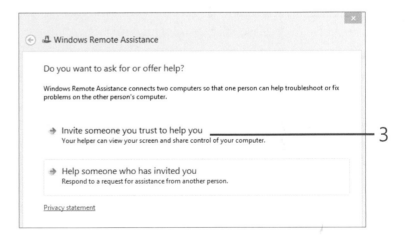

Get remote help   *(continued)*

4 If you've used Remote Assistance before, you'll see the name of the person that helped you. If this is the case, either select Invite Someone To Help You or click the name of the person listed.

5 Click either Save This Invitation As A File (if you use web-based email) or Use Email To Send An Invitation (if you have a program installed on your computer to send email).

(continued on next page)

4

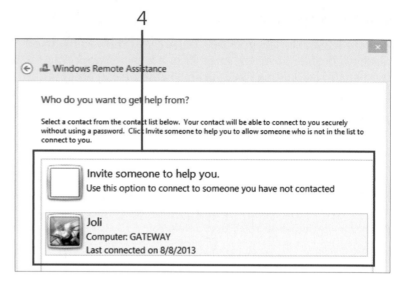

5

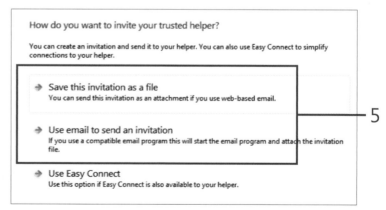

Get remote help *(continued)*

6 Your helper needs the password contained in the invitation, so either:

  a Complete the process to send the invitation via email, which will differ depending on the option you choose in step 5.

  b Call your helper on the phone or by using Skype, and give them the invitation password.

7 After your helper receives the invitation and responds, click Yes to allow access.

8 To end the session at any time, click the X in the top-right corner of the Windows Remote Assistance window.

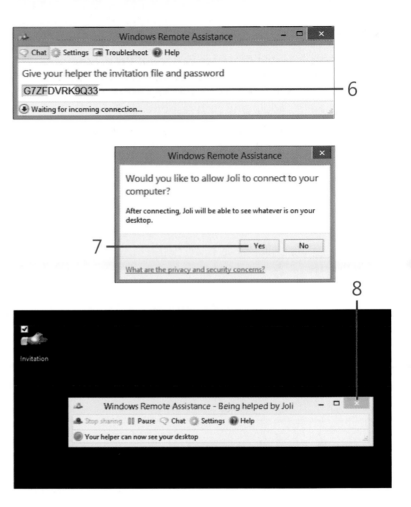

⚠ **CAUTION** Always make sure that you know and trust any person whom you allow to access your computer remotely. A clever hacker or scammer could pretend to be from a valid company like Microsoft and offer to resolve any problems you have over the Internet, when in reality they are not at all trustworthy or from the company they say they're from. Remote Assistance is safe only if you send the invitation to someone you know, and never if someone tries to access your computer without you initiating the session.

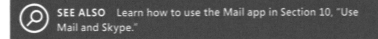

🔍 **SEE ALSO** Learn how to use the Mail app in Section 10, "Use Mail and Skype."

Troubleshooting with Windows Task Manager

Task Manager is a utility that keeps track of the various programs and processes that are running on your computer, and it offers you an option to end those programs and processes manually, should one stop responding. Task Manager is extremely useful to professional computer technicians, and there's a lot more that you can do with it than this. However, it's important to know how to end applications that don't respond to any attempt to close them, because this might save you from having to completely restart your computer. It might also resolve problems currently caused by the errant, albeit frozen, application.

Use Windows Task Manager to close an application

1 Press Ctrl+Shift+Esc.

2 Click More Details. (If it shows Fewer Details instead of More Details, skip this step.)

(continued on next page)

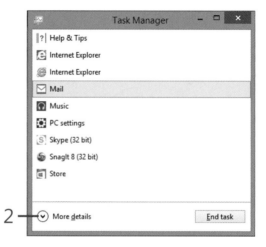

Use Windows Task Manager to close an application *(continued)*

3 On the Processes tab, click the item to close.

4 If you don't see what you want to close in the list, click the applicable down arrow to find it.

5 Click End Task.

6 Click the X in the top-right corner to close Task Manager.

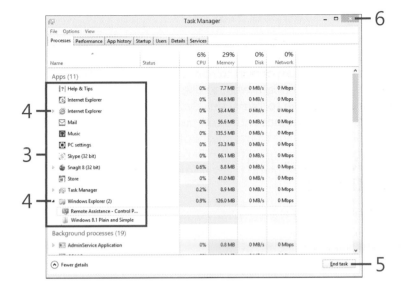

✅ **TIP** If you see the application that you want to close after opening Task Manager and before clicking More Details, you can select it and click End Task. You don't have to view the additional details if you don't want to. However, to see what Task Manager has to offer and to show how to access tasks hidden under down arrows, we clicked More Details in step 2.

✅ **TIP** To see what apps start when you boot your computer, in Task Manager, click the Startup tab. If there are several desktop applications listed that you recognize, consider disabling them. Your computer will boot faster and perform better without unnecessary applications running in the background. Don't worry; those applications will start when you click their icons.

Using Advanced Startup

Sometimes you'll need to start your computer in a way other than booting to the hard disk. For example, if the computer won't start, you might need to boot it with a Windows 8.1 DVD or USB drive. You might want to use Advanced Startup options to make use of the recovery drive you created at the beginning of this section to recover the computer if it's having problems. You might also want to troubleshoot your PC by selecting tools such as System Restore, Startup Repair, and Startup Settings. These tools can help you recover from all kinds of startup problems.

Here are a few of the items you might want to try if you've been unable to repair your computer successfully by using other techniques:

- **System Restore** To restore your computer to an earlier time, when the computer was stable. Windows automatically creates restore points that you can use to do this.

- **System Image Recovery** To restore your computer by using a system image recovery that you might have created with backup software.

- **Startup Repair** To run an automated fix to check for and repair common startup problems.

- **Startup Settings** To troubleshoot startup by starting minimally with a low-resolution video display, in Safe Mode, and enable boot logging, among other things.

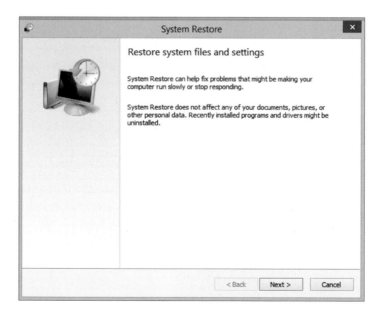

Access Advanced Startup

1 From the Start screen, type **Recovery**.

2 Click Recovery Options in the results.

3 Under Advanced Startup, click Restart Now.

(continued on next page)

Access Advanced Startup *(continued)*

4 After the computer restarts, choose either Use A Device or Troubleshoot.

5 If you choose Use A Device, select the device to use in the resulting list (not shown). The computer will reboot using this device.

6 If you choose Troubleshoot, you can select one of the following:

   a Refresh Your PC–to refresh your PC as outlined in the next task in this section.

   b Reset Your PC–to reset your PC to factory defaults, as outlined in the last task in this section.

   c Advanced Options–to access additional options.

(continued on next page)

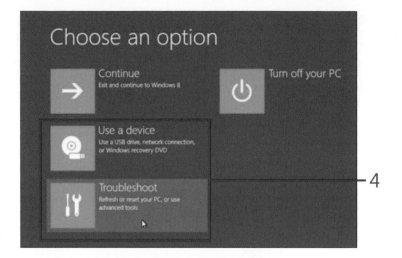

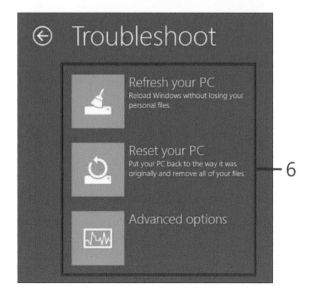

Access Advanced Startup *(continued)*

7 If you chose Advanced Options in step 6, select from one of the following:

   a System Restore

   b System Image Recovery

   c Automatic Repair

   d Windows Startup Settings

8 Follow the prompts that appear, which will differ based on previous choices, to complete the process.

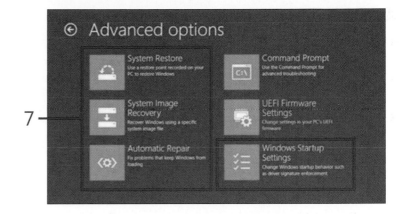

Refreshing your PC

If your computer has so many problems that the only way you know how to resolve them is to completely start over by formatting your computer or restoring from your computer's recovery drive (and you've already tried System Restore, Startup Repair, and similar options), try refreshing your PC. When you refresh your PC, only third-party programs, web browser add-ons, printer software, scanner software, and other desktop apps are removed, but apps from the Windows Store, your personal settings, and your personal data (documents, music, videos, pictures, and so on) will remain intact.

Refresh your PC

1 From the Start screen, type **Refresh**.

2 In the results, click Refresh Your PC Without Affecting Your Files.

3 Under Refresh Your PC Without Affecting Your Files, click Get Started.

4 Read the information and click Next.

5 Wait while the computer refreshes, and respond to any prompts as applicable.

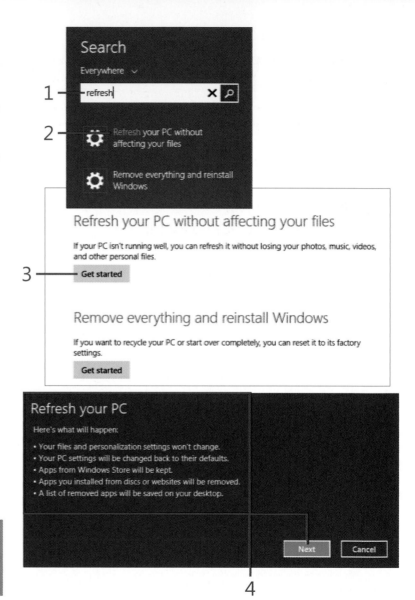

> ⚠️ **CAUTION** After the refresh procedure is complete, you'll have to reinstall third-party applications. You'll likely need product and activation codes, and the installation will take some time. Perform a refresh only if you've tried everything else that you can think of.

Resetting your PC

If your computer has so many problems that the computer is extremely unstable, and if you've tried all of the troubleshooting techniques outlined here, including refreshing your PC, you might have to reset your PC. However, for the most part, you'll use this feature only when you want to give your computer away or recycle it. When you do, the computer is reset to factory defaults. All of your apps, data, and desktop applications will be removed from your computer, as will your personal (local) settings, network information, and data about connected hardware. Your PC will be formatted. You will be able to log in with your Microsoft account, and restore your apps and saved settings and access data from SkyDrive, but this is still a major step to take. Try everything else first.

Reset your PC

1 From the Start screen, type **Remove Everything**.

2 Click Remove Everything And Reinstall Windows.

3 Under Remove Everything And Reinstall Windows, click Get Started.

(continued on next page)

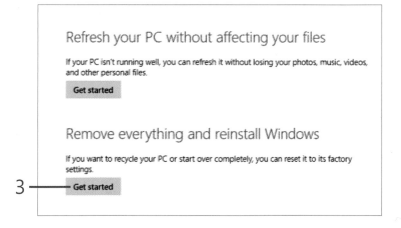

Reset your PC *(continued)*

4 Read the information and click Next.

5 Wait while the computer refreshes, and respond to any prompts as applicable.

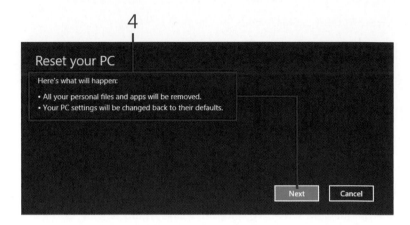

TIP Reset your PC before you sell it or give it away.

 CAUTION After the reset is complete, your computer will look and perform the way it did on the day that you purchased it. You'll be starting from scratch.

Upgrading to Windows 8.1

21

Windows 8.1 comes in several editions, but you'll be concerned with only two. You'll choose Windows 8.1 or Windows 8.1 Pro. Beyond that you can opt to purchase the full edition or an upgrade. Here you'll learn about upgrading. Finally, you can install a 32-bit version of the software or a 64-bit version, based on your system's hardware properties.

However, before you make the purchase or start the installation, you need to check several things. Your computer will either need to already be running Windows 8, or will need to have enough available hard drive space to install the new operating system, enough memory to run it, and a compatible processor that meets the processor requirements listed for the edition of Windows 8.1 that you select. If you're unsure about making these comparison, you can run the Windows 8.1 Upgrade Assistant.

After your decisions are made, you will perform the upgrade and then resolve any problems that arise after installation is complete.

In this section:

- Understanding differences among Windows 8.1 editions
- Upgrading Windows 8 to Windows 8.1
- Determining system requirements
- View basic information about your computer
- Using the Upgrade Assistant
- Performing the installation
- Using the Program Compatibility Troubleshooter
- Updating drivers

Understanding differences among Windows 8.1 editions

There are four editions of Windows 8.1. You'll probably purchase the first option, Windows 8.1, but you might opt for Windows 8.1 Pro.

Here's an overview of the various editions of Windows 8.1:

- **Windows 8.1**   The mainstream consumer edition of Windows 8.1. This edition has all the features most people need when using the operating system in a home setting, including everything introduced in this book (and more).

- **Windows 8.1 Pro**   Designed for tech enthusiasts and business/technical professionals. Windows 8.1 Pro adds additional features including BitLocker and BitLocker to Go, the ability to serve as a Remote Desktop host, and the ability to join a domain, among other things.

- **Windows 8.1 Enterprise**   A version that is available only through Microsoft's volume licensing subscription program. Enterprise includes features that are useful to those using Windows 8.1 in a Windows server environment and who require more management tools and security, an available virtual desktop infrastructure, Direct Access, BranchCache, and other enterprise features.

- **Windows RT**   Preinstalled on tablets running on ARM-based processors. This version doesn't include all of the features of other versions of Windows 8.1, and you can't purchase it as a stand-alone product. It is available preinstalled only on compatible devices. Additionally, Windows RT has limitations: you can't install software from CDs, DVDs, or the Internet, for starters; you can install only software from the Windows Store. It does come with a tablet version of Microsoft Office, which is quite useful.

In addition to choosing one of these editions of Windows, you should select either a 32-bit or a 64-bit version. You'll learn how to determine which of these is right for you in the section titled "View basic information about your computer."

Determining system requirements

If you want to run Windows 8.1 on your PC, here's what it takes:

- **Processor**   1 gigahertz (GHz) or faster with support for PAE, NX, and SSE2
- **RAM**   1 GB (32-bit) or 2 GB (64-bit)
- **Hard disk space**   16 GB (32-bit) or 20 GB (64-bit)
- **Graphics card**   Microsoft DirectX 9 graphics device with WDDM driver

Additional requirements to use certain features include the following:

- To use touch, you need a tablet or a monitor that supports multitouch.
- To access the Windows Store and to download and run apps, you need an active Internet connection and a screen resolution of at least 1024 x 768.
- To snap apps, you need a screen resolution of at least 1366 x 768.
- Internet access (ISP fees might apply).
- Secure boot requires firmware that supports UEFI v2.3.1 Errata B and has the Microsoft Windows Certification Authority in the UEFI signature database.

- Some games and programs might require a graphics card compatible with DirectX 10 or higher for optimal performance.
- Microsoft account required for some features.
- Watching DVDs requires separate playback software.
- Windows Media Center license sold separately.
- BitLocker To Go requires a USB flash drive (Windows 8 Pro only).
- BitLocker requires either Trusted Platform Module (TPM) 1.2 or a USB flash drive (Windows 8 Pro only).
- Client Hyper-V requires a 64-bit system with second level address translation (SLAT) capabilities and additional 2 GB of RAM (Windows 8 Pro only).
- A TV tuner is required to play and record live TV in Windows Media Center (Windows 8 Pro Pack and Windows 8 Media Center Pack only).
- Free Internet TV content varies by geography, some content might require additional fees (Windows 8 Pro Pack and Windows 8 Media Center Pack only).

To determine whetheryour PC meets these requirements, you can run the Upgrade Assistant: *http://windows.microsoft.com/ en-us/windows-8/upgrade-to-windows-8*. You'll learn how to use this assistant in the section titled "Use the Upgrade Assistant."

Upgrading from Windows 8 to Windows 8.1

If your computer already has Windows 8 installed, you might not need to read any further in this section. Your computer, laptop, or tablet is already compatible and ready for the installation. You can simply install the Windows 8.1 update that is available through the Windows Store. Before you start, close any desktop applications and save your work if applicable. Also, note that the installation can take some time (most likely an hour, but possibly much longer), and that your device will restart several times. Make sure your tablet or laptop is plugged in to a power source too.

Upgrade from Windows 8 to Windows 8.1

1 On the Start screen, click Store.

2 Click the option to update to Windows 8.1 for free.

3 Click Download.

4 Click Restart Now when prompted, and wait for setup to complete (not shown). At the end of the installation process, answer the prompts outlined next.

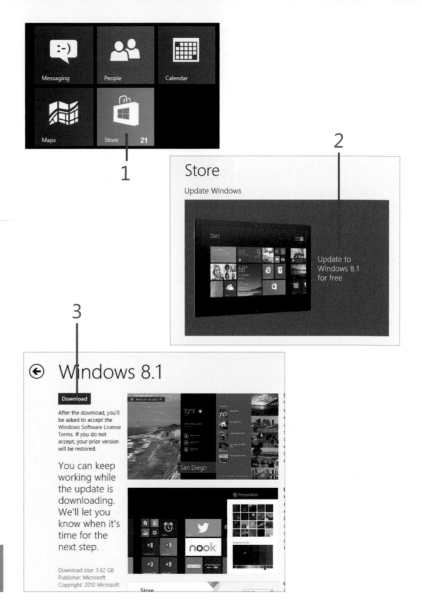

1

2

3

Store
Update Windows

Update to
Windows 8.1
for free

⊙ Windows 8.1

Download

After the download, you'll be asked to accept the Windows Software License Terms. If you do not accept, your prior version will be restored.

You can keep working while the update is downloading. We'll let you know when it's time for the next step.

Download size: 3.62 GB
Publisher: Microsoft
Copyright: 2013 Microsoft

> **CAUTION** Make sure that laptops and tablets are plugged in to a power outlet before starting the installation.

Windows 8.1 installation prompts

Once the installation of Windows 8.1 is getting close to being finalized, you'll be prompted to do a few things and answer a few questions to complete set up. Here are a list of the prompts you'll see:

- **Agree to License Terms**   Click I Accept to agree to these terms to continue the set up process.

- **Configure default settings**   Click Use Express Settings to quickly move through the setup process.

- **Sign in to your account**   Type the password associated with your Microsoft Account. If you don't use one or aren't connected to the internet, follow any prompts to log in to your local account.

- **Choose a method to verify your account**   Choose to receive a text to your mobile phone or an email to verify your account. The communication will contain a code. Enter the code after it arrives and click Next.

- **Opt to use SkyDrive**   Click Next to use SkyDrive. If you don't want to use SkyDrive, click Turn Off These SkyDrive Settings (Not Recommended).

- **Access the new Start screen**   When installation and setup is complete, you'll see the new Start screen. It will be configured as it was with Windows 8, with the Windows 8.1 changes applied (which includes, among other things, the Messaging app having been removed).

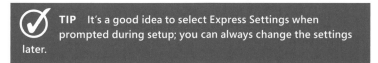

TIP   It's a good idea to select Express Settings when prompted during setup; you can always change the settings later.

View basic information about your computer

To find out what your computer consists of, specifically what kind of processor is installed, whether the system is 32-bit or 64-bit, the amount of installed memory, available hard drive space, you can locate and view the system properties for your device. If you have Windows 8 installed on your device, checking to see whether your computer meets the minimum requirements for Windows 8.1 isn't necessary. However, it might be necessary if you're currently running Windows 7.

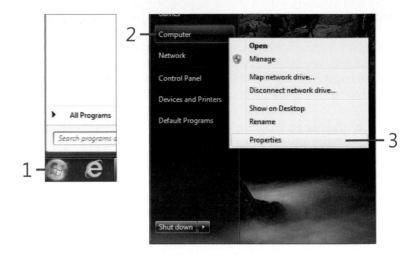

View basic information about your computer

1 On your Windows 7-based computer (performing this task on Vista is similar), click the Start button in the lower-left corner of the screen.

2 Right-click Computer.

3 Click Properties.

4 Note the edition of Windows you have.

5 Verify that you have a compatible processor and enough memory.

6 Note what type of system you have (32-bit or 64-bit).

7 Check for touch capabilities.

8 Click the Close button.

(continued on next page)

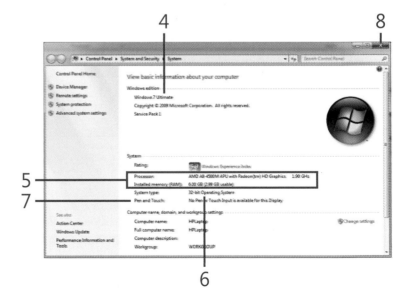

View basic information about your computer

(continued)

9 Click the Start button again, and click Computer.

10 Verify that you have the required hard drive space on your primary drive.

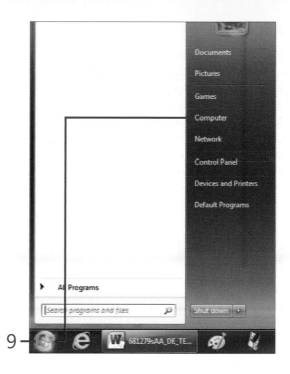

Using the Upgrade Assistant

Even if you know that your current computer system has enough hard drive space, memory, and processor capacity, there could still be problems with upgrading it to Windows 8.1. You might have desktop applications that aren't compatible with the newer operating system, hardware that won't work properly because the manufacturer has not provided an updated device driver, or other issues. So, even if you think your system is ready for Windows 8.1, run the Upgrade Assistant anyway.

Use the Upgrade Assistant

1 Using Internet Explorer on the computer you'd like to install Windows 8.1 on, navigate here: *http://windows.microsoft.com/en-US/windows-8/upgrade-to-windows-8*.

2 Click Download Upgrade Assistant.

3 Click Run.

4 Click See Compatibility Details.

(continued on next page)

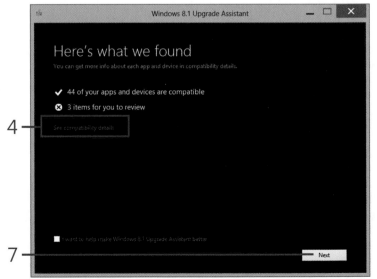

Use the Upgrade Assistant *(continued)*

5 Make a note of what needs to be resolved before you can successfully install Windows 8.1.

6 Click Close.

7 Click Next (shown on previous page).

8 Read the information provided in the resulting screen (not shown).
   You may be prompted to open the Windows Store to perform the
   upgrade or purchase and download it from Microsoft's website.
   Follow the prompts as needed.

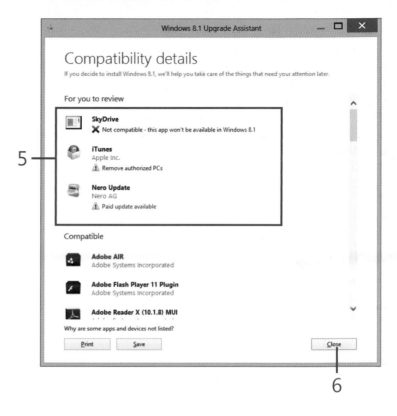

TIP   If you are running Windows 8, you will perform the
   upgrade using the Windows Store. If you are using Windows 7
or earlier, follow the prompts to purchase and download the product.

Performing the installation

If your computer is installed with Windows 8, you can upgrade to Windows 8.1 from the Windows Store. If it is running Windows 7 or earlier, it's more complicated. Thus, it is much easier to purchase a computer with Windows 8.1 on it than it is to buy and install it yourself. Installation requires several steps, and there are too many steps and configurations to outline here. That said, the process will take some time and you'll have some decisions to make during the upgrade, so you'll want to set aside an afternoon for it if you want to do it yourself.

When you're ready to install Windows 8.1, you must perform several tasks, including the following:

- Purchase Windows 8.1. You can make the purchase from the Buy Windows 8.1 webpage: *http://windows.microsoft.com/en-us/windows/buy*.

- Download Windows 8.1 when prompted.

- Start the installation of Windows 8.1. You'll have two options, Install Now or Install Later. It's best to choose Install Now.

- Choose to keep Windows Settings, Personal Files, and Apps; Just Personal Files; or Nothing. These choices vary based on which version of Windows you upgrade from. It's easiest to choose the first option to keep all of your apps and files intact.

- Wait while installation completes. Your computer will reboot several times.

- Set up Windows 8.1 by answering questions when prompted. You'll choose a Start screen color, join a network if applicable, get and/or sign in with a Microsoft account, and more.

> **TIP** Be aware that if you're upgrading from Windows XP, the upgrade will transfer only apps, but no settings or user account files. For this reason, it's a good idea to back up or make note of those system and file settings.

Using the Program Compatibility Troubleshooter

After installing Windows 8.1, you might experience problems with older desktop applications that have yet to be updated to be compatible with Windows 8.1. However, you can configure these applications to run in the mode they were designed to run in, using the Program Compatibility Troubleshooter.

Run the Windows Program Compatibility Troubleshooter

1 From the Start screen, type **Compatibility**.

2 In the results, click Run Programs Made For Previous Versions Of Windows.

3 Click Next.

4 Select the problematic software in the list. If the software isn't listed, click Not Listed and browse to the program before continuing.

5 Click Next.

(continued on next page)

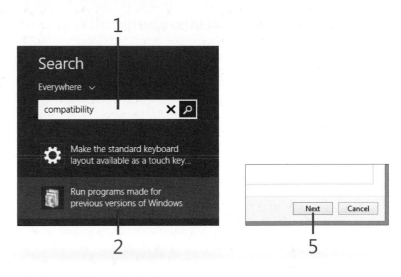

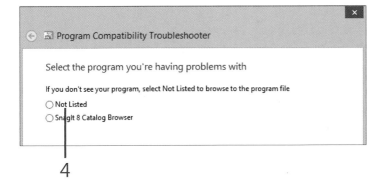

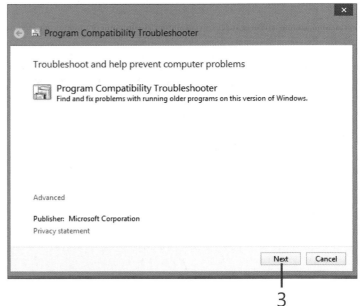

Run the Windows Program Compatibility Troubleshooter *(continued)*

6 Click Try Recommended Settings. (Select Troubleshoot Program only if you've worked through these steps before and the recommended settings didn't work.)

7 Click Test The Program.

8 Try the program (not shown).

9 Click Next.

(continued on next page)

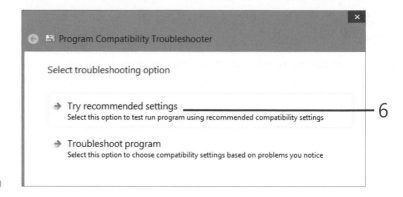

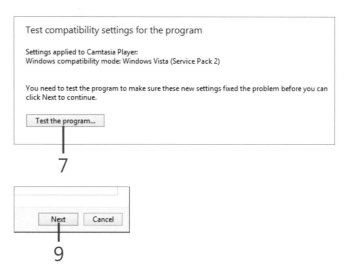

Run the Windows Program Compatibility Troubleshooter *(continued)*

10 Select an appropriate option regarding the fix.

11 Click Close (or repeat these steps to run the troubleshooter again and try different settings).

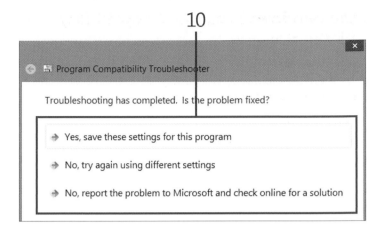

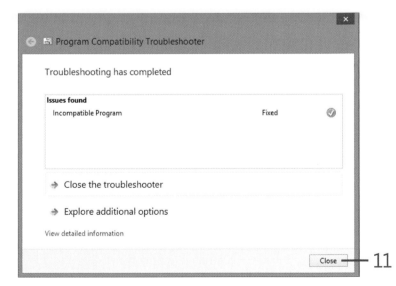

> ⚠ **CAUTION** If you don't see the problematic application in step 4, click Not Listed and use the displayed options to browse to the program and select it.

Updating drivers

Device drivers are software programs that enable your computer to communicate with hardware (and vice versa) such as printers, scanners, cameras, phones, and so on. After installing Windows 8.1, you might find that you're having issues with specific devices and need to update their drivers.

You might be prompted by Windows 8.1 to search for a driver the first time you try (unsuccessfully) to use the hardware. If so, follow the prompts to do so. You might be prompted at some later date by the Action Center that a new driver is available. If so, follow the instructions in the Action Center to perform the upgrade. Device drivers might also be installed automatically from Windows Update.

However, sometimes a problem needs immediate attention, such as an issue with internal hardware such as wireless network cards, sound devices, or display adapters. In these cases, you can update device drivers manually with Device Manager.

Update device drivers manually

1 From the Start screen, type **Device Manager**.

2 Click Device Manager in the results.

(continued on next page)

TIP   If you are experiencing problems with software or hardware compatibility, go to the Windows 8 Compatibility Center: *www.microsoft.com/en-us/windows/compatibility*.

Update device drivers manually *(continued)*

3 Double-click a problematic device.

4 Click the Update Driver button.

5 Click Search Automatically For Updated Driver Software.

6 If Windows states that your driver is up to date or that a driver was unavailable, click Close. If Windows reports that a newer driver is available, follow the instructions to upgrade.

7 Click Close again (not shown).

8 Click the x to close Device Manager.

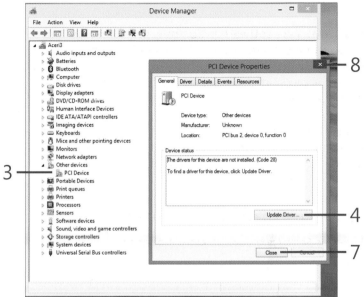

3

8

4

7

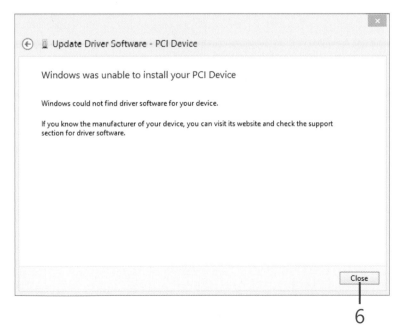

6

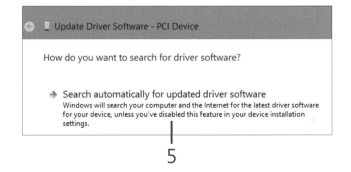

5

Getting help

22

Even though Windows 8.1 provides many intuitive ways to get things done, this new approach can present a learning curve even for those who have used previous versions of Windows. When you run into something you can't figure out, you can use the built-in tools to get help. There are three ways presented here: Using the Help + Tips app on the Start screen, using Microsoft's Support website, and using the more traditional Help and Support window.

In this section:

- Using the Help + Tips app
- Getting support at the Microsoft Support website
- Using desktop help
- Accessing specific desktop help

Using the Help + Tips app

There's a new Help + Tips app available on the Start screen. This app offers a list of the most common questions asked by Windows 8.1 users. The Help + Tips app has 6 sections, each containing related information.

Use the Help + Tips app

1 From the Start screen, click Help + Tips.

2 Note the following options:

  a Start And Apps

  b Get Around

  c Basic Actions

  d Your Account And Files

  e Settings

  f What's New

3 Click any link to learn more about an item.

4 Use the Back button to return to the main screen.

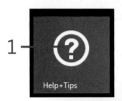

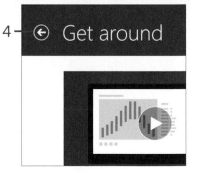

> **→ TRY THIS** Right-click an empty area of the screen from anywhere inside the app to see the Help + Tips app bar. This offers easy access to the app categories.

> **⊙ SEE ALSO** Refer to the tasks "Using Microsoft Fix It," "Using troubleshooting wizards," and "Asking for Remote Assistance," in Section 20, "Maintaining and troubleshooting your computer."

Getting support at the Microsoft Support website

The Microsoft Support website offers help for all Microsoft products. After navigating to the site. you can choose the product you need help with—in this case, Windows. You can select a topic (such as Email & Communication, Repair & Recovery, Hardware & Drivers, and so on). After you've made that selection, you can select a subtopic. Following that, you'll be presented with a list of solutions to the most commonly asked questions.

Get support at the Microsoft Support website

1 From the Start screen, click Internet Explorer.

2 Right-click the screen if you can't see the Address bar.

3 Type *support.microsoft.com,* and press Enter on the keyboard.

(continued on next page)

Get support at the Microsoft Support website

(continued)

4 On the Find It Myself tab, click Windows.

5 Click Windows 8.1.

6 Click a topic.

7 Click a subtopic.

8 Browse the solutions.

4
5

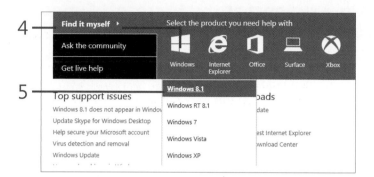

6

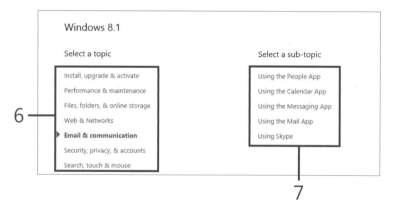

7

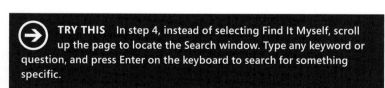

> **TRY THIS**   In step 4, instead of selecting Find It Myself, scroll up the page to locate the Search window. Type any keyword or question, and press Enter on the keyboard to search for something specific.

> **TRY THIS**   In step 4, instead of selecting Find It Myself, click Ask The Community to peruse community forums where users like yourself ask questions of others and offer solutions. Click Get Live Help to communicate with a person via instant messaging.

8

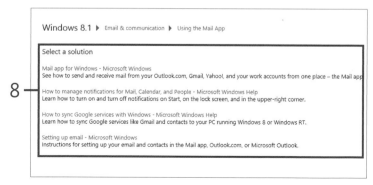

Using desktop help

The Help feature (which you can access from the desktop) gives you the option of using offline help or online help (or both). Offline help doesn't require an Internet connection, but the online help will be more up-to-date. It's best to use the online help, so if possible, connect to the Internet before continuing here.

Use general desktop help

1 From the desktop, press Windows logo key+I to show the Settings charm, and click Help.

2 Note the three main options: Get Started, Internet & Networking, and Security, Privacy, & Accounts; click an option.

(continued on next page)

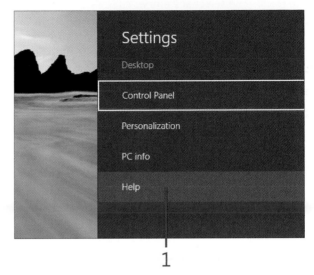

1

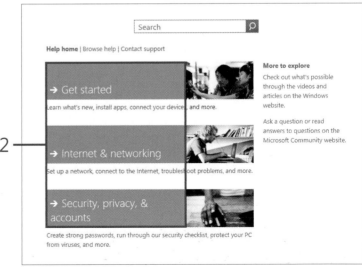

2

Use general desktop help *(continued)*

3 Browse the results and select any entry.

4 Use the back and forward arrows to navigate to previously viewed page.

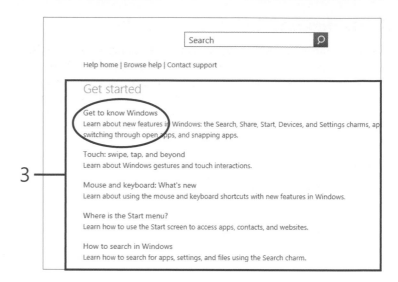

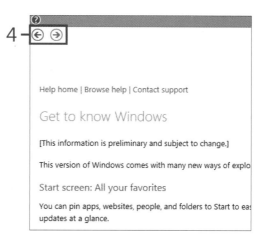

✓ **TIP** Note the Search window in step 3. You can use it to search for help on a specific topic.

Accessing specific desktop help

Almost every window that opens on the desktop offers a help option in the form of a question mark in the top-right corner, provided that the window is the result of opening a Microsoft product or feature (such as Control Panel, Paint, File Explorer, and so on). Virtually all third-party applications offer one too,

if not in the form of a blue question mark at least from a menu option named Help. Help options might also appear in dialog boxes in the form of a link. Whatever the case, when you click a help option that is offered from inside a Microsoft application or window, desktop help opens to that specific topic.

Access specific desktop help

1 From the desktop, open File Explorer.

2 In the navigation pane, click This PC.

3 Click the blue Help icon in the top-right corner.

4 Note that the results have to do with what's selected and the Help And Support window does not open to the generic Desktop Help page.

5 Close the Help And Support window.

6 Close File Explorer.

(continued on next page)

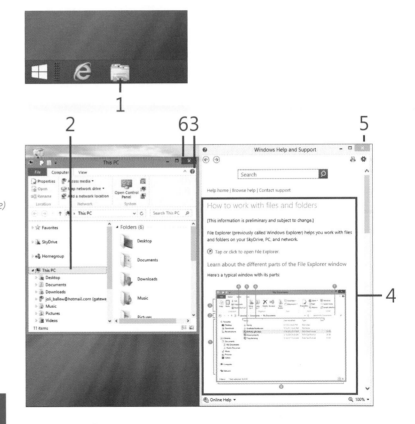

 TIP   Note the Search window in step 3. You can use it to search for help on a specific topic.

Access specific desktop help *(continued)*

7 Press the Windows key to return to the Start screen, and type **Windows Defender**.

8 Click Windows Defender in the results.

9 Click the Help icon in the top-right corner.

10 Note that the results have to do with what's selected and the Help And Support window does not open to the generic desktop help page.

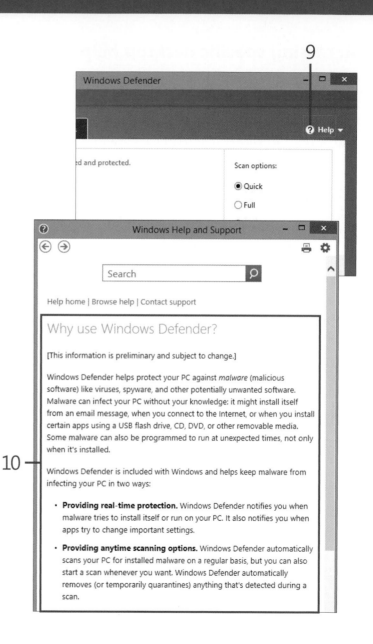

TIP Remember, you can search Help by using keywords. If you can't find what you want by browsing or opening the Help And Support window from inside an application, use this method.

Appendix

Windows 8.1 keyboard shortcuts

Rather than using menus, toolbars, or ribbon buttons to get things done in Windows 8.1, you can use keyboard shortcuts. A keyboard shortcut is either a function key, such as F1, or a combination of keys, such as Ctrl+C (hold down the first key and, without letting go, press the second key), that performs an action such as opening help or copying selected text. Mastering keyboard shortcuts can make you a more efficient computer user.

Some shortcuts work in the Windows Start screen or desktop or in File Explorer, while others work in software programs such as Microsoft Word or Microsoft Excel. The tables in this chapter list keyboard shortcuts that work with the Windows user interface displayed, and general shortcuts are grouped into categories such as Editing and Accessibility.

Windows 8.1 user interface shortcuts

Use This Keystroke Combination	To Do This
Windows logo key+B, D, M, and T	Go to the desktop
Windows logo key+C	Open the charms
Windows logo key+E	Open File Explorer
Windows logo key+F	Open the Search charm with Files selected
Windows logo key+H	Open the Share charm
Windows logo key+I	Open the Settings charm
Windows logo key+K	Open the Devices charm
Windows logo key+L	Access the lock screen
Windows logo key+P	Access the second screen settings
Windows logo key+Q	Open the Search charm with Everywhere selected
Windows logo key+R	Desktop with Run dialog open
Windows logo key+U	Open the Ease of Access Center
Windows logo key+W	Open the Search charm with Settings selected
Windows logo key+X	Show the Power User menu displays in lower-left corner
Windows logo key+Z	When at the Start screen, opens the toolbar that offers Customize
Windows logo key+Enter	Launch Narrator (Caps Lock+Esc to close)

Traditional Windows shortcuts

Use This Keystroke Combination	To Do This
F1	Display Help for the active app
Ctrl+Esc	Toggle between the Start screen and desktop
Alt+Tab	Switch between open programs
Shift+Delete	Delete item permanently by using File Explorer
Ctrl+Shift+Esc	Open Windows Task Manager

Editing shortcuts

Use This Keystroke Combination	To Do This
Ctrl+C	Copy
Ctrl+X	Cut
Ctrl+V	Paste
Ctrl+B	Bold
Ctrl+U	Underline
Ctrl+I	Italic
Ctrl+Z	Undo last command or last text entry
Ctrl+A	Select all items in active window

File Explorer shortcuts

Use This Keystroke Combination	To Do This
F2	Rename selected object
F3	In File Explorer, opens the Search tab to search for all files
Alt+Enter	Open properties for selected object
Right-click while dragging a file to the desktop or a folder	Create a shortcut, copy, or move an item
F5	Refresh active window
F6 or Tab	Cycle through items in File Explorer

Accessibility shortcuts

Use This Keystroke Combination	To Do This
Press Shift five times	Toggle StickyKeys on and off
Press left mouse button and hold the right Shift key for eight seconds	Toggle FilterKeys on and off
Press down and hold the Num Lock key for five seconds	Toggle ToggleKeys on and off
Left Alt+left Shift+Num+Lock	Toggle MouseKeys on and off
Left Alt+left Shift+Print Screen	Toggle high contrast on and off

Desktop shortcuts

Use This Keystroke Combination	To Do This
Windows logo key+M	Minimize all
Windows logo key+F1	Help
Shift+Windows logo key+M	Undo minimize all
Windows logo key+Tab	Cycle through open apps
Ctrl+Windows logo key+F	Find computer

Dialog box keyboard commands

Use This Keystroke Combination	To Do This
Tab	Move to the next control in the dialog box.
Shift+Tab	Move to the previous control in the dialog box.
Spacebar	If the current control is a button, this clicks the button. If the current control is a check box, this toggles the check box. If the current control is an option, this selects the option.
Enter	Equivalent to clicking the selected button (the button with the outline).
Esc	Equivalent to clicking the Cancel button.
Alt+underlined letter in dialog box item	Move to the corresponding item.

Glossary

A

Action Center A feature in Windows 8.1 that lets you view and fix problems and run automated troubleshooters, among other things. The Action Center is represented by a white flag on the desktop taskbar.

Activation The process you must complete to verify that you have a valid copy of Windows 8.1, which includes a Product ID. You usually activate Windows 8.1 online the first time that you turn on your computer or device, but there are other activation options. Activation is mandatory.

Active window The window that is in the foreground and currently in use. The active window has a red x for a close button, while inactive windows do not.

Address bar In Internet Explorer or any web browser, the area in which you type Internet addresses, also known as URLs (uniform resource locators). Often, an Internet address takes the form of *http://www.companyname.com*.

Administrator account A type of Windows user account with access to all system files and settings and with permission to perform all operations. Every computer must have at least one administrator account. This account type is not recommended for daily use. See also **standard user account**.

App An application available from the Start screen (and the Windows Store) that is created to use the entire screen (or snapped to a portion of it) and is tailored to work well on desktop computers, laptops, tablets, and Windows Phones. Some apps have desktop counterparts, including Internet Explorer 11. The app has fewer features than its desktop counterpart but is more streamlined and often easier to use.

App bar A toolbar (available in virtually all apps) that is typically hidden until needed. The App bar holds commands that might enable the user to configure the app, input a location, add an event, delete an item, view properties, and more.

Application Software that you or the computer's manufacturer install or have installed on your computer or device other than the operating system (Windows 8.1). Some applications come preinstalled on Windows 8.1, such as Paint, Notepad, Snipping Tool, and Windows Defender, whereas others can be third-party applications or software that you purchase separately and install yourself, such as Adobe Photoshop. Applications (also called desktop apps) differ from apps in several ways; most notably, they run on the desktop and in a window, as traditional programs have always run, and not in full-screen mode as the new apps do.

Attachment Data that you add to an email, such as a photograph, a short video, a sound recording, a document, or other data. Attachments can be dangerous to open because they can contain viruses.

B

BCC Abbreviation for *blind carbon copy* (a secret copy). If you want to send an email to someone and you don't want other recipients to know that you included that person in the email, add them to the BCC line.

Bitmap (.bmp) A patent-free digital image file format. A bitmap image consists of pixels in a grid. Each pixel is a specific color; the colors within the color palette are governed by the specific bitmap format. Common formats include monochrome bitmap, 16-color bitmap, 256-color bitmap, and 24-bit bitmap. The bitmap file format does not support transparency.

Browse The process of navigating into the operating system's folder structure to locate a desired item, such as a file, folder, picture, video, song, or program (among other things). *Browse* can also describe the act of surfing the Internet.

Burn A term that describes the process of copying music from a computer to a CD or DVD. The term originated because data is actually burned onto this media with a laser. In many cases, music is burned to CDs because CDs can be played in cars and generic DVD players, and videos are burned to DVDs because videos require much more space and DVDs can be played on DVD players.

C

CC Abbreviation for *carbon copy*. If you want to send an email to someone and you don't need that person to respond, you can put that person on the CC line. (BCC is a blind carbon copy; other recipients cannot see the BCC field address.)

Charm An icon that appears when you swipe from the right side of the screen to the left or use the key combination Windows key+C. The default icons are Search, Share, Start, Devices, and Settings. Apps have their own charms, generally available from the App bar found there.

Click To point to an interface element and then press the primary mouse button one time, usually for the purpose of selecting an item or positioning a cursor.

Cloud A broad term that represents the Internet, specifically Internet servers and data centers where data can be stored and applications hosted. A cloud is called a *Public cloud* when the services are rendered over a network that is open for public use. Personal cloud is cloud computing for individuals.

Cloud computing A technology where groups of computers are connected through a network for the purpose of accessing and sharing resources that are available off-site. Cloud computing can minimize the cost that companies pay for application management and on-site hosting.

Cloud storage The ability to save data off-site and to have it managed by a third party. In doing so, companies can save money by outsourcing data storage. Tablet, laptop, and even desktop users can store data in the cloud (rather than on their devices) and on Internet servers to make it accessible from anywhere. SkyDrive is cloud storage. You must be able to connect to the Internet to access data stored in the cloud.

Command An instruction that you give to a computer program.

Compress To reduce the size of a set of data, such as a folder, a file, or group of files, inside a compressed folder that can be stored in less space or transmitted with less bandwidth.

Compressed folder A folder containing folders, a file, or multiple files whose contents have been compressed.

Content pane In File Explorer, the pane that displays files and folders stored in the currently selected folder or storage device.

Control Panel The window from which you can change computer settings related to system and maintenance, networks, and the Internet; user accounts; appearance; security; hardware; and sounds; among others. Control Panel opens on the desktop and is not an app, bit is a desktop app (application).

Cookies Small text files that include data that identify your preferences when you visit particular websites. Cookies are generally harmless and enable websites such as Amazon.com to greet you by name when you navigate there.

Copy Copies data to a virtual clipboard, which is a temporary holding area for data. You generally copy data so that you can paste it somewhere else.

Cursor The point at which text or graphics will be inserted. The cursor usually appears on the screen as a blinking vertical line.

Cut To remove the selected text, picture, or object and place it on the Clipboard. After it's pasted, the item is deleted from its original location.

D

Desktop Where programs and desktop applications run; where windows open; where you browse File Explorer; and where you work with desktop programs to write letters, create spreadsheets, manage files and folders, install and uninstall programs, and do everything else you're used to doing on Windows 7, Windows Vista, and other earlier operating systems.

Desktop folder Contains icons that represent what's on your desktop. You can access this folder from File Explorer.

Desktop computer A computer designed for use at one location. A typical desktop computer system includes the computer case containing the actual computer components, a monitor, a keyboard, a mouse, and speakers.

Details pane In File Explorer, an optional pane that displays details about the folder or selected items.

Dialog box A box from which to make changes to default settings in an application, make decisions when installing programs, set print options for a selected printer, configure sharing options for a file or folder, and perform similar tasks. A dialog box is not a window and does not include minimize and maximize buttons.

Disk Cleanup An application included with Windows 8.1 that offers a safe and effective way to remove unwanted and unnecessary data. You can remove temporary files, downloaded program files, and offline webpages; empty the Recycle Bin; and more, all in a single process.

Disk Defragmenter An application included with Windows 8.1 that improves performance by analyzing the data stored on your hard disk drive and consolidating files that are not stored together. Disk Defragmenter runs automatically on a schedule, so you should (theoretically) never have to invoke it manually.

Double-click To point to an interface element and press the primary mouse button two times in rapid succession, usually for the purpose of starting a program or opening a window, folder, or file.

Drag To move an item to another location on the screen by pointing to it, holding down the primary mouse button, and then moving the mouse.

Drafts A folder that holds email messages that you've started and saved but not yet completed and sent.

Driver A program that enables Windows to communicate with a hardware device (such as a printer, mouse, or keyboard) that is attached to your computer or located inside it. Every device needs a driver for it to work. Many drivers, such as the keyboard driver, are built into Windows.

E

Ethernet A technology that uses Ethernet cables to connect computers to routers and similar hardware to transmit data and connect multiple computers to form a network.

Executable file A computer file that starts a program, such as a word processor, game, or Windows utility. Executable files can often be identified by the file name extension .exe.

Expansion card A printed circuit board that, when inserted into an expansion slot of a computer, provides additional functionality. There are many types of expansion cards, including audio cards, modems, network cards, security device cards, TV tuner cards, video cards, and video processing expansion cards.

Expansion slot A socket on a computer's motherboard designed to establish the electrical contact between the electronics on an expansion card and on the motherboard. Many form factors (physical dimensions) and standards for expansion slots are available, including AGP, PC Card, PCI, and PCI Express. An expansion slot accepts only expansion cards of the same form factor.

F

Favorite A webpage for which you've created a shortcut in Internet Explorer. You can click a favorite instead of typing the web address to visit a website quickly.

Favorites bar In Internet Explorer, a toolbar located below the Address bar that provides buttons for storing web locations for easy future access, obtaining add-ons, and accessing sites that match your browsing history.

Favorites Center In Internet Explorer, a pane with three tabs: Favorites, on which you can save and organize links to websites and webpages; Feeds, on which you can save and organize RSS feeds; and History, on which you can view your browsing history.

File A distinct piece of data. A file can be a single Word document, a spreadsheet, a song, a movie, a picture, or even a very large single backup.

File Explorer A window that enables you to browse all the data stored on your computer and your network. You use File Explorer to access your data libraries, personal and public folders, and networked computers.

File name extension Characters appended to the name of a file by the program that created it and separated from the file name by a period. Some file name extensions identify the program that can open the file, such as .xlsx for Microsoft Office Excel 2010 or newer files, and some represent formats that more than one program can work with, such as .jpg graphics files.

File recovery The backup feature included with Windows 8.1 with which you can perform backups and, in the case of a computer failure, restore the backed-up data.

Filter To display only items that match specified criteria.

Flash drive See **USB flash drive**.

Flick A gesture performed with a single finger by swiping quickly left, right, up, or down.

Flip A way to move through open windows and open applications, as well as running apps graphically instead of clicking the item on the desktop or flicking to it. You invoke this by pressing Alt+Tab.

Folder A data unit (similar to a folder in a filing cabinet) that holds files and subfolders. You use folders to organize data. Some folders come with Windows 8.1, including but not limited to Documents, Public Pictures, Videos, Downloads, Contacts, Favorites, and Searches.

Form data In Internet Explorer, this is personal data, such as your name and address, that's been saved using the Internet Explorer autocomplete form data functionality. If you don't want forms to be filled out automatically, disable this.

G

Gesture A movement you that make with your finger to perform a task. Flick, swipe, tap, double-tap, and others are considered gestures. See also **multi-touch gesture**.

Gigabyte (GB) 1,024 megabytes of data storage; often interpreted as approximately 1 billion bytes.

Graphics Interchange Format (.gif) A digital image file format developed by CompuServe that is used for transmitting raster images on the Internet. An image in this format might contain up to 256 colors, including a transparent color. The size of the file depends on the number of colors used.

Guest account A built-in Windows user account that allows limited use of the computer. When logged on to a computer with the Guest account, a user can't install software or hardware, change settings, or create a password. The Guest account is turned off (unavailable) by default; you can turn it on from the User Accounts window of Control Panel.

H

Hardware Physical computing devices that you connect externally to the computer and the physical items inside it. Common hardware includes printers, external USB drives, network interface cards, CPUs, RAM, and more.

Hibernate A power option by which the computer is still powered on but is using very little power.

History In Internet Explorer, the list of websites you've visited or typed in the Address bar. Anyone who has access to your computer or device and to your user account can look at your History list to see where you've been, and often it's advisable to clear your History list if you share a computer and do not have separate user accounts.

Homegroup A group of computers running Windows 7, Windows 8, and Windows 8.1 that have been configured to join the homegroup. Homegroups make sharing easier because the most common sharing settings are already configured. After a homegroup is set up, one needs only the proper operating system, access to the local network, and the homegroup password to join.

Home page The webpage that opens when you open Internet Explorer 11. You can set the home page and configure additional pages to open as well.

Hotspot A wireless public network where you can connect to the Internet without being tethered to an Ethernet cable. Sometimes access to a wireless hotspot service is free, provided that you have the required wireless hardware and are at a location with an open connection. You'll find wireless hotspots in libraries, coffee shops, hotels, bars, and so on.

Hyperlink A link from a text, graphic, audio, or video element to a target location in the same document, another document, or a webpage.

I

Icon A visual representation of a file, folder, or program that you can click or double-click as applicable, and which then opens the item the icon represents. *Icon* is a term generally associated with the desktop and items that you find in folders, whereas **tile** is a term generally used to represent the items available from the Start screen.

InPrivate Browsing A browsing mode that opens a separate Internet Explorer window in which the places you visit are not tracked. The pages and sites do not appear on the History tab, and temporary files and cookies are not saved on your computer.

Input device A piece of hardware that enables you to type, select, open, or otherwise interact with the computer. Common input devices include mice and keyboards. However, your finger can be an input device, and there are several specialty input devices for people with disabilities.

Instant messaging A way to communicate that is similar to email but is instantaneous—the recipient gets the message right after you send it. It is a real-time electronic communication system that you can use to "chat" and interact in other ways with other people by typing in a window on your computer screen. Instant messaging is the term generally reserved for text communications between two or more computers; text messaging is a term generally referring to communication between two cell phones.

Interface What you see on the screen when working in a window. For example, in the WordPad interface, you see the ribbon, tabs, and the page itself.

Internet Explorer 11 The newest version of the Microsoft web browser. It's available as an app and a desktop app.

Internet Message Access Protocol (IMAP) A method computers use to send and receive email messages. It allows you to access email without downloading it to your computer.

Internet server A computer that stores data off-site, such as one that might store your email before you download it or hold backups that you store in the cloud. Through Internet servers, you can access information from any computer that can access the Internet.

Internet service provider (ISP) A company that provides Internet access to individuals or companies. An ISP provides the connection information necessary for users to access the Internet through the ISP's computers. An ISP typically charges a monthly connection fee.

J

JPEG (.jpg) file format A digital image file format designed for compressing either full-color or grayscale still images. It works well on photographs, naturalistic artwork, and similar material. Images saved in this format have .jpg or .jpeg file extensions.

K

Kbps Kilobits per second; a unit of data transfer equal to around 1,000 bits per second or 125 bytes per second.

Keyword A word or phrase assigned to a file or webpage so that it can be located in searches for that word or phrase.

Kilobyte (KB) 1,024 bytes of data storage; in reference to data transfer rates, 1,000 bytes.

L

Laptop An older term for a portable computer, referring to the fact that portable computers are small enough to set on your lap. See also **netbook**, **notebook**, and **portable computer**.

Library A virtual data unit that offers access to related data. Links to libraries are no longer part of the navigation pane of File Explorer but can be added.

Link A shortcut to a webpage. It might be contained in an email, document, or webpage and offers access to a site without actually typing the site's name.

Local area network (LAN) A computer network covering a small physical area, like a home or office, with a central connection point such as a network router and a shared Internet connection.

Local printer A printer that is directly connected to one of the ports on a computer. See also **remote printer**.

Lock To make your Windows computing session unavailable to other people. Locking is most effective when your user account is protected by a password.

Lock screen The Windows 8.1 welcome screen, which appears when the computer first starts. It features the time, date, and a series of notification glyphs; the screen can be personalized with your own background picture and the glyphs shown.

Log off To stop your computing session without affecting other users' sessions.

Log on To start a computing session.

M

Magnifier A tool in the Ease of Access suite of applications. You use Magnifier to increase the size of the information shown on the screen; three options are available for doing so. By default, you use your mouse to enlarge what's under it, and you can choose to what degree the material is magnified.

Mail server A computer that your ISP configures to transmit email. It often includes a POP3 incoming mail server and an SMTP outgoing mail server. You'll need to know the names of these servers if you use an ISP to configure Mail. Often, the server names look similar to *pop.yourispnamehere.com* and *smtp. yourispnamehere.com*.

Malware Malicious software. Malware includes viruses, worms, spyware, and so on.

Mbps Megabits per second; a unit of data transfer equal to about 1,000 Kbps (kilobits per second).

Media Materials on which data is recorded or stored, such as CDs, DVDs, floppy disks, or USB flash drives.

Megabyte (MB) 1,024 kilobytes of data storage; often interpreted as approximately 1 million bytes; in reference to data transfer rates, 1,000 kilobytes.

Menu A title on a menu bar (such as File, Edit, View). Clicking a menu name opens a drop-down list with additional choices (Open, Save, Print). Menus are being phased out by the ribbon in many applications, including those included with Windows 8.1, such as WordPad and Paint, among others.

Menu bar A toolbar from which you can access menus of commands.

Metadata Descriptive information, including keywords and properties, about a file or webpage. Title, subject, author, and size are examples of a file's metadata.

Microsoft account A sign-in option that lets you sync settings and other data across PCs, which are applied when you log on with the account. You need to be connected to the Internet when logging in for this to work effectively.

Modem A device that allows computer information to be transmitted and received over a telephone line or through a broadband service such as cable or DSL.

Multi-monitor A term used when more than one monitor is configured on a Windows 8.1–based computer. There are multi-monitor capabilities that are new to Windows 8.1, for both the Start screen and the classic Windows desktop.

Multi-touch gestures Gestures that require two (or more) fingers to perform, such as pinching to zoom in and out of the computer screen.

N

Narrator A basic screen reader included with Windows 8.1 and part of the Ease of Access suite of applications. This application will read aloud text that appears on the screen while you navigate using the keyboard and mouse.

Navigate A term used to describe surfing the Internet by browsing webpages. It is the process of moving from one webpage to another or viewing items on a single webpage. You can also navigate the data on your computer with File Explorer.

Navigation pane In File Explorer, the left pane of a folder window. It displays favorite links, access to SkyDrive, access to your Homegroup, My PC, and an expandable list of drives and folders.

NET Passport See **Windows Live ID or Microsoft account**.

Netbook A small, lightweight portable computer designed primarily for web browsing and simple computing. Most netbooks have limited internal resources and a screen size of less than 11 inches.

Network A group of computers, printers, and other devices that communicate wirelessly or through wired connections, often for the purpose of sharing both data and physical resources (such as printers). Networks often contain routers, cable modems, hubs, switches, or similar hardware to connect the computers and offer them all access to the Internet.

Network adapter A piece of hardware that connects your computer to a network such as the Internet or a local network. Network adapters can offer wired capabilities, wireless capabilities, or both.

Network And Sharing Center A place in Windows 8.1 where you can view your basic network information and set up connections. You can also diagnose problems here, change adapter settings, and change advanced sharing settings.

Network discovery A feature that must be enabled so that computers can find other computers on the network. When connected to public networks, this feature is disabled by default.

Network drive A shared folder or drive on your network to which you assign a drive letter so that it appears in the My PC window as a named drive.

Network hub A device used to connect computers on a network. The computers are connected to the hub with cables. The hub sends information received from one computer to all other computers on the network.

Network printer A printer that is connected directly to a network through a wired (Ethernet) or wireless network connection or through a print server or printer hub.

Network profile Information about a specific network connection, such as the network name, type, and settings.

Network router A hardware device connecting computers on a network or connecting multiple networks (for example, connecting a LAN to an ISP).

Network share A shared folder on a computer on your network

Notebook A standard portable computer designed for all types of computing. Notebooks have technical specifications that are comparable to those of desktop computers. Most notebooks have a screen size ranging from 11 to 17 inches.

Notification area The area at the right end of the Windows taskbar. It contains shortcuts to programs and important status information.

O

Office 365 A product and services bundle from Microsoft that includes Microsoft Online Services as well as domain administration tools, additional account storage space and increased vendor support.

Online Connected to a network or to the Internet. Also used to describe time that you will be working on your computer.

On-Screen Keyboard A feature that is available as part of Windows 8.1 that enables you to input text and interact with the computer by using a virtual keyboard.

Operating system The underlying program that tells your computer what to do and how to do it. The operating system coordinates interactions among the computer system components, acts as the interface between you and your computer, enables your computer to communicate with other computers and peripheral devices, and interacts with programs installed on your computer.

Option One of a group of mutually exclusive values for a setting, usually in a dialog box.

Option button A standard Windows control that you use to select one from a set of options.

P

Partition A certain amount of space to store data on a hard drive. That can be 120 GB, 500 GB, or 1 or 2 TB, among other sizes. Sometimes people or computer manufacturers separate this space into two or three distinct spaces called partitions (or drives or volumes). The purpose is to separate system files, data files, and application files, among other reasons. Windows 8.1 creates a small partition at the beginning of the hard disk to hold files needed to repair the computer if something goes wrong.

Password A security feature in which the user is required to input a personal password to access the computer, specific files, websites, and other data.

Password hint An entry you record when you create or change your password to remind you what the password is. Windows displays the password hint if you enter an incorrect password.

Path A sequence of names of drives, directories, or folders, separated by backslashes (\), that leads to a specific file or folder.

Paste To place previously copied or cut data in a new location. You can cut, copy, and paste a single word, sentence, paragraph, or page; a file; a folder; a web link; and more.

PC Settings A pared-down Control Panel that offers access to the most-configured settings, including changing the picture on the lock screen, adding users, viewing installed devices, and configuring Windows Update.

Peek To see what's on the desktop behind open windows and applications. To use Peek, you position your mouse in the lower-right corner. Peek must be enabled to work.

Peer-to-peer A network, such as a workgroup, where computers and resources are connected directly and are not centrally managed by a server.

Peripheral device A device, such as a disk drive, printer, modem, or game controller, that is connected to a computer and is controlled by the computer's microprocessor but is not necessary to the computer's operation. See also **external peripheral** and **internal peripheral**.

Permissions Rules associated with a shared resource, such as a folder, file, or printer, that define who can use it and what he or she can do after he or she has access to it. For example, you can set permissions to allow a user to print to a printer only during certain hours.

Personal folder In Windows, a storage folder created by Windows for each user account and containing subfolders and information that is specific to the user profile, such as Documents and Pictures. The personal folder is labeled with the name used to log on to the computer.

Phishing A hacking technique to entice you to divulge personal information such as bank account numbers. Internet Explorer 11 has a phishing filter to warn you of potential phishing websites.

Picture password A method of logging on to Windows 8.1. Instead of typing a password or PIN, you can use a series of touch gestures on a particular part of a photo that you select.

PIN password A method of logging on to Windows 8.1. The PIN is similar to what you type in an ATM machine and is a four-digit numeric password.

Pinned taskbar button A button representing a program, which appears permanently at the left end of the taskbar. A button that is not pinned appears only when its program is running.

Pinning Attaching a program, folder, or file shortcut to a user interface element such as the taskbar.

Playlist A group of songs that you can save and then listen to as a group. You can also burn a playlist to a CD, copy a playlist to a portable music player, and more.

Plug and play A technology that enables the computer to automatically discover and configure settings for a device connected to the computer through a USB or IEEE 1394 connection.

Pointer The on-screen image that moves around the screen when you move your mouse. Depending on the current action, the pointer might resemble an arrow, a hand, an I-beam, or another shape.

Pointing device A device such as a mouse that controls a pointer with which you can interact with items displayed on the screen.

POP3 A standard method that computers use to send and receive email messages. POP3 messages are typically held on an email server until you download them to your computer, and then they are deleted from the server. With other email protocols, such as IMAP, email messages are held on the server until you delete them.

Pop-up window A small web browser window that opens on top of (or sometimes below) the web browser window when you display a website or click an advertising link.

Portable computer A computer, such as a notebook or netbook, with a built-in monitor, keyboard, and pointing device, designed to be mobile and used in multiple locations.

Portable Network Graphic (.png) A digital image file format that uses lossless compression (compression that doesn't lose data) and was created as a patent-free alternative to the .gif file format.

Power plan A group of settings that denote when and whether to turn off the computer monitor or display and when or whether to put the computer to sleep. You can create your own power plan if desired.

Preview pane In Windows Explorer, an optional pane used to show a preview of a file selected in the content pane. See also **Content pane**, **Details pane**, and **Navigation pane**.

Primary display In a multiple-monitor system, the monitor that displays the Welcome screen and taskbar. Most program windows appear on the primary display when they first open. See also **secondary display**.

Product key A unique registration code issued by the manufacturer of a program. The key must be supplied during the setup process to verify that you have a valid license to install and use the program.

Public folder Folders from which you can easily share data with other users. Anyone with an account on the computer can access the data here.

R

ReadyBoost A technology in which you can use a USB drive or memory card as additional system cache, which acts like RAM, to improve computer performance.

Really Simple Syndication (RSS) A method of distributing information from a website or blog to subscribers for display in an RSS reader or aggregator.

Recycle Bin A system folder that holds deleted files until you manually empty it. The Recycle Bin is a safeguard and enables you to recover items that you've accidentally deleted or items that you thought you no longer wanted but later decide you need. Note that after you empty the Recycle Bin, the items in it are gone forever.

Refresh Your PC A service in Windows 8.1 that, when invoked, automatically backs up all your photos, music, videos, and other personal files, reinstalls your PC with new operating system files, and then puts your data back on it for you. It also backs up and restores your customizations, changes you've made to apps, and more. It enables you to completely reinstall Windows and then easily put your data back on your machine.

Remote Desktop Connection A program included in Windows 8.1 by which you can access your computer from somewhere else, such as an office or hotel room.

Reset Your PC A service in Windows 8.1 that returns your PC to its factory settings. It does this by wiping all the data from it and reinstalling Windows, after which the computer will appear as it did the first time you turned it on, right out of the box.

Resolution The number of pixels shown on a computer screen. A pixel is a very small square unit of display. Choosing 1024 × 768 pixels means that the desktop is shown to you with 1024 pixels across and 768 pixels down. When you increase the resolution, you increase the number of pixels on the screen, making images sharper and making everything on the screen appear smaller.

Restore point A snapshot of your computer system settings taken by Windows at a scheduled time as well as before any major change, such as installing a program or updating system files. If you experience problems with your system, you can restore it to any saved restore point without undoing changes to your personal files.

Ribbon A feature that appeared in Microsoft Office programs a few years ago and is now part of the Windows 8.1 graphical user interface. The ribbon contains tabs that, when selected, show a related set of tools and features underneath. The ribbon replaces the older menu bar, menus, and drop-down menu lists.

Right-click To point to an interface element and press the secondary mouse button one time.

Rip A term that describes the process of copying files from a physical CD to your hard drive. Generally, the term is used to describe the process of copying music CDs to the music library on your computer.

Router A piece of equipment that connects two dissimilar networks and sends data from computer to computer on a local area network. A router routes the data to the correct PC and rejects data that is deemed harmful.

S

Screen resolution The fineness or coarseness of detail attained by a monitor in producing an image, measured in pixels, expressed as the number of pixels wide by the number of pixels high. For example, 1024 × 768. See also **pixel**.

ScreenTip Information that sometimes appears when you point to an item in a software program's interface.

Scroll bar A bar that appears when what is available to show on the screen is more than can be viewed on it. You'll see a scroll bar on the Start screen, on webpages, in long documents, and in other places.

Scroll up and scroll down A process of using the mouse, the arrow keys on a keyboard, or a flick of your finger to scroll when a scroll bar is available.

Search A Windows 8.1 feature that provides searching capabilities. You can use this feature to search through apps, settings, files, emails, web entries, and more. Search is available as a charm, available from the right side of the screen when called on.

Search provider A company that provides a search engine, which you can use to find information on the web.

Search term The term you type in the Search box of the Start menu, search box of a search engine like Bing, or any folder window. Pressing Enter on the keyboard generally provides search results.

Secondary display In a multiple-monitor system, the monitor onto which you can expand programs so that you can increase your work area. See also **primary display**.

Semantic zoom The technical term for the technology that enables you to pinch with two fingers to zoom in and out of the screen.

Shared drive A drive that has been made available for other people on a network to access.

Shared folder A folder that has been made available for other people on a network to access.

Shared printer A printer connected to a computer and made available from that computer for use by other computers on a network.

Share A charm that is available from the right side of the screen that, when invoked, enables you to share information in one app with another app and, possibly, with other people (for example, by Mail). This charm can also make local files or resources available to other users of the same computer or other computers on a network.

Shortcut An icon with an arrow on it that offers access to a particular item on the hard disk drive. For example, you can put shortcuts on your desktop, that, when double-clicked, open programs, files, and folders stored in places other than the desktop.

Shortcut menu A menu displayed when you right-click an object, showing a list of commands relevant to that object. This is also called a contextual menu.

Shut down To initiate the process that closes all your open programs and files, ends your computing session, closes network connections, stops system processes, stops the hard disk, and turns off the computer.

Shut-down options Ways in which you can disconnect from the current computing session. You can shut down the computer, switch to a different user account, log off from the computer, lock the computer, restart the computer, or put the computer into Sleep mode or Hibernate mode.

Simple Mail Transfer Protocol (SMTP) A protocol for sending messages from one computer to another on a network. This protocol is used on the Internet to route email.

SkyDrive A location in the cloud offered by Microsoft where you can store data, including documents and pictures, among other things. Data you save is saved on Internet servers, enabling you to access the data from an Internet-enabled compatible device.

Snap The process by which two to four apps can be displayed side by side in Windows 8.1. This enables you to work with multiple apps at once.

Snipping tool A feature in Windows 8.1 by which you can drag your cursor around any area on the screen to copy and capture it. You can then save the captured data to edit it or attach it to an email.

Software Programs that you use to do things with hardware.

Sound recorder A tool included with Windows 8.1 that offers three options: Start Recording, Stop Recording, and Resume Recording. You can save recorded clips for use with other programs.

Spam Unwanted email; junk email.

Speech Recognition A program included with Windows 8.1 by which you control your computer with your voice. Speech Recognition provides a wizard to help you set up your microphone and use the program.

Spyware Software that can display advertisements (such as pop-up ads), collect information about you, or change settings on your computer, generally without appropriately obtaining your consent.

Standard toolbar A toolbar that is often underneath a menu bar in applications that do not offer a ribbon, which contains icons or pictures of common commands. You might already be familiar with the graphic icons for Save, Print, Cut, Copy, Paste, Undo, and others. These toolbars are being phased out and are being replaced by the ribbon.

Standard user account A type of Windows user account that allows the user to install software and change system settings that do not affect other users or the security of the computer. This account type is recommended for daily use.

Start button A button now available in the lower-right corner that, when clicked, takes you to the Start screen. You can right-click this button to access a contextual menu with shutdown options, access to Control Panel, and more.

Start screen A Windows 8.1 graphical user experience that offers access to apps, desktop programs, the desktop itself, and more. You can type while at the Start screen to locate something on it or elsewhere on your computer.

Status bar A toolbar that often appears at the bottom of an application window (such as the desktop version of Internet Explorer 11) and offers information about what is happening at the moment.

Store See **Windows Store**.

Subfolder A folder inside another folder. You often create subfolders to further organize data that is stored in folders.

Sync To compare data in one location to the data in another. Syncing is the act of performing the tasks required to match up the data. When data is synced, the data in both places matches.

System Restore If enabled, creates and stores restore points on your computer or device's hard disk drive. If something goes wrong, you can run System Restore and revert to a pre-problem date by selecting the desired point in time. System Restore deals with system data only, so none of your personal data will be changed when you run the program.

T

Tab An element that indicates separate pages of settings within the dialog box window, options in PC Settings, and in other places. The tab title indicates the nature of the group. You can display the settings by clicking the tab. In Internet Explorer, when tabbed browsing is turned on, tabs indicate separate webpages displayed within one browser window. You can display a page by clicking its tab or display a shortcut menu of options for working with a page by right-clicking its tab.

Tabbed browsing An Internet Explorer feature that enables you to open and view multiple webpages or files by displaying them on different tabs. You can easily switch among pages or files by clicking the tabs.

Tags Metadata included with a file, such as the date a photo was taken or the artist who sang a particular song. You can create your own tags in compatible programs and then sort data by using those tags.

Tap (Touch) A gesture you perform with your finger or a pen or stylus. A tap or touch is often the equivalent of a single left-click with a mouse.

Taskbar The bar that runs horizontally across the bottom of the Windows 8.1 desktop. It contains icons for running programs, your user folder, and Internet Explorer, and it offers the notification area, among other things. You can access open files, folders, and applications from the taskbar, too.

Taskbar button A button on the taskbar representing an open window, file, or program. See also **pinned taskbar button**.

Task Manager A way to access, manage, stop, or start running applications, processes, and services. You often use Task Manager to close something that has stopped working and is unresponsive, such as a program or process.

Task pane A fixed pane that appears on one side of a program window, which contains options related to the completion of a specific task.

Theme A set of visual elements and sounds that applies a unified look to the computer user interface. A theme can include a desktop background, screen saver, window colors, and sounds. Some themes might also change the look of icons and mouse pointers.

This PC An entry in the navigation pane of File Explorer that offers access to installed hard disk drives, CD and DVD drives, connected external drives, network locations (drives), network media servers, and similar connected media and locations.

Tiles Graphical user interface elements on the Windows 8.1 Start screen. Some can offer live information, such as news headlines or the number of unread emails. Tiles are said to be pinned to the Start screen.

Title bar The horizontal area at the top of a window on the desktop that displays the title of the program or file displayed in the window and buttons for controlling the display of the window.

Toolbar A horizontal or vertical bar that displays buttons representing commands that can be used with the content of the current window. When more commands are available than can fit on the toolbar, a chevron (>>) appears at the right end of the toolbar; clicking the chevron displays the additional commands.

U

Uniform Resource Locator (URL) An address that uniquely identifies the location of a website or webpage. A URL is usually preceded by http://, as in *http://www.microsoft.com*. URLs are used by web browsers to locate Internet resources.

Universal Serial Bus (USB) A connection that provides data transfer capabilities and power to a peripheral device. See also **USB hub** and **USB port**.

Upgrade To replace older hardware with newer hardware or an earlier version of a program with the current version.

USB flash drive A portable flash memory card that plugs into a computer's USB port. You can store data on a USB flash drive or, if the USB flash drive supports ReadyBoost, use all or part of the available drive space to increase the operating system speed. See also **ReadyBoost**.

USB hub A device used to connect multiple USB devices to a single USB port or to connect one or more USB devices to USB ports on multiple computers. The latter type of USB hub, called a sharing hub, operates as a switch box to give control of the hub-connected devices to one computer at a time.

USB port A connection that provides both power and data transfer capabilities to a hardware device.

User account On a Windows computer, a uniquely named account that allows an individual to gain access to the system and to specific resources and settings. Each user account includes a collection of information that describes the way the computer environment looks and operates for that particular user, as well as a private folder not accessible by other people using the computer, in which personal documents, pictures, media, and other files can be stored. See also **administrator account** and **standard user account**.

User Account Control (UAC) A Windows security feature that allows or restricts actions by the user and the system to prevent malicious programs from damaging the computer.

User account name A unique name identifying a user account to Windows.

User account picture An image representing a user account.

User interface (UI) The portion of a program with which a user interacts. Types of user interfaces include command-line interfaces, menu-driven interfaces, and graphical user interfaces.

V

Virus A self-replicating program that infects computers with intent to do harm. Viruses can come as an attachment in an email, from a USB stick, from a macro in a Microsoft Office program, through a network connection, and even in instant messages.

W

Wallpaper The picture that appears on the desktop. Windows 8.1 comes with several options, but you can use your own picture(s) or graphics if desired.

Web An abbreviation of *World Wide Web*. A worldwide network consisting of millions of smaller networks that exchange data.

Web browser A software program that displays webpage content and enables you to interact with webpage content and navigate the Internet. Internet Explorer is a web browser.

Webcam A camera that can send live images over the Internet. Windows 8.1 comes with a camera app that should be able to find and use your camera without any setup.

Website A webpage or a group of webpages that contain related information. The Microsoft website contains information about Microsoft products, for instance.

Wi-Fi A technology that allows an electronic device to exchange data or connect to the Internet *wirelessly* using *radio waves*. Public hotspots often offer free Wi-Fi connections to the internet.

Window Programs, documents, pictures, videos, folders, and so on that open a window of their own. Window, as it is used here, has nothing to do with the name of the operating system Windows 8.1; it is a generic term. Windows have minimize, restore, and maximize buttons so you can resize them. Windows open on the desktop.

Windows Defender A built-in tool that provides antivirus and antimalware functionality.

Windows Live ID An older term for an email address, registered with the Windows Live ID authentication service, that identifies you to sites and services that use Windows Live ID authentication. This has been replaced with the Microsoft account.

Windows Firewall If enabled, helps to lessen the ability of unauthorized users to access your computer or device and its data. The firewall blocks the programs that can be a threat. You can allow programs through the firewall or create exceptions if the need arises.

Windows Media Center A full-fledged media and media management application. You can view and manage photos, music, videos, and even television here. This is not included with Windows 8.1 by default; it is an add-on.

Windows Store The Microsoft online store for Windows 8.1 apps. You can also shop for music, videos, and more.

Windows Update When set to use the recommended settings, checks for security updates automatically and installs them. You can choose which optional updates to install.

Wizard A tool that walks you through the steps necessary to accomplish a particular task.

Workgroup A peer-to-peer computer network through which computers can share resources, such as files, printers, and Internet connections.

Index